# ANDROGYNY

Other books by June Singer

*The Unholy Bible: Blake, Jung & the Collective Unconscious*

*Boundaries of the Soul: The Practice of Jung's Psychology*

*Love's Energies*

# ANDROGYNY
## THE OPPOSITES WITHIN

June Singer

SECOND EDITION

### SIGO PRESS
BOSTON

Printing history
    Originally published by Anchor Press/Doubleday, 1976

 SIGO PRESS
25 New Chardon Street, #8748
Boston, Massachusetts 02114

Publisher and Editor: Sisa Sternback

International Standard Book Number: 0-938434-29-2 (cloth)
    0-938434-30-6 (paperback)
Library of Congress Cataloging in Publication Data
Singer, June.
    Androgyny: the opposites within.

    Bibliography: p.
    Includes index.
    1. Androgyny (Psychology) I. Title.
BF692.2.S55    1989    155.3'3            88-15779

Printed in the United States of America

# TABLE OF CONTENTS

# PREFACE

More than a decade has passed since Androgyny first appeared in bookstores. When it was written, "androgyny" was still an unfamiliar word to most people, and others held the misconception that the term referred to someone not quite normal either because of sexual preference or some abnormality of the genitals. Between that time and this, "androgyny" has become a familiar term with a multitude of connotations — some denoting a healthy personality with a balance of masculine and feminine attributes, others suggesting a special kind of weirdness, and everything in between. Furthermore, in the intervening years, the sexual climate has undergone at least two one-hundred-and-eighty degree turns: first, from the unconscious sexual freedoms of the sixties to the more aware sexual liberation of the seventies; and second, to the eighties with its watered-down awareness of responsible sexual practice and, as an inevitable backlash, ultraconservatives' attempts to persuade or enforce a clearly stated moral standard. Why now, when changes in sexual practice are occurring so rapidly and are so widespread, should Androgyny be revised and republished?

The message of the book was clear enough, but in certain respects it was ahead of its time. Androgyny appeared in the early stages of the Women's Liberation Movement. It was an exciting time, a thrilling time, in which women were beginning to feel their own potency. The leaders of the Movement foresaw the possibilities for greater numbers of women to discover their independent identities and individual strengths. The leaders also saw the necessity for women to pool their energies in joint efforts to modify social structures in ways that would allow greater opportunities for women in their work and more choices in their personal lives. Nor did those leaders of the Movement underestimate the strength and resistance of the existing power structure. There existed, of necessity, an adversarial relationship consisting of the "victims of society" (read "women") and the "oppressors" (read "men"). The resulting polarization of interests, as seen by the women who were beginning to assert their rights, left little room for the flexibility of goals and behavior that androgyny advocated. It was as though in the heat of battle someone had said, "Now what you ought to do is sit down to a dinner-table conversation with the ene-my and find out how he feels about the situation in which you are both em-broiled." Not much chance!

Women who had accepted their gender-assigned roles in society over the years with more or less pleasure, more or less irritation, now were roused into anger by the possibilities for change that were held out to them. It was not only the Women's Movement that offered them a variety of new opportuni-ties, but also the new technologies which freed an ever-growing mass of the female population from unwanted chores which could include anything from childbearing to nursing to scrubbing clothes to preparing meals from scratch. One would have thought that the opportunities now available to women would have engendered in them a gradual trend toward developing those talents, capacities and inclinations that in the past had been more closely associated with the masculine role. In other words, woman had before her an opportu-nity to develop her "animus," Jung's term for the more active, assertive initiat-ing aspects of her personality which had, for the most part, remained unconscious because they did not fit in well with the "feminine" role she was supposed to play. In many cases this development toward androgyny did oc-cur, but more often it was held back by one of two factors. The first was that these newly liberated women had been reared by women whose conscious-ness had developed a generation earlier, and they had bred into their daugh-ters a strong sense of what "femininity" meant, based on an earlier time. While logic militated against accepting the parental viewpoint when it was no longer applicable, the strong emotional impact of early training still refuses to relin-quish its hold upon the mature adult. Added to this was the natural resis-tance of men to the new development in distaff side; for, with the family as a closed system, where one side gains in power, the other correspondingly loses. Whatever women might gain, men felt they might have to give up some-thing in return. The time was yet to come when both women and men would realize that what was good for one sex would eventually be good for the other. But we are getting ahead of our story.

If many of the people who were desperately trying to break out of a societally-imposed status failed to find the idea of androgyny appealing, there were those on the fringes of mainstream tradition who found much comfort in it. The chapter "Androgyny Experienced in Homosexuality, Bisexuality and Heter-osexuality" brought heartwarming responses from people who had fallen into one or another of those categories and had felt bound to be members of it for once and for all, with no possibility of crossing or recrossing the invisible barriers that the groups themselves had erected. *Androgyny* showed them that sexual energy was simply energy that people channeled into various kinds of behavior, and that such behavior was not cast in concrete but could be altered if there were sufficient motivation. Nor need one remain in any of these categories unless one desired to do so. Energy itself was neutral; it could be channeled into various kinds of behavior according to the individual's inclination. Before reading *Androgyny,* many people believed that they were alone in their discomfort at being typed according to their sexual preference at a given time. They were greatly relieved to discover that they were not alone in these feelings, and that there could be release from their self-imposed prison of the mind.

The chapter "Androgyny Experienced in Masturbation, Celibacy and Marriage" found resonance in particular with individuals who, for one reason or another, had to find peace and acceptance of the opposites within, in the absence of any satisfactory intimate relationship out in the world. These people discovered that through the recognition of their own androgyny, they could find wholeness in themselves and feel complete in themselves. They could realize the essential fact that androgyny exists as a model for resolving disunion, both within the individual and in society.

*Androgyny* came out at a time when ambiguous sexuality was one of the shockers of the popular culture. Male rock stars appeared as caricatures of the most offensive female features, ranging from the heavily made up whore-types all the way to the most ridiculously sissified images. Meanwhile, on the streets, fashion favored the ubiquitous blue jeans, and the body's trend was to litheness and leanness, long hair and heavy shoes, so that sex of a young person was often difficult to determine from the rear and one was thankful for a mustache or a beard when the person turned around, to resolve the mystery. For many, androgyny came to mean a hopeless and hapless confusion of the sexes. This was the furthest possible departure from the actual intent of the book. Over the past decade this, too, has changed. Images of masculinity and femininity in fashion reflect a sense of clear difference between the sexes, not in the stereotyped fashions of earlier times, but with a new sense of style that reflects the individual man's or woman's unique being. This is an outward sign that suggests an inner condition — the freedom to be one's own person, enjoying the particular aspects of personhood which include sex and gender.

It may be through our own personal experience that we come to consider the meaning of androgyny, but we soon discover that the personal aspects are rooted in something far deeper than our immediate concerns. Androgyny is described in this book as an archetype, rather that as merely a social phenomenon. Social phenomena come and go like the season's fashions, but an archetype is a consistent core idea that expresses itself in a variety of images and behaviors which depend upon the cultures in which they exist for their content. Thus, the archetype of androgyny as it appeared in Plato's *Symposium* expresses the human being's aspiration to the power of the gods, while the archetype of androgyny as it appeared in the *Tao te Ching,* comes as an expression of the yin/yang opposites of ancient Chinese Taoist philosophy. In whatever form this archetype appears, it raises issues around the separation of the inner opposites and the challenge to reunite them in a harmonious way.

The prime issue is the same as that in the ancient creation myth, where the first entities to tumble out of the cosmic egg when it was broken were Love and Strife. Love and Strife are twins who eternally struggle in the mother's womb; and when the mother is Earth, our world is caught in the struggle. Love represents one kind of energy: drawing together, conserving, holding, nurturing, trusting, protecting. Strife represents the other: pulling apart, separating, discriminating, penetrating, dispersing, attacking, judging, achieving. Although, at first glance, it may appear that the archetype of Love comes closer to the traditional image of the Feminine, and that of Strife comes closer to the traditional image of the Masculine, in closer observation it becomes clear that these opposites exist within every person. Moreover, they are needed by all of us, for were we to be only an expression of Love, we would be utterly vulnerable, and were we to be only an expression of Strife, we would be at odds with everyone, including ourselves. The archetype of androgyny is the expression of the two-in-the-one, the paradox that an inner union requires an ongoing dynamic relationship of the opposites within. Wholeness can only be achieved if nothing is left out. The androgyne accepts the inner opposites — not necessarily as points of internal conflict, but rather as parts that need each other to function, in order to maintain the whole.

It is in the nature of the archetype that it is not restricted to individual experience, but that it applies to the human condition in general. With archetypal phenomena, we tend to move from our subjective experience of the archetype to its deeper, collective meaning. With reference to the archetype of androgyny, once we have learned to recognize and accept the seemingly disparate aspects within ourselves, it naturally follows that we need to extend this openness, this attitude of friendship and cooperation of parts and whole, to the wider human community. That means that androgynes (by which I mean persons who are conscious of their androgyny) will not see themselves in conflict with "them" out there, even though "they" may represent a different way of being than "we." Androgyny demands a meeting of the opposites outside as well as within the individual, even though the other may be very different from ourselves or from our self-concept. We need to recognize that each of us is a part of a larger system, whether it be family, corporation, community, nation, or the whole planet. The phrase, "No man is an island," now takes on enormous proportions. If someone pours contaminants into a river upstream, a people perishes downstream. If someone causes an accident in a nuclear plant in the Soviet Union, reindeer die of radiation sickness and Laplanders starve. We begin to think like this: If I buy abusive drugs and take them, I do not only disturb my own precious consciousness, I lend support to the international criminals who get rich at the expense of the health and sanity of the public. If I take one drink too many and get into the driver's seat of my automobile, I may kill someone or maim someone for life. If I engage in promiscuous sexual practices, I am personally responsible for risking an increase in the incidence of a fatal disease that is threatening to assume epidemic proportions.

In the not too distant past, one could do as one pleased and assume "my body is my own and it is my business what I do with it." No longer. Nor can I regard the other as my enemy, and engage in behaviors that will annihilate that other person, that other nation. The world is too small. The direction of the wind shifts freely and what I send out will sooner or later blow back into my face. The truth is that I am a part of all humanity, and what I do to the least of them I do unto myself.

Androgyny comes from two Greek words meaning male and female. In a wider sense, this particular dichotomy is one of many possible expressions of all dichotomies, as the Greek philosophers have taught us—thesis and antitheses. To resolve a problem, an issue, or a war, it is necessary to bring together the opposites into a harmonious relationship, synthesis. It does not mean that the issues no longer exist, but that they exist as clearly defined and workable entities within a working system. Likewise, masculinity and femininity enter into a cooperative system under the rubric of androgyny. The idea, clearly is as old as philosophy and myth—and we have brought together here some sources that illustrate this contention. It is an idea that is also so new, that it is only now being rediscovered. It is the author's hope that this book will add greater depth to the concept of androgyny which is so relevant to many issues that divide our world today.

June Singer
Palo Alto, California
1988

# PREFACE TO FIRST EDITION

*Androgyny* is the outcome of my concern over unfinished business in my last book, *Boundaries of the Soul*. In the earlier work I had struggled over a chapter about inner images of men that are experienced by women, and inner images of women that are experienced by men. Starting as I had from a position in the twentieth century, I found it difficult to comprehend the meaning behind the rapidly shifting views of individuals regarding their own sexuality, and it was still more difficult to interpret the changes in the ways they viewed the sexuality of the opposite sex. After rewriting several times a chapter titled, "Will one sex ever understand the other?" I had to conclude that I could come to no conclusion. Nevertheless, if books are ever to be published, there comes a point at which the author has to stop. Although I ended the chapter with the Masculine and the Feminine clasped together in a well-fitted embrace like Yang and Yin, unresolved issues still stuck out like the white spot in the midst of Yin and the black spot in the midst of Yang. These spots, the contending opposites within the contented opposites, were the seeds of what was to become the new work, *Androgyny*.

The dynamism inherent in the masculine-feminine interaction is born not only of the embrace of the two within the one, but also of the germ of opposition within the opposites. Worlds within worlds, worlds embracing worlds. There no longer seems to be a need for more studies of masculine psychology or the psychology of the feminine. We are dealing with Eros here, and Eros — the double-sexed god — knows no boundaries. Nor does Eros willingly accept limitations, regardless of how energetically societies attempt to impose them. Love will have its way; and people everywhere are attempting anew to understand that way.

I have searched the pages of history and mythology to discover what people have thought about Love, and everywhere I found the androgyne gazing up at me with that curious smile which is neither altogether masculine nor altogether feminine. Are books the mirror of the soul, or only the mirror of my *soul* as I look into them? I have asked myself this question but will leave it to the reader to decide the answer. It has been possible in this book to deal only with a few examples of androgyny out of the man that periodically emerge out of darkness and repression. Doubtless, other instances of the harmonious coexistence of masculinity and femininity within a single individual could have been chosen, and they would have been equally convincing. But this work, like the one before it, had to have an end. This time I have concluded by pointing out some new pathways to an understanding of Love, pathways that go beyond considerations of relations between individuals. The new pathways must lead inwards, so that the individual can experience the relations of the parts of his or her own organic being within the psyche, and also outwardly, so that the individual can find a loving relationship with all that exists in the universe outside of herself or himself. The new pathways lead inevitably to a theory of human sexuality based on androgyny, because theories founded on the dominance of one sex and the compliance of the other have brought about an imbalance in society that needs to be remedied. Although today's sexual revolution appears to be a reaction against the injustices of the past, I will try to show that this is merely a surface manifestation of a fundamental principle that has existed for so long that it may be said to be inherent in the nature of the human organism. Androgyny is not reactive, but intrinsic to human nature.

In my work on Androgyny, I have been aided and encouraged by good friends, whom I wish to thank. Werner H. Engel read the manuscript as it moved along, discussed many of the issues with me, and offered helpful ideas from his storehouse of wisdom. Louise Bode listened to my litany of frustrations and helped to clear my head with good questions and innumerable cups of tea. Lee Roloff lent his skill to tighten up the language and suggest stylistic and other changes. Reginald Ray advised me on Chapter 14. Anne Wilmot prepared the manuscript and amused me with her extravagant reactions to the text.

I acknowledged my indebtedness to my analysands, who shared with me their secret doubts and fears about their own sexuality and helped me to deepen my convictions about the tyranny of convention. Many of them discovered their psychological androgyny, then denied it because they knew of no ideological context into which it could fit. For them, and for myself, I had to find reasons for what the feelings pronounced to be true: that Love is a boundless energy which, when truly free, overflows all the ideological vessels that society constructs to contain it

June Singer
1976

# ACKNOWLEDGEMENTS

The use of the following illustrations is gratefully acknowledged: O Great Eye from *Loka: A Journal from
Naropa Institute* published by Anchor Press/Double-
day, New York. The Aristotelian Concept of the Four
Humors from *Astrology, the Celestial Mirror,* published
by Thames and Hudson, London, and Avon Books,
New York. Ophion and the Universal Egg, The
Sefiroth Depicted as the Androgynous Adam Kadmon, The Kabbalistic Tree of Life, The Sefiroth as
the Tree Pillars, and The Path of Kundalini from
*Kabbalah,* copyright © 1973 by Charles Ponc, published by Straight Arrow Books. Abraxas from *A Fan-
tastic Bestiary* published by Leon Amiel Publishers,
New York. The Taoist Form of Interanl Alchemy
British Museum. The chart for Two Modes of Con-
sciousness from *The Psychology fo Consciousness* by Robert
E. Ornstein published by W.H. Freeman and Company, San Francisco. Copyright © 1972.
The quotation from "East Coker" in *Four Quartets* by
T. S. Eliot is reprinted with permission from Har-
court Brace Jovanovich, Inc., New York, and Faber
& Faber, Ltd., London.

O great Eye
of the Universe,
'round which I am but a
speck of dust swirling,
help me
to know that in my smallness
I participate in Your Greatness,
and in Your greatness
You participate in
my smallness.

# PART 1

## Yesterday

# Chapter 1

## Androgyny as Guiding Principle of the New Age

Soaring into space.

Taking off in a jet liner heading westward from Chicago. Feeling the exhilaration that comes from doing something totally against human nature. An *opus contra naturam,* as the alchemists called their work. The excitement of flying, something that a human being was not meant to do, allows consciousness to shift to another level. Ascending to thirty-five thousand feet, I find myself willing to think that the apparently impossible may not be impossible after all. I remember Blake's *Proverb:* "What is now proved was once only imagin'd."[1]

Human sexuality is natural enough. It begins with the proposition that we are male or we are female, which is surely incontrovertible. Androgyny is a work against nature, or seems to be. The sky over mid-America is an appropriate place to begin a consideration of the androgyne.

I suddenly recall that I started my first novel (unpublished) while traveling also, in the late 1950's. I was taking my first step toward freedom from the circumscribed existence of housewife and mother. My life was less limited, for my personal aspirations in the direction of a career were encouraged, at least as long as my aspirations did not interfere with anyone else's. Something was driving me to see what I could accomplish in the world as an individual. I had been living out the feminine role true to the stereotypes in vogue at the time, and repressing most of the qualities our society said were "masculine." I was awakening to the realization that I have been living only half a life with any immediacy, and the rest vicariously through my family, my friends, and my fantasies. No longer satisfied with staying at home, I took a job in the city.

The hour in transit, morning and evening, was the only time in my day that I could call my own. I did not owe it to anyone, home, husband, family, employer. I claimed that time to write in my notebook as I sat on the shabby green velvet upholstered seat of the commuter train that chugged along on a bumpy roadbed.

Today, as my pen moves across the page, I ride in a shiny aluminum needle swinging westward through the clouds. My state of consciousness is as different now from what it was then as is the vehicle in which I write about it. The change in my consciousness is largely a reflection of the change in the collective consciousness that is preparing the way for a new age. Astrologers refer to it as the "Age of Aquarius." Perhaps, in the distant future, social critics will look back upon the time we are approaching and will call it the "Age of Androgyny."

I enjoy flying.

There is no fear. Awe, perhaps, as I look out of the window and find myself in a bright, churning space in which nothing is defined. There is neither distance nor closeness, neither earth nor sky.

There is no thing. There is nothing.

There is nothing to fear, because I am suspended in the universe. Since the universe is universal, therefore everywhere, I cannot fall out of it. I was in it before I was born. I shall be in it after I am dead. My being, in this form as a passenger on this plane, is only one constellation of molecules that have come together in the process of becoming one person, namely, myself. I shall be here until the form in which I find myself is transformed into something else. Then the structure of molecules which I know as myself will disintegrate and become diffused throughout the universe, and after that, the particles will join with other particles and regroup in new ways, forming other beings, other things, another "I."

Life seems very beautiful up here, far above the surface of the earth. I love life, yet am not afraid of the ending of my personal existence. I recall a Japanese proverb often quoted by Alan Watts: "Flowering branches grow naturally, some short, some long." While the flower lasts it is enjoyed, but it does not cling to the bough. Fear of flying is fear of death. Death is seen as an enemy only by those who set themselves in opposition to Nature. If, however, death is a stage in the cycle of life wherein an organism undergoes transformation, then what is there to fear?

Outside, there is only the impenetrable whiteness, the void. All is One, and even the One-ness is so blindingly bright that I cannot look directly into it.

Now, we rise above the cloud bank and I witness a startlingly beautiful miracle of nature. The firmament above is separated from the firmament below. Above, I see an expanse of azure clarity; below it is pure white softly blended with pale gray, like a dove's breast feathers.

If in my own inner space I am experiencing the first and second days of creation, then nature is providing the perfect images for the ideas I want to communicate. A moment ago I was deep in the midst of unfathomable space perceiving the great and endless vastness that has been called "the cloud of unknowing." A complete and undifferentiated One-ness encompassed all I could see, and all that I am, flying through space. What is more ecstatic than to be at once suspended in the midst of the universe and at the same time warm and comfortable in the belly of a supernal aluminum mother?

In the moment that the One became Two, I knew the wrenching beauty of the primal separation. Before, sailing through the white cloud, I was able to look beyond it to the curved horizon and the blue sky arching over it. Now I find myself in the blue space, looking down upon the cloud. The human organism, psyche and soma, can move swiftly back and forth between the two that are, in reality, one — if it finds the proper vehicle.

The theme of my writing presents itself in eidetic imagery. The theme is androgyny, which in its broadest sense can be defined as the One which contains the Two; namely, the male (*andro-*) and the female (*gyne*). Androgyny is an *archetype* inherent in the human psyche. C. G. Jung has stated that his use of the term *archetype* is an explanatory paraphrase of Plato's *eidos*, and this is the sense in which I am using it here. The term *archetype* is helpful in this context because it indicates the presence of an archaic or primordial type, a universal and collective image that has existed since the remotest time. Archetypes give rise to images in primitive tribal lore, in myths and fairy tales, and in the contemporary media. They are, by definition, unconscious; their presence can only be intuited in the powerful motifs and symbols that give definite form to psychic contents.[2] Androgyny is just such an archetype; it continually represents itself in myths and symbols, which have the capacity — if recognized and invoked — to energize the creative potency of men and women in ways that most people hardly imagine today.

Androgyny may be the oldest archetype of which we have any experience. It derives from, and is second only to, the archetype of the Absolute, which is beyond the possibility of human experience and must remain forever unknowable. The archetype of androgyny appears in us as an innate sense of a primordial cosmic unity, having existed in oneness or wholeness before any separation was made. The human psyche is witness to the primordial unity; therefore, the psyche is the vehicle through which we can attain awareness of the awe-inspiring totality.

First, there is nothing in existence except the indescribable void, the ineffable nothingness. Second comes the primordial unity, the One in which all the opposites are contained, but not as yet differentiated. Like the yolk and the white in an egg, they are locked together, imprisoned and immovable. When the appointed time comes the primordial unity is broken open; then there exist the Two, as opposites. Only when the Two have become established as separate entities can they move apart and then join together in a new way to create the many and to disperse them. In time, pairs of opposites tend to polarize. The polarities are expressed in a variety of ways; for example — light and dark, positive and negative, eternal and temporal, hot and cold, spirit and matter, mind and body, art and science, war and peace.

One pair, male and female, serves as the symbolic expression of the energic power behind all of the other polarities. It does not matter what the order, for as creating principles, one is invalid without the other. For the spark of creation to be engendered, the male and the female must come together in all their sexual maleness and femaleness. Before they can be joined they must first have been apart, differentiated, separated from one another. Before they were separated they were bound together in one body, and that body was the Primordial Androgyne.

The idea of a Divine Androgyne is a consequence of the concept that the Ultimate Being consists of a unity-totality. Within this unity-totality are seen to exist all the conjoined pairs of opposites at all levels of potentiality. Creation occurs when the cosmogonic egg is broken. Then the world is born. Or it occurs when male and female, having been incorporated in one spherical body, are separated by the supreme power of creation. Cosmic energy is generated by the surge of longing in each one of the two for the other.

We have come to know about the primal quality of the androgyne from its traces in the myths and legends and sacred traditions of many primitive peoples. Ancient mythology abounds with tales of a time when the eternal male and the eternal female where locked in an unending embrace. A Greek myth tells of a time when out of Chaos were born Night and also Erebus, the unfathomable depth where Death dwelt. From Darkness and from Death, Love was born, and from Love, Light. Then Mother Earth emerged and lay in union with Father Sky. There they remained for eons in an unending embrace. In other versions, Earth-Sky was seen as an androgynous deity. This non-dual constitution of the Primal Being, which contains within itself the potentialities of duality and multiplicity, has come down to us by way of the more sophisticated religions also, especially in elements of Hinduism, Taoism and Buddhism, as well as in the Platonic tradition of the West.

The Androgyne has been nearly totally expunged from the Judeo-Christian tradition, for it apparently threatens the idea of a patriarchal God-image. Male dominance has been the keystone of the Judeo-Christian civilization. Our major institutions outside the home have been conceived and operated primarily by men, and they function according to certain kinds of principles and behavior that we commonly designate as "masculine." Androgyny, however, corresponds more faithfully to the guiding human archetype than does a societal structure based on a dominantly patriarchal mode of functioning with women in a subordinate role. Despite the expunging, androgyny continues to assert itself—sometimes fiercely—challenging all attempts to suppress it.

Androgyny refers to a specific way of joining the "masculine" and "feminine" aspects of a single human being. We see much evidence of the trend toward androgyny in our Western world today in social customs, manners, morals, and also in the awareness of millions of people who are searching out ways to expand their consciousness of themselves and their world. The deeply moving spirit of androgyny is not yet obvious or familiar in our time and place, even though it is older than history itself. Everywhere, it has existed as the "hidden river."[3] It has nourished religion and literature. From time to time it has emerged, sometimes as the spring of a new idea, sometimes as a torrent of reaction against an overwhelmingly one-sided political situation.

Even in the Judeo-Christian culture androgyny has periodically come to light, but until now it has not gained sufficient understanding, and therefore strength, to reassume its original primacy over the patriarchal powers in our society. The recent expansion of androgynous consciousness, brought about largely through the catalytic effect of the Women's Movement, has increased our awareness of the necessity for questioning the nearly impregnable fortress of male-oriented values. The Women's Movement has confronted us with the historic undermining of women and has challenged us to utilize the potency of the female in our society. The Women's Movement may turn out to be the decisive step in the direction of androgyny, inasmuch as it confronts directly some of the obstacles that lie in the path toward androgyny. I am not sure that many women know where the path is leading, specifically in terms of their own inner development, but they are led on by the archetype deep in the psyche, the archetype that in its own way constructs reality at least as much as do the events in the external environment.

Only in the present century have women effectively begun to challenge this state of affairs on any large scale, although often in the past certain women held positions of power and influence in affairs of state. Until recently a woman's challenge to the existing power structures had been of a token nature and had met with very limited success. Beginning, however, with the last half of the twentieth century, the assertiveness of some women has begun to make an impression. Those women who have been freed from the most pressing of their domestic tasks, who have been afforded opportunities for good educations, and who have taken the option of deciding for themselves when and whether to bear children, have been able to turn some time and energy to the consideration of their condition as women. Growing dissatisfaction with the subordinate role of women in our society has stimulated the contemporary feminist movement, with its goal of raising the level of freedom and opportunity for women closer to that of men.

Despite the gradual nature of the impact it is making now, the Women's Movement is revolutionary in nature. Its aims are radical; its cutting edge is to enable woman to conceive of herself as possessing the inner potential to become economically and spiritually independent. The radical feminist of today recalls the mythic Amazon, a fearsome warrior who could defeat man at his own game. The rationale of the Movement, as the more liberal wing recognizes, is that if woman can get beyond a position of subservience to man, she can then begin to relate to him in a much more satisfying way for both, and that is as an equal. They say that the woman of the coming era will be able to choose far more freely the ways in which she will participate in her relationships with men. Indeed, this potential is already being realized by many women, especially by those who were born after the mid-century.

I am in touch with the collective and individual struggles of the feminist movement because for more than a decade I have been actively engaged in attempting to find my standpoint as a psychotherapist and as a woman. This includes defining myself in new ways. Still, there is something about the feminist movement that makes me uncomfortable, even while I acknowledge with appreciation the many gains it has already made toward improving the status of women. The Movement supports the independent position of woman in contrast to her former position of subservience to man; but this often tends to polarize further the images we have now of the male and the female, and of "masculinity" and "femininity." The questions are no longer primarily about dominance and subservience, but they are being transformed into questions of politics, pressure groups and public relations. A few women are becoming more and more competent at what men have been doing for centuries. Some women are already arrogating to themselves the patriarchal model by attempting to be as much like men as it is possible for a woman to be. But there is a limit beyond which it cannot work, for at some point a woman is basically different, and she feels that difference as a tidal wave arising from within. If she does not heed it, it may eventually overwhelm her whole person.

What the Women's Movement has already achieved, and what it is planning for the future, points to an improvement in the quality of life for millions of women and, it is hoped, for the men with whom they are involved. The Movement represents a conversion from a situation in which woman was inevitably expected to be the compliant partner in a male-female relationship, into one in which woman need not be afraid to assert herself, her beliefs and her values. But we must realize that a battle-line has been drawn—and for the next several years it is likely to be a violent struggle.

Beyond the contest for dominance, beyond the polarization of *masculine* consciousness and *feminine* consciousness, lies the intuition that there must be something else, a further development in *human* consciousness. This intuition leads to questions that seem to apply in our own times but, in fact, have been asked many times in ages past:

*What are the sources for our concepts of the ideal masculine personality and the ideal feminine personality?*

*Do women possess the so-called "masculine" qualities of consciousness and men the so-called "feminine" qualities?*

*What are the potentials in recognizing these apparently divergent elements within the single personality?*

*Where does the longing for the opposite other come from that human beings have always recognized in the many forms of love?*

*Can a new alchemy bring into being a union or reunion of opposing elements, a conjunction that may produce a new guiding image?*

*What may be the nature of an image that can bridge the masculine/feminine opposites in human consciousness?*

The image of the androgyne begins to take new form before the eyes of many people. The androgyne will not be discovered by turning outward into the world, but by turning inward into ourselves. It is a subtle body, that is to say "non-material," buried in the deep unconscious realm that all humans collectively share. The collective unconscious yields up its treasures slowly. The androgyne rests in its murky depths and will not easily be imagined, let alone comprehended. It rarely enters awareness, or if it does, it is usually repressed, and for two important reasons. First, androgyny is a state of consciousness that is far from ordinary, and therefore it threatens many people's state of equilibrium. Second, androgyny threatens many presuppositions about individuals' identity as men or as women, and hence threatens the security of those people, including most of us, who have vested interests in the conventional attitudes toward sex (maleness and femaleness) and gender (masculinity and femininity).

The images of the androgyne are many. They may be drawn up out of a network of esoteric and mystical speculations in which one discipline often feeds upon and supports the others. Alchemy, for example, is related in a large degree to Kabbalistic literature, as is Gnosticism, and all draw upon astrological speculations. Wherever orthodoxies have been promulgated and enforced, philosophers and mystics have thought differently and have devised their own systems, systems that in conflict with orthodoxies often became "heresies." Their esoteric writings were deliberately couched in abstruse terms so that they could be understood only by the student who had made a serious commitment to their study and who was prepared to tolerate considerable ambiguity.

Uncovering the sources of the principle of androgyny in many esoteric disciplines and investigating the implications of this principle for contemporary consciousness does not depend upon logical thinking or linear reasoning. The recognitions come through immersion in the material, contemplation of the images and meditation on their significance. Suddenly a pattern becomes clearly visible, and the insight brings a joy such as that Buckminster Fuller has so clearly described:

> When mind discovers a generalized principle permeating whole fields of special-case experiences, the discovered relationship is awesomely and elatingly beautiful to the discoverer personally, not only because to the best of his knowledge it has been heretofore unknown, but also because of the intuitively sensed potential of its effect upon knowledge and the consequently improved advantages accruing to humanity's survival and growth struggle in Universe.[4]

The joy is like the experience of flying itself. It comes about through leaving the conventional, earthbound ideas and finding a perspective up in space from which to look down upon what was formerly so close at hand. Looked on from an airplane, one is not covering mile by mile the distance between two cities. One is a participant in a miracle of technology which transforms before one's eyes the future (where one is going) to the past (where one has been); and all the while the earth moves along under the shadow of the winged needle. Miles and hours, time and space, transform themselves in terms of distance and one can see it happening almost as if from some cosmic point outside the system.

The plane itself a structure; it is matter, the matter in which this transformation of time and place occurs. The plane has function; the function is the flying, an expenditure of energy through which the relative distance ahead is constantly being converted into a relative distance already covered. The "future" is being converted into the "past," and all the while an equilibrium is being maintained. In the plane, I am in the "eternal now," and the distance from place to place is just as great as it ever was, no more and no less.

The journey of the plane could be seen as a metaphor for the way toward androgyny. One might say that the qualities of maleness and femaleness are structure, they themselves do not change in an individual, although sexually related changes may take place in men and women. Men and women function in certain ways; each has masculine and feminine functioning capacities. In the process of living, these qualities, which for want of a better name we call "masculine" and "feminine," are also convertible. The difference is that the conversions may proceed in a single direction as with our plane, or the conversions may move backwards and forwards, oscillating so swiftly that it is impossible to discern when "masculine" functioning is in the superior position, and when "feminine." In the case of oscillation, the functioning can be so smooth as to bring into being a personality of unusual grace, adapting itself to every situation out of an inner guiding mechanism that senses what is needed at any particular moment. The guiding mechanism might be said to be operating on the principle of androgyny. Through this dynamism a sense of equilibrium could be achieved.

My purpose here is not to explicate a method for getting in touch with an abstract principle. Instead, it is to pursue the exploration of a path from a chaotic, diffuse primordial image of androgyny toward a new and differentiated consciousness that is androgynous in nature. The hope is to move from chaos toward clarity. In setting this task I am aware that any attempt to leave the usual reference point, which is solid by reason of its being earth-bound, in order to employ a new perspective, invites the devils of logical mistakes and human fallibility. Since it is an exploration, and since much of the territory is strange, the path may be plagued by trial and error and we may often retrace our steps. Yet there is much to be learned from the searching, and the quest summons up its own energy. It is a special kind of energy, as will become clearer as we proceed.

The movement toward androgyny that is emerging today grows out of the tensions between the "masculine" and the "feminine" elements in contemporary Western society. It spirals back upon itself to discover the older androgyny that is revealed in the mythology of that primordial time when the masculine and the feminine were not yet separated in the Godhead. To attempt to deal with the nascent, contemporary androgyny without taking into account the old androgyny, would be to deal only with the isolated and symptomatic manifestations without noticing their archetypal bases which we have inherited from generations long passed into oblivion.

# Chapter 2

## Hermaphrodites, Bisexuals, Androgynes
## and the Uncarved Block

A new consciousness is rising out of the morass of a declining society that has bent too far toward rationalism, toward technology and toward the acquisition of power through unbridled competition — or whatever other means have been considered necessary by those in charge to achieve dominance and control over less sophisticated people. The new consciousness takes note that our society has become overbalanced in favor of the so-called "masculine" qualities of character.

The new orientation that is gaining in influence may be characterized as emphasizing "feminine" values, or values that in the past, at least, have been associated more with the feminine than with the masculine. Among these values is a preference for co-operation rather than competition, for a team approach to problems rather than a strictly individualistic approach, for giving credit to intuition at times over and above a deliberate thinking process, and for emphasizing sexuality and relationship over and above power and violence. Men and women are sensitive to issues of masculine or feminine values as social and political determinants.

If another argument in the war between the sexes is to be avoided, or if the battle we now have on our hands is to be resolved, it will be necessary to take a fresh view of our notions of the masculine and the feminine character. Both notions are challenged by an overriding principle, androgyny. When we begin to recognize androgyny as an essential reality of human nature, we begin to move toward a world in which individual roles and the modes of personal behavior can be freely chosen. Androgyny has the power to liberate the individual from the confines of the "appropriate."

In order to understand what androgyny is, we may begin by suggesting what it is not. It is not hermaphroditism and it is not bisexuality, although sometimes it gets confused with one or the other.

*Hermaphroditism* refers to a *physiological* abnormality in which sex characteristics of the opposite sex are found in an individual. Hermaphrodites belong to the classification of *intersexuals,* in whom there is a significant shift of one

11

or more of the sex qualities in the direction of the opposite sex. These qualities include the external genitals, the internal sexual apparatuses, the nature
of the chromosomes, the hormonal states and the secondary sexual characteristics. In general usage, hermaphroditism refers primarily to the appearance of abnormally formed external genitals which resemble those of the
opposite sex. In literature or mythology, hermaphrodites are weaklings or mon-
sters; in any case, anomalies. Hermaphroditus, a son of Aphrodite, served
the goddess and took responsibility only as her deputy. His womanish breasts
and long hair, and sometimes his wearing of women's skirts, bore witness to
his subservience. This freakish, little-respected figure was a product of a period of transition from a goddess-worshipping society into one in which the young
male gods, heretofore subordinated, would begin to assume powers of their
own.

   *Bisexuality,* as I am using the term here, refers to a *psychological* condition.
While *hermaphroditism* referred to a lack of differentiation in *physical* sex characteristics; that is, maleness or femaleness; *bisexuality* refers to a lack of clarity
in gender identification; that is, to confusion about masculinity or femininity. Bisexuality refers to people who at one time or another in their adult lives
have felt strong sexual attraction for members of both sexes. Freud equated
overt homosexuality with bisexuality and also included the latent homosexuality of heterosexuals in this category.[1] Classically, however, bisexuality refers
to people who select *both* male and female sexual partners.

   Today we tend to exclude from this grouping people who are exclusively
homosexual, both in their fantasy and in their sexual behavior. However, while
working with many people in my analytic practice who consider themselves
unalterably homosexual, I have rarely found a person whose dreams or fantasies did not give some indication of bisexuality. The same may be said for
people who consider themselves to be exclusively heterosexual. A young man
made this observation:

> Bisexuality is a fad now. I'm not so sure how it works out. I'm not so sure it
> has to do with sexual behavior as much as it does with empathizing with people.
> Even more, I believe it has to do with one's attitude toward oneself. If you try
> to act it out, there's a confusion; neither you nor the others know exactly who
> you are. You don't go anywhere. It just loses its edge.

   When we explore sexual material at the deeper levels of the psyche, we inevitably arrive at a state in which sexual feelings are far more loose and free-
flowing than the individual normally would be willing to admit. Bisexuality
may or may not involve actual engagement in sexual relations with members
of both sexes; the psychological inclination to do so is the factor that determines bisexuality. If it is not a matter of overt behavior, it is certainly a matter of inclination.

   The question may be asked as to whether we are not all bisexuals by this
definition. The question does not lend itself to a theoretical answer, and my
clinical experience suggests that a bisexual orientation is far more widespread

than most people recognize. There are not many people who have not at some time experienced erotic feelings toward actual or potential partners of both sexes.

And yet, bisexuality goes beyond this. It includes feelings directed toward all people, feelings that do not fit into the exclusive categories that many psychotherapists apply to sexual behavior. Many bisexual people seem intent upon breaking through boundaries of sexual conventions, and "bi-lib" is widely proclaimed as an expression of liberated life style. Some who call themselves bisexual realize that sexual relationships and sexual satisfactions are not only goals in and of themselves, but are also expressions of a total personality structure. What a man or woman believes about human relationships and human values is given form and expression in the sexual encounter. Bisexuality concerns itself primarily with interpersonal relationships. Bisexuality is by no means the same as androgyny.

The new androgyny also suffers through confusion with an image that used to be popular in Romantic literature and art. The word *androgyne* has been mistakenly applied to effete young men who wore foppish clothes or to women with boyish figures and facade. The following quotation from Susan Sontag is typical of that genre:

> The androgyne is certainly one of the great images of Camp sensibility. Examples: the swooning slim sinuous figures of pre-Raphaelite painting and poetry in the Art Nouveau style, the thin, flowing, sexless bodies in prints and posters, presented in relief on lamps and ashtrays; the haunting androgynous vacancy behind the perfect beauty of Greta Garbo.[2]

Sontag's definition represents a transitory style that bears little relationship to the quality of the person who will claim the designation of *androgyne* in the times ahead. It recalls the tasteless novels of the Romantic era in England and France dealing with sexual pathology, the macabre and the diabolical. I refer to such works as Oscar Wilde's *Salomé* dramatizing a vampire passion, the *Hérodiade* of Mallarmé, the writings of Péladan and Gautier — obsessed as they were with the hermaphrodite, the celebration of Lesbian love in Baudelaire, the morbid interest in sexual flagellation in Marquis de Sade and in Swinburne; and there were many others.[3]

The androgyne was understood by the decadent writers simply as a hermaphrodite in whom both sexes exist anatomically and physiologically. These writers were not concerned with a "wholeness and fusion of the sexes but with a superabundance of erotic possibilities," according to Mircea Eliade:

> Their subject is not the appearance of a new type of humanity in which the fusion of the sexes produces a new unpolarized consciousness, but a self-styled sensual perfection, resulting from the active presence of both sexes in one.
>
> This idea of the hermaphrodite had probably been encouraged by the study of certain ancient sculptures. But the decadent writers did not know that the hermaphrodite represented in antiquity an ideal condition which men endeavored to achieve by spiritual means of imitative rites; but that if a child showed at

birth any signs of hermaphroditism, it was killed by its own parents. In other
words, the actual, anatomical hermaphrodite was considered an aberration of
Nature or a sign of the gods' anger and consequently destroyed out of hand. Only
the ritual androgyne provided a model, because it implied not an augmentation
of anatomical organs but, symbolically, the union of the magicoreligious powers
belonging to both sexes.[4]

The new androgyne is not confused about his or her sexual identity. Androgynous men express a natural, unforced and uninhibited male sexuality,
while androgynous women can be totally female in their own sexuality. Yet
neither tends to extremes: Men do not need to exude machismo, or women
to pretend a naive and dependent character. Excessively polarized personality types thrive in a culture that demands the repression of certain natural
tendencies while people are developing the so-called "masculine" and the so-
called "feminine" traits which that society considers to be appropriate for each
sex. Androgynous individuals allow these repressions in themselves to be lift-
ed; not in order to prepare a way for living out sexual impulses so much as
in order to permit what has been repressed to return and to be reintegrated
into conscious awareness.

It may be argued that when a modality of being is repressed and is no longer
conscious, it cannot be recovered by simply "permitting" it to return again.
Yet in my experience of working with people in the area of their sexual repressions I have come to believe that the line between consciousness and the unconscious is not as rigid a boundary as I had once thought. Openness to dreams
and fantasies, respect for other manifestations of the nonrational sphere of
functioning, invite the formerly unknown contents to pass easily through the
gates into consciousness. In the 1960s, our culture was introduced en masse,
through the agency of psychedelic drugs, to the dissolution of boundaries that
were once thought to be impermeable. It is now well known that there are
many states or levels of consciousness. Much of what was formerly thought
to belong to the realm of the unconscious had already crossed the boundary
and needed only to be activated to come into full awareness. And awareness,
far from being a static state of "knowing," is capable of being expanded and
deepened and refined.

The principles called "masculine" and "feminine," respectively, are well
defined within our particular social structure. Or at least they were well defined
until the sexual revolution plunged many people into a state of perplexity.
One could ask any group of people to list qualities they thought would fall
into the masculine and feminine stereotypes. The masculine stereotype would
invariably include aggressivity, dominance, hardness, logic, competitiveness,
achievement orientation, thinking, inventiveness, reason; while the feminine
stereotype would include passivity, compliance, softness, and tenderness. There
would be little variation in the response from group to group. Always, when
I have lectured and put such a list on the blackboard, it has become apparent
to both men and women that each person possesses a mixture of qualities from

both lists. For most people, it seems important that these "masculine" qualities be in the forefront in men and those "feminine" qualities be in the forefront in women. The contrasexual qualities have traditionally been thought best kept in the background in order to establish and preserve a strong gender identity. But the old values do not carry much weight any more, and new values have yet to become established in the realms of sex and gender.

The androgyne approaches the problem by seeing that true change begins primarily *within the psychic structure of the individual*. Here is where the androgyne differs fundamentally from the bisexual. If the concerns of the bisexual are mainly *interpersonal*, those of the androgyne are mainly *intrapsychic*. The androgyne consciously accepts the interplay of the masculine and feminine aspects of the individual psyche. One is the complement of the other, in the same sense that the active, probing sperm is the complement of the waiting, yielding ovum. In conception, the two principles are combined; in the individual, the active and receptive natures coexist throughout the span of life. They do not always exist in the same relationship to one another, however.

·From puberty through the childbearing years, sex and gender have traditionally tended to be more closely related (i.e., men are more masculine, and women more feminine) than they were in early childhood or would be in middle age and old age. Here again, this is the stereotype; in reality there are many exceptions. During the courting and childbearing years, the biological impetus toward reproduction is strong. Often, just *because* of this, many young women resent being classified according to their sexual, reproductive and childbearing capacities. Without necessarily negating these, some women make special efforts to develop a sense of independence and to increase their intellectual functioning in these years so that their personal autonomy will be preserved. At the same time, men may assist their partners in some of the more traditionally "feminine" tasks, especially during the child-rearing period, and so come in touch with the contrasexual potentialities within themselves. Neither does the stereotype of the "sexually latent" period of childhood always work out into a lack of differentiation of masculinity and femininity in children. How "masculine" little boys will become, or how "feminine" little girls, depends to a large extent upon parental attitudes and upon the influence of peers. Nor do older people necessarily develop the wisdom of maturity which recognizes the contrasexual side of the personality. Despite the innate or biological tendency toward androgyny in the earliest and latest years of life, the impress of circumstance often leads people into one of the polar opposites. Still, the androgynous potential is always present in each person, ready to be tapped as a source of energy. The androgyny principle is intuitively experienced as the key that can unlock the prison of sex and gender — a key that is available to anyone who has the courage and imagination to make use of it.

A warning is in order. The state of awareness that nourishes and fosters the symbolic sexual union within the individual has been an anathema to adherents of the Judeo-Christian tradition. Where this awareness has come to consciousness, it has been accepted as valid mostly by people and groups outside the mainstreams of the culture — e.g., the alchemists, the Kabbalists, the mystics. Those who understood its complexity learned when and where to keep silent about it; while those who misunderstood it — and gave overt expression to what they thought it was — found themselves the objects of scorn or mystified glances or social ostracism or even legal discrimination. The warning is this: Be aware that the society in which we live is not yet prepared to accept the value, much less the necessity, of personal and political androgyny.

Fortunately, the new androgyny does not need to be acted out in the world in order to survive and evolve. It is an inner process through which, in the long run, behavior changes. The new development of the individual comes out of a perspective in which men and women view themselves as whole and complete particles of Being, functioning within an ordered cosmic unity. A new consciousness in individuals inevitably has its effect on the collective consciousness.

A sense of belonging to a cosmic order and reflecting that vast macrocosm in human microcosm is essential to understanding the concept of androgyny. For those who feel isolated in an alien world, the concept may appear radical, but it is no more new than a green shoot that springs up from a tangled mass of roots buried deep in the ground. Androgyny is stirring in our depths, and we are in the cycle of eternal return. One who is in touch with his own wholeness finds a resonance in those esoteric works of literature and art that reveal the androgynous nature of the primordial wholeness and the power inherent in that androgyny. The *Tao Tê Ching* speaks of that "power," but it is not power in the Western sense. The meaning of the word comes closer to "potency" or "inner strength":

> He who knows the male, yet cleaves to what is female
> Becomes like a ravine, receiving all things under heaven,
> And being such a ravine
> He knows all the time a power that he never calls upon in vain.
> This is returning to the state of infancy.
> He who knows the white, yet cleaves to the black
> Becomes the standard by which all things are tested;
> And being such a standard
> He has all the time a power that never errs,
> He returns to the Limitless.
> He who knows glory, yet cleaves to ignominy
> Becomes like a valley that receives into it all things under heaven,
> And being such a valley
> He has all the time a power that suffices;
> He returns to the state of the Uncarved Block...[5]

These lines express with exquisite simplicity the paradoxical nature of the androgynous. The two must be united with the one. Power (potency) is synonymous with returning to the state of innocence. Yet we cannot return to innocence; it is only when we are old and wise that we may be able to put aside the knowledge that we have learned and to act spontaneously out of what we are.

Power (potency) that never errs is possible only in the sphere of the Limitless; that is, before birth or after death. It is beyond human consciousness and therefore implies a trust in the unconscious, a willingness to flow with nature, in Tao, "the water-course way." [6]

Once formed and shaped, how is it possible to return to the state of the Uncarved Block? The power (inner strength) lies in the openness to the opposites within oneself — not by an effort to integrate that which is strange or foreign, but by awakening to the reality that the opposites have been there all along, and would coexist in harmony if only we did not drive a wedge between them.

# Chapter 3

## The Two in the One: Pathology or Mythology?

The tradition of Western thought is primarily linear and analytical. When faced with opposites, we tend to see them as irreconcilable or, at the very least, as problematical. It is difficult to accept holistic thinking, in which opposition is only apparent, and opposing forces are only aspects of the same things seen from different points of view. And so we drive wedges between the black and the white, between consciousness and the unconscious, between the masculine principle and the feminine principle. The tendency of Western thought to separate out, dissect, examine and reassemble, reached its zenith in the psychoanalytic movement that began just before the turn of the twentieth century.

Sigmund Freud was born in 1856 into a world in which the alienation of the sexes from each other had become a searing, tearing and painful experience for many people. Those who consulted Freud as a doctor revealed to him physical symptoms that had no apparent organic basis, or they came with peculiar ideas that clearly did not make sense when taken a face value. In almost every case, the presenting symptoms of Freud's patients served to mask the real problems. These arose out of personal experiences and their residues that were so painful that the sufferers were unable to acknowledge them even to themselves, or indeed to face the reality of their existence. It would be even more difficult to make these experiences conscious enough so that they could be divulged to another person, the doctor. As Freud believed, most of the "illnesses" stemmed from problems associated with sexuality, and especially from traumatic experiences that had occurred in early childhood.

If the premise is accepted that at this time in central Europe there was a true psychological and spiritual alienation between men and women—and especially between the fairly well-educated men and women of the middle and upper-middle classes who came to Freud—then it would follow quite reasonably that this sort of alienation would find in sexuality its target for expression. If a wife were, for example, out of true spiritual contact with her husband, if they did not think alike or feel alike—if they had different interests, differ-

19

ent needs and different goals, and if the conventions of their society were such that these dissatisfactions were not openly talked about — where was her misery and unhappiness most likely to find its outer expression? Quite naturally, it would have to be on the one battlefield where the man and woman did confront each other most directly, if not in words then in another and equally direct form of communication. I refer, of course, to the marriage bed. And, equally naturally, the confrontations would be re-evoked on that analogue of the marriage bed — the analyst's couch.

I do not believe that all the problems that appeared as sexual problems were, fundamentally, sexual problems. To make such an assumption would be like suggesting that a person who goes on a hunger strike as a passive-aggressive way of demonstrating a political inequity has a problem that is fundamentally nutritional. Here the nutritional problem is only a symptom, as were often the sexual problems which emerged in Freud's consulting room. The important question is, what is *really* going on in the innermost depths of the individual who comes for psychotherapy? It is necessary to concentrate more upon the causes for this war than upon the maneuvers of the battlefield.

Freud's treatment of the neurotic problems of men and women, which appeared to him as problems concerned primarily with their sexuality, were highly creative attempts on his part to come to terms with the issues of his times. In confronting those issues he tuned directly into the major illness of society — the growing chasm between the sexes and between masculine psychology and feminine psychology. Responding to what he saw as the crucial questions of his age, he made important investigations which led to his formulating the theoretical structure of psychoanalysis. The new discipline profoundly affected the course of human development over more than three quarters of a century. Much of Freud's work was the product of society's reaction to the widest extremes of the pendulum's swing between masculine psychology and feminine psychology.

Carl Gustav Jung, Freud's beloved and most promising disciple from their meeting in 1907 until shortly before their parting in 1913, was younger than Freud by nineteen years. There was just enough difference in their ages so that Jung belonged to a generation that was beginning to see the most subtle modulation in the pendulum's swing away from the polarized opposites. Jung's views on the relative importance of sexuality as a causative factor in neurosis were to differ markedly from Freud's absolute view. Disagreements in ideology as well as the clash of the two powerful personality structures led to the dissolution of the Freud-Jung relationship in 1913. At the time Freud was approaching the height of his fame, and Jung was only at the threshold of his own most creative work.

By 1916, after Jung had reflected on the essence of his difference with Freud, he wrote in an essay titled "The Structure of the Unconscious:"

Since we parted company with the Viennese school upon the question of the nature of the interpretative principle in psychoanalysis, which in our view is not the *sexual impulse*, but simply *energy*, our concepts have undergone considerable development. (Italics Jung's.)[1]

For Jung, the energy principle in itself was neutral; it could find its expression through sexuality, intellectual activity, spiritual discipline, physical expression, creative artistry, business or professional life. The use to which the energy was directed was what endowed it with meaning. There was no such thing as "sexual energy" *per se* for Jung, only a psychic energy that would be directed into sexual or other aims.

Jung's ideas were close to those of his elder colleague in their first years together, but as time went on Jung's ideas diverged and he began to formulate his own position, as an eminently creative student inevitably will. As times, changes and circumstances alter the social fabric, students must first learn the teaching of the master and then be willing to detach themselves from it so that they can approach each new situation with a freshness and freedom from bias, dealing with every problem according to its demands. I believe that it is more important to proceed in the spirit of a great teacher than to adhere literally to the teachings themselves, and furthermore, that Jung would have approved of such a procedure. This is said by way of apologia for some of my own assertions throughout this work that may take issue with certain teachings of my spiritual mentor, although not with his trust in the capacity of each individual to find his or her own natural way of being. This is, after all, what androgyny is about.

My interest in the problem of androgyny grew out of my discomfort with certain of each of their views concerning the nature of sexual impulses and sexual behavior. I began by asking questions about bisexuality because, in my own analytic practice, I have heard over and over again that people who were living heterosexual lives often expressed longings for intimacy with members of their own sex, or for expressing feelings or behaving in ways that were generally considered "appropriate" for people of the opposite sex. And, at the same time, I was hearing from people who were committed homosexuals that they experienced a longing to be accepted as normal human beings who could move about freely in a "straight" society, even from time to time having sexual relations with members of the opposite sex, without having to face the censure of their fellow members of the homosexual subculture. The anomie experience by people who are living as heterosexuals as well as by those who are living as homosexuals has a resonant sameness — people in each category seem to suffer by being categorized. Categorizing is experienced as unnatural, as forced, as constricting and often as compelling individuals to remain in unloving relationships and to deny themselves other relationships that could possibly offer deeply affectionate companionship.

All of this led me to direct questions about bisexuality to the people with whom I worked therapeutically. I compared the answers I received with the theoretical statements of Freud and Jung. My studies led me to the inescapa-

ble conclusion that the phenomenon of bisexuality, whether acted out or intuitively and privately sensed within one's own personality, was the avenue
through which the more fundamental problem could be approached. That
problem had to be, of course, the psychological realization of the essentially
androgynous nature of each human personality. However, it is a long way
from bisexuality to androgyny. The journey should begin with a brief inquiry
into the positions of Freud and Jung on the matter of bisexuality as it stood
in the years of their association and those immediately following, as these were
the creative years for both of them. From all that I have determined, Jung
was fully in accord with Freud's contention that we are all by nature bisexual,
and also with Freud's assumption that each individual combines in his or her
nature elements of both maleness and femaleness.

Robert J. Stoller, in summarizing Freud's concept of bisexuality, stated that
when Freud first began constructing the edifice of psychoanalytic theory, he
placed the concept of bisexuality in the center, and that from those early days
until the end, it remained there.[2] I believe that the same may be said of the
centrality of Jung's concept of the dual nature of human sexuality. There is,
however, a great difference between the viewpoints of the two men. Freud
predicated the most important tenets of his theoretical formulations on the
*biological* basis of human behavior. For example, he wrote, "Psycho-analysis
has a common basis with biology, in that it presupposes an original bisexuality in human beings [as in animals]."[3] For Freud, the observation that bisexuality was a biological universal warranted the assumption that it necessarily
exerted its influence on the psychological, "which at bottom, is in itself a reflection of biology."[4] The biological basis of bisexuality, as Freud saw it, led logi-
cally to his central thesis — that *bisexuality is at the heart of all psychopathology.*

Jung, like Freud, was a physician and a psychiatrist, and was, of course,
thoroughly trained in the biological sciences. Physiology, however, was not
the primary goal of departure for Jung's explorations into psychology. He preferred to look more closely into the sources of human behavior as they were
derived from the artifacts and manuscripts recovered by archaeologists from
past civilizations. He was especially interested, also, in the psychological functioning of peoples living today, unaffected or minimally affected by contemporary Western civilization, and he was an ardent student of anthropology,
mythology and comparative religion.

On the basis of his studies as well as his clinical observations, Jung developed a view of bisexuality[5] that differed radically from Freud's. Well acquainted
with the lore of societies where bisexuality was practiced openly and considered natural and normal, Jung came to regard *bisexuality* as a phenomenon
that one should understand, rather than as a disease that one should try to
cure.* Another significant difference in their approach was that Freud

---

*In this connection it is interesting to note that not until 1974, and against many ob-
jections, did the American Psychiatric Association pass a resolution to remove homosexuality from its list of "mental disorders."

emphasized the interpersonal aspect of sexuality and posited as a primary goal of psychoanalysis the achievement of a mature relationship with a member of the opposite sex, while Jung was more concerned with the *interplay* between the masculine and feminine components of the *individual psyche*.

Furthermore, Jung's view of the importance of the biological element in bisexuality was as understated as Freud's was overstated. Jung regarded bisexuality as an archetypal element of the collective unconscious that surfaced under certain conditions in normative cultural practice. Acceptance of the bisexual — or, rather, androgynous — potential has been an absolute requirement for admission as a full member of the adult community in some societies. An example of this is the practice of subincision, an initiatory ceremonial among Australian aborigines. The youths who would be accepted into the society of men submit to a ritual in which the underside of the penis is slit, so that the initiate acquires a penis-wound which is also a "penis-womb." Among other primitive groups, for example, in Africa among the Masai, the Nandi and the Nuba, the novices are dressed as girls; while among the South African Sotho, girls who are being initiated are dressed in men's clothing.[6]

Jung found himself in close agreement with Mircea Eliade's suggestion as to the religious meaning of all these customs. Eliade writes:

> The novice has a better chance of attaining to a particular mode of being — for example, becoming a man, a woman — if he first symbolically becomes a totality. For mythical thought, a particular mode of being is necessarily preceded by a *total* mode of being. The androgyne is considered superior to the two sexes just because it incarnates totality and hence perfection.[7]

The writings of Jung are filled with examples from myth and custom that point to the importance and value of recognizing the qualities of the two sexes within each person. Far from being seen as pathological, the fullest human potential of men and women, in Jung's view, could be realized only through a process that included the recognition of the contrasexual aspect.

What cannot be stressed too strongly is that in Jung *this recognition was neither associated with heterosexual behavior between men and women nor with so-called homosexual behavior, but rather with an individual's intrapsychic functioning.* This points up the crucial difference between bisexuality and androgyny. Bisexuality, in common parlance, refers to acting out maleness and femaleness in sexual behavior. But Jung seems to imply that bisexuality in the contemporary Western world is an expression, usually misunderstood, of a natural but unconscious thrust toward androgyny. Androgyny begins with our *conscious* recognition of the masculine and feminine potential in every individual and is realized as we develop our capacity to establish harmonious relations between the two aspects within the single individual. These aspects may interact competitively with each other and thereby produce conflict, or co-operatively, and thereby release the energy that would otherwise be dissipated in reducing conflict.

Jung's writings provide clues that show that he was familiar with a body of mythological material pointing to androgyny as a residual element in the human psyche. This idea comes from the mythic theology, which is nearly universally diffused, about an androgynous god or goddess as creator-creatrix. Humanity was supposed to be modeled after this divine image, but somehow mankind fell away from or was severed from the original wholeness and degenerated into the imperfect men and women of this world—ever in search of completion through integration of the alienated opposite. The representation of human androgyny as an ideal state of being is but a mythic image today, lost in the remoteness of forgotten eons. Yet, traces still remain.

It may be that Jung developed his core concepts of *anima* and *animus* from the evidence of these traces. Anima, the Latin word for "soul," is in the feminine gender. It refers to the feminine element that exists in man and remains, according to Jung, largely unconscious. As a man's "normal" consciousness is masculine for the most part, his soul, or anima, becomes the container for the unconscious processes that are constantly taking place in him. Likewise, Jung posited a masculine soul, or animus, for woman, as the carrier of her unconscious. Anima and animus are the contrasexual opposites that form the basics of Jung's psychosexual theory, and rank in importance with Freud's concept of bisexuality.

It must be remembered that both Freud and Jung came out of a society that was strongly patriarchal in tenor and monotheistic in belief and practice. In it the Father God was the ruling deity, and masculine consciousness was considered the more valuable consciousness, associated as it was with light, while feminine consciousness was subordinated and associated with darkness.

In the Vienna Circle, Freud certainly assumed the role of the patriarch, one might even say the Father God. If he were the spokesman for masculine consciousness as the highest social value and for adaptation to a world constructed on the masculine principle, it is no wonder that a gifted disciple, in attempting to rescue his own identity from the dominating influence of the master, should occupy much of his concern with the role of the feminine principle in a man's psyche. If Freud took the first steps away from bisexuality in his sexual theory, one might observe that Jung took the first steps toward androgyny in his own sexual theory.

# Chapter 4

## Becoming Liberated from Sex and Gender:
## Risks and Challenges

In *analytical psychology,* as Jung called his discipline, masculinity and femininity describe the attitudes of *consciousness* of men and women, respectively. *Unconscious attitudes,* according to Jung, stand in a compensatory relationship to those of consciousness. In a society in which the modes of consciousness tend to be polarized, one would expect to find polarization in the unconscious as well. It follows, then, that if Jung conceives masculine consciousness as being radically different from feminine consciousness, in the unconscious the man's anima will differ correspondingly from woman's animus.

Jung claims not to ascribe an inferior consciousness to women; he merely points out the differences as he sees them. Here is one example:

> Just as a woman is often clearly conscious of things which a man is still groping for in the dark, so there are naturally fields of experience in a man which, for woman, are still wrapped in the shadows of non-differentiation, chiefly things in which she has little interest.[1]

Of the contrasexual side, he says:

> We must therefore expect the unconscious of woman to show aspects essentially different from those found in man. . . as the anima produces *moods,* so the animus produces *opinions.*[2]

For Jung, "opinions" when expressed by women, are hardly worth ignoring. He makes this kind of generalization:

> Animus opinions often have the character of solid convictions whose validity is seemingly unassailable. If we analyze these opinions, we immediately come upon the unconscious assumptions. . . In reality the opinions are not thought out at all. . .[3]

It will be no surprise that many modern women become incensed on reading

25

this kind of statement! Jung also advises woman that she:

> ...must learn to criticize and hold her opinions at a distance; not in order to repress them, but, by investigating their origins, to penetrate more deeply into the background, where she will recover the primordial images, just as the man does in dealing with the anima. The animus is the deposit, as it were, of all woman's ancestral experiences of man — and not only that, he is also a creative and productive being, not in the sense of masculine creativity, but in the sense that he brings forth something that we call *logos spermaticos,* the spermatic word.[4]

The implications of Jung's polarized notion of anima and animus do not suggest a "separate but equal" view of the sexes:

> Just as a man brings forth *his work* as a complete creation out of his feminine nature, so the inner masculine side of a woman brings forth creative seeds which have the power to fertilize the feminine side *of the man.* [Emphasis mine.][5]

Although Jung asserts that both men and women draw their creative energies from the unconscious, there is a subtle — or perhaps not so subtle — difference. The man's anima helps *him* to produce *his* creative work. The woman's animus is supposed to inseminate the man's anima, which thereupon inspires him to produce his creative work. Fortunate, but rare indeed, is the woman whose active creative animus is furthered by the tender nurturing of a man's anima.

Jung stressed the necessity of woman's integrating the animus into the totality of her personality. In order to accomplish this, she would first have to recognize the functioning of the animus when it appeared. The animus manifests itself in independence, assertiveness, ambition, intellectual striving and other kinds of behavior that did not seem quite appropriate for women — as viewed by men, who considered these qualities virtues when possessed by themselves. What was appropriate was for woman to keep her animus under firm control, subordinated to her "feminine ego." If a woman were desirous of a well-functioning relationship with a man, subordination of animus was not only "appropriate," it was essential. This position, as stated by Jung in the 1920s, was not seriously challenged until the 1970s.

As women began to turn their efforts toward a revision of this state of affairs, the Women's Movement became extremely vocal. One of the first of the feminist psychologists to attack the double standard that exists in determining normality or mental health was Phyllis Chesler. In her book, *Women and Madness: when is a woman mad and who is it who decides?*, Dr. Chesler showed how the subject of women has traditionally elicited the most sentimental pronouncements from clinicians. For example, she cites Freud (in 1925) as saying:

> [Women] refused to accept the fact of being castrated and have hope of someday obtaining a penis in spite of everything...I cannot escape the notion (though I hesitate to give it expression) that for a woman the level of what is ethically

normal is different from what it is in a man. We must not allow ourselves to be deflected from such conclusions by the denials of the feminists who are anxious to force us to regard the two sexes as completely equal in position and worth.[6]

And, from Freud in 1933:

We say also of women that their social interests are weaker than those of men and that their capacity for the sublimation of their interests is less. . .the difficult development which leads to feminine [seems to] exhaust all the possibilities of the individual.[7]

Lest the assumption be made that these ideas of Freud have become obsolete, a report on a recent meeting in New York of the American Academy of Psychoanalysis published in *Science News* notes:

[Abram] Kardiner, the most outspoken of the senior analysts present, discussed his own analysis by the Viennese master and then went on the say that Freudian analysis is in serious need of revisions in important areas. 'For 50 years it has not moved one iota,' he charged. 'And as a discipline,' he went on, 'Freudian analysis has no claim on the future if it does not begin to grow and produce usable knowledge—knowledge that can be used as a sociological tool.'[8]

Bruno Bettelheim provides another example of the male clinician's attitude toward the emergence of the woman who is oriented in the direction of greater freedom to pursue her interests and talents. The occasion was a symposium on American Women in Engineering, at the Massachusetts Institute of Technology in 1965. It is unlikely that Dr. Bettelheim would be permitted this statement today: ". . .as much as women want to be good scientists and engineers, they want, first and foremost, to be womanly companions of men and to be mothers."[9]

Nor is Jung immune from charges of being bound by the patriarchal tradition. He states:

No one can evade the fact, that in taking up a masculine calling, studying and working in a man's way, woman is doing something not wholly in agreement with, if not directly injurious to, her feminine nature. . .[Female] psychology is founded on the principle of Eros, the great binder and deliverer; while age-old wisdom has ascribed Logos to man as his ruling principle.[10]

It has been not only the male clinicians, however, who have stressed psychological differences between the sexes as to their effective functioning in business or professional life. Women analysts have accepted the stereotypes too, or at least they have until recently. M. Esther Harding, one of Jung's disciples and a founding member of the Jungian analytic movement in the United States, recognized as early as 1933 that women might rise to a high level in their careers, but she said this could occur "only through the exercise of those masculine qualities which are ordinarily latent or unconscious."[11] Dr. Harding believed that a woman achieves success in the world only at the risk of sacrificing her love life completely. The only hope, as Harding saw it, was that woman would have to manage her career and her home with equal capability and efficiency. No word is mentioned about a man's responsibility to his working wife to serve as an "enabling" factor in her life, in ways similar to what is taken for granted that a woman will do for her husband. For Harding, it is woman's responsibility alone to discover how to function in the impersonal way demanded by business and professional life without losing touch with the personal warmth and relatedness that Harding identifies with the feminine nature.

I find myself with women today, and with a growing number of men, who regard the sex and gender stereotypes of Freud, of Bettelheim, of Jung and Harding—and also those of the currently popular sexist magazines and many television images—as outdated, demeaning to women, and as vestigial remnants of a polarized consciousness that has been with us far too long. The behavioral models of the past are not viable models for where the boundaries of the soul are today. Man is no longer as unconscious of his anima as he used to be, *or* woman of her animus, which is not to say that *no* aspect of either of these is unconscious. In these days, when life has lost its linear quality and stimuli from an ever-increasing multitude of sources bombard our every sense simultaneously, we lose our lust for the slow process of coming to consciousness step by step. We lose patience with the idea of a frail and tiny ego differentiating itself, step by step, out of the boundless Self, finding its identity as man or woman, and in the process accepting the stereotypes belonging to the gender role. There are intimations of the Divine Self within ourselves, and the desire to experience more of this draws us forward with increasing energy and speed toward an inner unity.

While it is true that our ways of functioning in the world continue to be limited by our biology, the limitations need not be so crucial to our lives as they once were. There are few positions in our society today that could not be filled equally well by women as by men *if women were but given the opportunity.* The need for sheer physical strength has in most places yielded to technology. But it is woman alone who is able to conceive and bear children, despite the assertion of Apollo in Aeschylus' drama *Euminides.* Unless, perhaps, the lines below contain a fearful premonition of what may come to pass only in our own generation!

> APOLLO: To be called mother is no wise to be
> Parent, but rather nurse of seed new-sown.
> The male begets: she's host to her small guest;
> Preserves the plant, except it please God blight it.
> I'll furnish reasons for my argument.
> There hath been and there can be fatherhood
> Though there should be no mother; witness here
> Olympian Zeus' own self-created child,
> That grew not in the womb's dark coverture;
> A branch so goodly never Goddess bore.[12]

In the spirit of Zeus, we read today that fetal life has been maintained and developed in a test tube for a short time. So far the laboratory has produced no Athena, but some technology for genetic engineering is already developed and more is being researched. Soon we will choose the sexes of our children. This alone has awesome implications.

If biology places less of a limitation upon us than it did in the past, psychological preconceptions are becoming correspondingly free from stricture. Life is no longer seen as a lumbering process, moving progressively through developmental stage after stage.[13] It is typical of our times that questions arise during the period of youth that formerly were relegated to maturity or old age. In the past, young people (except for the few adolescent Romantics meeting early with questions of meaning) were primarily concerned about making a living; today many people are concerned earlier with the meaning in life; that is, with questions of philosophy, religion, metaphysics.

There are today many lives within a life; not simply birth, growth and death. Within these many lives are possibilities unheard of a few years ago. It is not uncommon for people to change their vocations two or three or even four times within a span of a lifetime. Women return to higher education after their childbearing years and then enter careers that would not have been open to them a few years ago. Men married to such women are assuming a share of household responsibility and a role in child rearing. They are discovering that you don't have to be able to bear a child in order to nurture it. Older people are taking advantage of university programs for "returning scholars." Psychological research has shown that IQ does not begin to deteriorate when youth fades, but that it holds up remarkably well into the sixth and seventh decades.[14] In our changing civilization, even the possibility of changing sexes is here. Christine Jorgensen was a sensation a few years ago. More recently, James Morris, the British journalist who accompanied Sir Edmund Hillary on his conquest of Mt. Everest, wrote a book called *Conundrum,* which created little stir. It is the personal report of his transformation into a woman, Jan Morris, through hormonal treatment and transsexual surgery.[15]

However, the whole point is lost, it seems to me, when people become obsessed with the idea that they have to prove to the world, by making *visible* changes in themselves, that they have undergone a process of psychological adaptation. If, as it has now come to be accepted generally, each person has a variety of psychological tendencies and capabilities that fall into both "masculine" and "feminine" categories, then the question, "Which is predominant?" is the wrong question. What needs to be asked is, "How are these aspects within myself relating to each other?" If peace about this is established within the individual, there will be no need for public proclamation.

A change of conscious attitude, however, inevitably has an effect upon the way an individual behaves in the outer world. This is apparent in some women who, in the process of becoming liberated from the conventions that accorded them a secondary role in a world dominated by men, attempt to take over the very power they resented when wielded by men. Instead of trying to imitate men, I believe that on a deep psychic level women need to become aware of themselves as women; but not only that, women need to become aware of themselves as whole and complete persons, and not as mutilated persons, in the Freudian sense.

Jung was not so quick as Freud to label behavior "pathological," especially the behavior of women when it veered from the norm. He discussed openly in his psychological writings those aspects of human nature which, until last decade or so, had been firmly suppressed in the Judeo-Christian culture myth. Yet it appears that he was not successful in solving this classical double-bind situation: a woman can be free to activate the side of her nature involved with intellect, creativity and assertiveness in the world, but a woman must preserve her "femininity" at all costs if she wishes to participate in a fully loving relationship with a man.

A prominent woman psychiatrist who hoped to do some consciousness raising among her colleagues, mostly male, lectured on the subject, "Sexism in Medicine." She said that in the course of their training, female medical students were sharply criticized for not being sufficiently active, decisive, firm and authoritative. Then, as soon as they began to make progress in developing those qualities they were criticized for being "unfeminine." During the open discussion that followed her lecture, one young male doctor, looking quite perplexed, made this comment, "I understand and appreciate all that my colleague has expressed and I agree with her one hundred per cent, *in my head;* but when I get home in the evening I still want my wife to have dinner ready for me." Following this lecture, the psychiatrist who had introduced the main speaker and led the discussion closed the meeting with the remark, "I want to thank our speaker and all you men and you *girls* who entered into this interesting discussion." The speaker gave him a piercing look, then shrugged her shoulders.

This only serves to illustrate the point that the problems of sexism in our time do not respond very effectively to recitals of the sociological ills people suffer on account of the inequities that are in practice between the sexes. What must be dealt with is far more deep-seated than the symptoms in our society. If symptomatic treatment is able to alleviate immediate distress, it serves a useful purpose, but the basic need for cure remains. This begins with the need to clarify the real issues, which have their foundations not so much in anatomy as in the ways, historically and culturally, that people have become used to regarding the differences between what is "masculine" and what is "feminine." It is these psychological attitudes that have been responsible for the formulation of the gender roles that openly and subtly, consciously and unconsciously, have been transmitted through the generations.

Jung's advice long ago that "woman must learn to criticize and hold her opinions at a distance; not in order to repress them, but, by investigating their origins, to penetrate more deeply into the background, where she will then discover the primordial images,"[16] provided the challenge that led me to the investigations which follow. The labyrinthine search was the outcome of a question I had to ask myself, if I believed that woman was truly oppressed and relegated to an inferior position. The question was this, "What has been behind woman's willingness to accept her limited and defined status over the years, on terms dictated largely by members of the dominant male sex?"

# Chapter 5

## In the Midst of Chaos the Woman Danced

There was a time long ago when men and women lived their myths. In doing so they knew that they were indissolubly bound to the cosmos, and that in their daily acts they were enacting the great cosmic dramas. They called forth the sun with their morning prayers, and made the earth fecund with their fertility rites. Then, little by little, they discovered that they were not bound to the cosmos, that all events occurred as a result of predictable causes, that history proceeded in a sequential way, that through information and reason one could gain the knowledge of all things. Theoretically, at least, it would become possible eventually to gain control over the things of this world. Therefore, men and women studied all their disciplines, their sciences, their philosophies and their arts until everything was on the way to becoming categorized and ordered, and each person knew his or her place. As people found out where they belonged and what tasks were assigned to them, they learned how to function efficiently and effectively. Things were beginning to get better, but somehow life had lost its color; and gradually some of the more soulful among the people began to take a renewed interest in the ancient mythologies. What they found out was not so very different from what today's nuclear physicists are also discovering—that all human beings are indissolubly bound to the cosmos, and that day by day people are enacting the great cosmic dramas.

This is a paraphrase of a Zen teaching.

Androgyny began in a mythic time so distant that one might almost say that Androgyny *was* the beginning of mythic time, for creation was not yet born when Androgyny was. *In illo tempore* there was only a Void, or Chaos, and no one knows what it was, although many have tried to describe the image they have of it. I had some hint, while flying in space in the midst of a cloud, but only when I was able to allow my fantasy to take me out of my body and out of the airplane, until I was totally enveloped in the impenetrable churning nothingness. Still, the cloud was bright, unlike the Void of primordial myth which was before there was even any light, nor was there cold nor

33

heat nor moisture nor dryness. The idea of Chaos, however, suggests a lack of order—yet what would there be to put in order if there were nothing but emptiness? Chaos, however, suggests a lack of order—yet what would there be to put in order if there were nothing but emptiness? Chaos is the potency that exists in the Void, the potentiality for energy within the potentiality for matter.

The Void or the Chaos is the starting point for nearly all creation mythology. People have always tried to imagine what it might have been like before anything of all they knew had come into existence. It is like trying to imagine what it was like before you were born, or even before conception. No entities of any kind were in awareness and then, in some mysterious way some bright spark, some principle, some idea, some image, emerged out of the nothingness. Within that spark, wholly undifferentiated, were contained principles that would eventually be distinguishable as opposites, opposites that would display masculine or feminine natures. Creation mythology has existed wherever people have questioned their own origins; and who has not? These myths depict the Chaos of infinite space, which is experienced by human beings as objective when they let their eyes wander over an oceanic horizon, or as subjective when the psyche remembers in an organic but non-conscious way the formation of the first embryonic cells in the vast wasteland of the womb.

Familiar examples from early Greek cosmogonic myths, so much a part of our Western cultural history, show how an archaic civilization imagined the beginning of the world. The myths provide clues that suggest a lost culture that was predominantly matriarchal. Since so many prehistoric societies are said to have begun under the aegis of the Great Mother, one needs to ask whether their mythologies do not reflect in cosmic scale the individual's early attachment to and dependence on the Mother, which is the common and archetypal experience of all human beings.

Only tantalizing fragments remain of the pre-Hellenic Pelasgian myth, in which the feminine principle calls the masculine principle into being and with his aid brings about the creation of the world. In the beginning the Goddess of All Things, Eurynome, rose naked from Chaos. Finding nothing substantial for her feet to rest upon, she made a separation between the sea and the sky and danced lonely upon the waves. As she danced toward the South she set the wind in motion behind her; then she felt the north wind and took it between her hands and rubbed it, and there was the great serpent, Ophion. Eurynome danced more and more wildly to warm herself, and Ophion grew lustful to see her and coiled himself about her limbs and coupled with her. This is the same north wind, also called Boreas, who is said to fertilize, which is why it is said that mares often turn their hindquarters to the wind and breed foals without the aid of a stallion. So Eurynome likewise became pregnant.

It is said that she then assumed the form of a dove, brooding on the waves. When the time was right, she laid the universal egg. Ophion the serpent coiled himself seven times around it, and remained there until it hatched and split into two parts. Out spilled all the things that exist, the children of Eurynome: the sun, moon, planets and stars, the earth and all that grows upon it. Eurynome and Ophion lived on Mount Olympus until the time when Ophion angered the Great Goddess by claiming that he was the creator of the universe. Furious, she bruised his head with her heel, kicked out his teeth and exiled him to the regions below the earth. Then she created the seven planetary powers, setting a Titan and a Titaness over each: Thetia and Hyperion for the Sun; Phoebe and Atlas for the Moon; Dione and Crius for the planet Mars; Metis and Coeus for the planet Mercury; Themis and Eurymedon for the planet Jupiter; Tethys and Oceanus for Venus; Rhea and Cronus for the planet Saturn. From Ophion's teeth were born the first man, Pelasgus and the race of Pelasgians.[1]

In those few lines are found many mythologems, that is to say, mythological motifs that appear repeatedly in the stories people tell each other in attempting to account for the beclouded past at the edge of history and to carry forward the fading tradition of a people. Is mythology — as Jung and others have thought — a vehicle through which a people projects the contents of the collective psyche upon the external world, in much the same way that an individual projects his personal psychic contents upon his immediate environment? Or might it just be possible that the structures and functions of individual organisms and of the wide cosmos can only be imperfectly perceived and inadequately understood because of the limitations of human consciousness — and that therefore where knowledge wears thin, mythology takes up as the language used to express the meaning of the mysterious in life?

If the language of myth is indeed the speech for the unspeakable and the approach to the unapproachable, what then is to happen to myth when, through the advance of science, more and more is learned about the universe? Will the mythologems become absorbed by the facts until they gradually lose their impact or disappear altogether? To me, this seems unlikely. As knowledge proceeds with spiraling movement to penetrate the vast universe of black mystery, one is continually astounded to discover that at the outer limit of awareness, where science interfaces with the unknown, there is nothing but a growing edge, where knowledge and ignorance meet. The more one learns, the more one discovers the increasing magnitude of the unknown, as anyone who has tried to do "exhaustive" research knows very well!

It is not necessary to be afraid of the awesome darkness. If science cannot penetrate it alone, perhaps intuition can receive light from it. Often when reason has been pushed as far as possible, reason must be suspended and the wisdom of the non-rational must be allowed to express itself. Myth springs from the intuitive faculties. Myth may be relegated to the area of the nonrational, but no one should underestimate the importance of this area in the objective world. Anyone who has the least conception of the workings of human nature knows that, in the long run, it is not the rational considerations that determine most of the decisions that are made in the world, either in the most personal matters or in the course of political events. The old statement about history could be paraphrased to read that he who does not know his *mythology* is forced to live it out in his life. It should not be — as Blake wrote:

That Man should Labour & sorrow, learn & forget, & return
To the dark valley whence he came, to begin his labour
anew.[2]

Creation mythologies yield themes that repeat themselves with endless variations all over the face of the earth. The recognition of certain patterns makes it possible to discover more about the archetypal substructure of the human psyche. The patterns provide a basis for rethinking the sexual theories that have prevailed in our society since the days of Freud and Jung but that in our day have been seriously attacked. It may be time for a radically different theory of human sexuality. Such a theory will be the outcome of much serious study and research, by a variety of scholars, psychologists and analysts, of the social condition. I believe the time is ripe for the development of a new sexual theory, but the magnitude of the task is too great to be undertaken by one person. I see my own role as that of one who may offer a few suggestions as to the direction in which the new sexual theory may evolve. Unless such a theory is based on the archetypal fundaments of the human personality, as shows over and over again in the myths people have told to each other in order to explain themselves and their world, the theory will be superficial and ephemeral. Any steps in the direction of revising sexual theory require at least a passing awareness of the pervasive mythological motifs. The Pelasgian creation myth just related contains several examples of such mythologems: The Great Mother, Primordial Separation, Loneliness, Dance, The Serpent and the Cosmic Egg.

*The Mother of All, the Supernal Mother, the Creatrix* appears in the very beginning in early matriarchal myths. In this one, she is Eurynome. She was also Rhea and Demeter; Ishtar and Astarte, goddesses of war and fertility; Mater Matuta of Etruria; Eileithyia, Mother of the Golden Dawn; and Isis. There is no end to her names or to the tales about her. In Sumer she appears as Iahu, the exalted dove. The Near East paid homage to her in an age before there were gods or priests. Woman was then the dominant sex, as the myths recount, and men feared women. The role of the father was not taken into consideration, or it was treated lightly, for people believe that women became pregnant through the wind, or the eating of a seed, or swallowing an insect. There are tales, also, of the overcoming of the Great Goddess. In the Babylonian spring festival, she is manifested in a dove, which is sliced in two by Marduk. Her all-powerful image had to be defeated and destroyed whenever and wherever the race of men sought their identity as independent beings no longer in servitude to the Great Mother. Thus destruction of the Goddess in ancient myth prepared the way for subordination of the feminine principle.

*The Separation of the Primordial Unity* is a mythologem that usually appears after the epiphany of the Creator God or Goddess, but sometimes before. The primal separation must take place before anything further can occur. It is the first step in organizing the Chaos. In the Pelasgian myth the division is between air and water, or dryness and moisture, or above and below. When there are two principles, there can be an interaction between them, and that interaction is the beginning of creation.

Another often-recurring theme is that of *Loneliness*. It was reason enough, the ancients believed, for the creation of a world. A Total Being who contains everything within himself or herself — not as reality but only *in potentia* — must be lonely indeed in the midst of endless emptiness. If, as in other myths, the world was created by thought, the One and Absolute Being's first thought must have been consciousness of utter Loneliness. The theme reappears in our own myth, when the God of the Old Testament realizes that it is not good for a man to be alone, and therefore makes Eve for the sake of Adam's well-being.

The creation of the world through *Dance* is a mythologem at least as old as Siva, the Cosmic Dancer. Heinrich Zimmer writes:

> . . . he embodies himself and simultaneously gives manifestation of Eternal Energy. The forces gathered and projected in his frantic and ever-enduring gyration, are the powers of the evolution, maintenance and dissolution of the world. Nature and all its creatures are the effects of this eternal dance.[3]

The mythologem of the Dance is also as new as the ever-moving atoms that modern physics sees as basic to the structure of the material world.

*The Serpent* is the consort of Eurynome. Often in myth the serpent is seen

in company with the Primordial Mother. Like the wind, he is filled to overflowing with energy. This phallic lord is sometimes the embodiment of the
demi-urge; sometimes he appears as the adversary of a god, sometimes as
the adversary of a man. The capacity for eternal renewal lies in his ability
to shed his skin (his "mortal evil") whenever he outgrows it; thus he is immortal. On ancient Greek frescoes, the serpent is often found near Demeter and
the other goddesses who carry the meaning of birth-giving and nourishing
and making the earth fruitful. His sinuous form is ever-present at the Eleusinian mystery rites, where the rhythms of birth and death in agriculture and
in man are performed in procession and dance in honor of Demeter. When
the sons of men return in death to the earth, their mother, it is the serpent
who offers them the hope of ever-lasting life. In our Judeo-Christian culture
myth the first woman becomes activated through the agency of the serpent.
Until his arrival, she is passive and withdrawn, langorously enjoying the
paradisiac luxury of innocence. Before Eve and after, the role of the wily serpent as a dynamic element penetrates the mythology of every land were ser-
pents dwell. He enters a situation and — often through doing mischief — brings
about a series of events that lead to transformation.

One more mythologem to touch upon with this archaic tale is the image
of the *Cosmic Egg,* that wonder of mysteries which demands faith and rewards
it. The delicate shell of the egg keeps its contents warm and safe from harm.
Within are contents that are becoming differentiated, even while resting together in perfect unity. The process can be trusted to develop in the way that
it will, for as long as it takes to happen. Then the shell that must not be broken prematurely, breaks of itself, and the new thing comes into being.

The Homeric version of the creation myth differs from the Pelasgian in that
all gods and all living creatures are said to have originated in the river of Oceanus, which circles the world. The Universal Female, Tethys, ruled the sea,
like Eurynome; and Oceanus wrapped himself about the Universe, like
Ophion.[4] But the Orphics says that the Mother of All was black-winged Night
who, embraced by the wind, laid a silver egg (the moon) in the womb of Darkness. Eros, who was also called Phanes, was hatched from this egg, and was
born double-sexed.This androgynous god of Love was golden-winged and had
four heads; he was the one who set the universe in motion.[5]

The matriarchal principle is evident in these earliest Greek myths, and it
is not until an invasion of northern Greece by Aryan peoples from the East
that evidence of a struggle for the recognition of the masculine principle is
reflected in the Olympian creation mythology. This myth in which Mother
Earth (Ge) lies in union with Father Sky (Uranus) allows the First Father to
be identified with the invading peoples of Varuna, one of the Aryan male trinity.
Although Uranus is identified with the pastoral god, his Greek name is the
masculine form of Ur-ana, the Goddess, in her orgiastic midsummer aspect.[6]
The androgynous nature of the original Greek God-concept is implicit here.

The continuous embrace of this primordial pair brought forth only mon-
sters and Cyclopes as offspring. Their father, disgusted, threw them down into

Tartarus, a place as far below the earth as the earth is below the sky, so that it takes a falling anvil nine days to reach the depths of it. The Great mother was angered by the loss of her children, ghastly as they were; and when the race of Titans had come into being and grown to adulthood she called upon Cronus, the youngest of the seven, to take revenge upon Uranus. Cronus lay in wait until his father was asleep, then grasping his father's genitals with his left hand—which has ever afterwards been known as the hand of ill omen—castrated his father with the flint sickle his mother had provided for him. He threw the genitals of Uranus into the sea which had been impregnated by them.

Cronus assumed power, and sometime later he released the monstrous Cyclopes. Then he married his sister Rhea. The two ruled the skies, together with their brother and sister Titans, who became the planetary powers. After a while Cronus again imprisoned the Cylopes. It had been prophesied by Mother Earth and her dying mate that Cronus would be dethroned by one of his own children; therefore each year as Rhea bore him a child, he swallowed it; Hestia, Demeter, Hades and Poseidon, in turn. But when Zeus was born Rhea would have no more of Cronus' fiendish destruction. She gave the child back to Mother Earth, who carried him to a cave to be reared by woodland nymphs with Goat-Pan for his foster brother.[7] Eventually Zeus grew up and fulfilled the prophecy—liberating the gods and goddesses from the belly of their father.

The interplay of anger and tenderness, of love and strife, was characteristic of the Great Mother as she appeared in these early creation myths. Her aspects of tenderness and love were stressed in the writings of Hesiod, who described a Golden Age following Creation as a time of paradise on earth, "an idealized, remote and unrecapturable dream of man's childhood, when the immortals walked the earth as human men and women."[8] It was the time of lost civilizations, of Atlantis and other fabled communities of which scarcely any traces remain except for the old myths.

After the passing of the Golden Age came a time called by Hesiod the "Silver Age," but the one which poets refer to as the Golden Age. Powerful gynocracies distinguished this civilization in which the Great Goddess was worshiped in her many forms in Sumer, Egypt and Crete. Again, Hesiod relates that in this age "men were utterly subject the their mothers, and dared not disobey them even though they lived to be a hundred years old. They never made sacrifices, never learned to hunt or kill, and never were sent forth to war."[9]

Erich Fromm, in a contemporary reading of Hesiod, attributed the sense of bliss that pervaded this age to the belief in the Great Mother. Diana of Ephesus with many breasts loved all her children equally, in contrast to the the later Father God whose love was conditional upon the behavior of the children: Unless they were totally obedient and conformed to his every dictate, they were subject to the cruelest punishment, even to death.[10]

J. J. Bachofen (1815-87), an attorney and historian of Roman law, became fascinated by the Great Mother and the legends about her rule in archaic

Greece. George Boas described him as "one of those men who see a problem in what is generally accepted as unproblematic."[11] Bachofen was not content with writing the history of law as a series of verbal changes; what intrigued him were the alternative in men's appraisals of human life and the revisions of social organization that necessitate changes in the law. Legal history presented and arranged the facts that were known to have brought about changes in the law, but legal history was not given to speculation about the broader sociological and political movements that formed a substructure for the facts and endowed them with meaning. He saw that the law was an attempt to reconcile opposing factors in a world of protagonists and antagonists, and realized that an understanding of something more basic than their differences might provide a meeting ground of commonality. Since the facts themselves did not provide this broader view, Bachofen turned to myth and symbol to explain the development of the strong patriarchal society and the authoritarian methods of government that expressed themselves through Roman law. The crucial extrapolation upon which his theory was based was this: "The strictness of the patriarchal system [in Rome] points to an earlier system that had to be combated and suppressed."[12] This older system had been deduced by Bachofen and others from its traces in mythology.[13]

Bachofen notes:

> The mythical tradition may be taken as a faithful reflection of the life in those time in which historical antiquity is rooted. It is a manifestation of primordial thinking, an immediate historical revelation, and consequently a highly reliable source.[14]

Bachofen's studies of myth may have convinced him that at one time matriarchal cultures were prevalent over much of the world, but his theory was generally discredited when it was first enunciated. Anthropologists were unable to find any primitive societies extant that corresponded to the mythological ones Bachofen had described, and so they assumed that none could have existed, or in any case not over the broad areas Bachofen had intimated.

While certain of the details of the presumed social movements of prehistoric times are still open to question, recent archaeological discoveries have established that a matriarchal society did in fact exist in at least some of the places Bachofen had mentioned. Joseph Campbell wrote in 1964, in his Introduction to *Myth, Religion and Mother Right*, that Bachofen's intuition of an age of mother-right has been irrefutably confirmed by such archaeological finds as the ruins of Cretan Knossos, uncovered by Sir Arthur Evans, and the subsequent deciphering by Michael Ventris of some of the writings discovered there. Evidence was also found from that pre-Hellenic treasure trove to substantiate Bachofen's recognition of Syria and Asia Minor as the proximate Asiatic provinces from which the agriculturally based, mother-right culture complex was transferred to the isles and peninsulas of Greece and Rome.[15] Since the time that Campbell wrote his Introduction to Bachofen's essay, archaeologist have been busily at work in Turkey uncovering incontrovertible facts that have caused historians to revise their entire concepts of the remote past of human history.

James Mellaart, the archaeologist in charge of the excavation of three prehistoric sites in Anatolia, chronicled his discoveries in Çatal Hüyük (a neolithic town), and they established firmly the existence of not only a matriarchal but also a utopian society.

> There had been no wars for a thousand years. There was an ordered pattern to society. There were no human or animal sacrifices. Vegetarianism prevailed, for domestic animals were kept for milk and wool—not for meat. There is no evidence of violent deaths. . .Above all, the supreme deity in all the temples was a goddess.[16]

Mellaart was able to draw sociological implications from his examination of remains of the houses, with their living quarters and their burial platforms. By studying the burial customs it was possible to affirm that the small corner platform belonged to the male, the master, while the much larger and main platform belonged to the mistress of the house. The woman's bed never changed its place, but the man's bed did.[17]

The woman was the center about whom the life of the family revolved. But her importance did not stop there.

Mellaart describes a shrine with its wall paintings:

> An enormous red bull occupied the great part of the north wall, once again emphasizing the strength of the religious tradition at Çatal Hüyük, where bulls always occupy this position facing the Taurus ("Bull") mountains, perhaps not a coincidence. The image of a great bull, over six feet long, dominates the decoration of the shrine. The awe inspired by this monster is clearly shown by the small size of the male figures that surround it.[18]

Taurus, the bull as a recurring symbol of gynocracy, was a strong sex symbol. It traditionally represented the male principle in a female-dominated world. The horns, a powerful sex symbol also, adorned many of the temples and shrines associated with the worship of the Great Goddess. The bull and the phallus, symbols of generation, were infallible indications of the presence of gynarchic societies in the age of Taurus.

# Chapter 6

## The Golden Age of the Mother and the Rebellion of Her Sons

Taurus gave its name to the astrological epoch that corresponds to the period from about 4000 B.C. to 2000 B.C., the time of the fabled gynocratic societies. If, as the old myths state, the long-lost Golden Age was the first and finest period, then each succeeding age has been more tarnished than the one that preceded it. Whatever the androgynous unity that appeared at the golden dawn of creation as a fantasy of pure paradise, that were none but the immortals to enjoy it. When human lives emerged from the womb of Eternal Life, mortality began, and with it the Age of Silver. The finite creatures were born frail and weak, unlike the goddesses who had sprung forth full-grown — Athena from the head of Zeus or Aphrodite from the bloody foam of the sea where Sky's severed member had fallen.

The human race was in its childhood; the children needed their mother. In the infancy of mankind the Great Mother cared for all. As her sons and daughters basked in her loving kindness they failed to notice the power of her utter domination. The Age of Taurus is the mythic history of humanity's awakening in the arms of the all-embracing Mother, of its trust in her undergoing transformation into worship and awe, of its awe being transformed into fear, of its fear becoming an impetus to growth and, at the end of the Age, human growth and development made possible the thrust toward independence from the nurturing Mother whose power had become so pervasive as to threaten the autonomy of her sons (although not that of her daughters, who stood to inherit her authority).

When we recall the archaic times we fuse history and myth, the two being indistinguishable in mythic memory. History is the impact upon us of the world outside of our own personal boundaries; myth is the voice of the collective psyche interpreting in its own way what a people perceives and experiences in the world. This relationship between history and myth is no less applicable when contemporary events are considered, although people may perhaps be less conscious of it because they are closed to the phenomena and consequently they experience the history in only one dimension. It becomes clearer when

one reads widely divergent newspaper accounts of some distant and emotionally charged event of international importance. Each reporter's interpretation
weaves its own myth of meaning in and out of the warp of facts. In any discussion of historic times, it becomes necessary to admit a tendency to combine perceived fact with experienced myth. Myth and history, which seem
to represent opposing approaches, actually may be complementary to each
other. Their interaction forms the very struggle that unites to construct reality. Both warp and woof are required to make a fabric, both inner and outer
to make a vessel, both male and female to create a human being. History
and myth are needed to give shape and dynamism to events; but often one
confounds the other. It is easier to recognize our myths when dealing with
ages long past. We tend to confuse the myths of the more recent past with
our view of history.

The Mother religions and the Taurean epoch continued into the Early
Bronze Age. A high degree of civilization was achieved at Mycenae in the
Peloponnesus and on the island of Crete, even before the Hellenes came into
the Greek peninsula soon after 2000 B.C. At Knossos excavations in the
ruins of the palace of the kings called "Minos" revealed may chambers beautifully tiled with mosaics depicting gracious ladies gowned in laces and em-
broidered robes, and fashionably coiffed. Their marble baths boasted a
plumbing system such as is hard to believe existed at so early a time. The
civilization was not limited to people of privilege. While most of Europe was
still in a primitive stage, the ordinary Cretan was living in a house of sun-
dried brick with a stone foundation and windows.

Here arose the legend of the Minotaur. The terrible monster, half man and
half bull, was the fruit of Queen Pasiphaë's passion for a magnificent white
bull. This was the same bull who had emerged from the sea at the command
of King Minos when that monarch had boasted that he could make the gods
do whatever he wanted. Some say Pasiphaë's monstrous lust was Poseidon's
way of punishing Minos for his effrontery to the god of the sea by not sacrificing the bull to him. Others say it was Zeus' wrath, while still others say that
it was Aphrodite, who Pasiphaë had failed to propitiate for several years. At
any rate, so great was the power of woman in those days that the husband
of the queen had to keep the Minotaur imprisoned in a labyrinth on the royal
estate, and to feed the Minotaur's insatiable appetite by sacrificing twelve of
the fairest youths and maidens from Greece each year. It was never quite clear
whether the Minotaur was prisoner of the King, or the other way around.

The overwhelming potency of the dazzling-white bull was known much earlier on the island of Crete. The tale is told of Europa, who lived near Tyre
in Canaan, a maiden of such exquisite charms that she caught the eye of Zeus
himself. Seeing her walking at the seashore, Zeus disguised himself as the
snow-white bull and joined the herd that was grazing nearby. He had small
gemlike horns, between which ran a single black streak. When Europa saw
him she was struck by his beauty and, finding him gentle, mastered her fear
and began to play with him. He knelt down and she climbed upon his back,

whereupon he ambled slowly toward the sea. When they arrived at the water's edge, he slipped swiftly into it and swam away with Europa on his back, across the sea to Crete where he was to rape her and "father upon her" Minos, who would become king, and two other sons. So runs the story as it was told in later times when the power of Zeus had been established. In that later patriarchal time, the expression "fathered upon" was used to describe the conception of a child, as though the mother were, in the true Apollonian sense, only the ground upon which the seed is sown and not of importance as parent. But in the earlier version of the tale, probably as recounted during the Taurian Age, it is Europa who seduces the noble bull with "crescent horns aglow like silver moons," and boldly rides him across the sea to the new land that will be her home. Myth always bears the psychic imprint of the teller of the tale.

In mainland Greece the cult of Demeter flowered in an agricultural civilization. Demeter was the second born of the Olympian goddesses, after Hestia, daughter of the union between Rhea and Cronus. Demeter was the Earth Goddess, and though she had no husband she had many lovers. She was Mater, she was maternal, and her legendary love and longing for her daughter, the Kore (which means simply "maiden" ), is well known. But Demeter was not only the mother of a beloved child, she was also the mother of matter, of all material things, and especially of all that grows from the earth. As such she was the exemplary feminine, she was womb, she was the one responsible for nurturing mankind, and her dominance over the matriarchal state was unquestioned. Demeter stood for the exclusivity of marriage for mortal beings, although as a goddess she herself was not subject to such rules. She fostered the regulation of motherhood and demanded the primacy of the generative womb.

There is a tradition that the matriarchal state, personified by Demeter, was a rebellion against the widespread promiscuity engaged in by *hetaerae* (courtesans) and sacred prostitutes before sexuality became regulated for the protection of women. But the theory of an earlier savage stage when women were supposed to have indulged in an unbridled expression of sexual lust may have no more historical basis than the other theory that a primal horde of males killed of a tribal father who supposedly kept all the women under his control for his exclusive sexual use. Nevertheless, the strict discipline of matriarchal rule under Demeter, and the conjugal chastity that was practiced then, makes sense only if we assume with Bachofen the existence of earlier, cruder conditions.

Even the virtuous life becomes a burden when carried to extremes. The purity of the cult of Demeter, growing overzealous, was no exception. Conventional behavior became rigid and eventually the strict observance broke down. Then, as now, alternatives arose and challenged the establishment's culture. Also, in other places other styles prevailed, for different people found different ways to solve a problem.

When a psychological need arises it seems that inevitably the deeper layers of the collective unconscious are activated, and sooner or later the memory of a myth, an event, or an earlier psychic state emerges into consciousness. The women of mainland Greece, becoming disenchanted with the constrict- ing demands of the worship of Demeter, recalled to each other the stories of the fabled Amazons who were supposed to have inhabited the Anatolian plain before their descendants, the Ionians, set forth to colonize the Greek islands and the Peloponnese, where the Myceanean civilization was born. Historians still doubt that a tribe of Amazons actually did exist, although the artifacts discovered by Mellaart and other archaeologist in the Çatal Haüyük area— which is now Turkey—show women as attacking in battle with sword in hand, or driving war chariots, or armed with bow and arrow.

The mythology of Greece, even of the later Hellenistic period, abounds with Amazon figures. If not explicitly Amazons, their behavior is characterized by a detachment from men, if not an outright hostility toward them. Queen Hypsipule, a descendant of the Amazon, Myrine, led her followers to kill their husbands and the other men of the island of Lemnos, and afterward assumed authority over the island. Other women of this category were Atalanta, the swift runner; Harpalyke, who was called "predatory wolf" and was the sub- ject of Virgil's writing; also Cammila, the "warrior woman," and Kyrene who tamed lions and whom Apollo eagerly sought; and Britomartis, who was chased for months by King Minos, until at last she eluded him by jumping into an ocean spring.[1]

Women of Greece who were inspired by the Amazon myths took Artemis as their goddess. The divine huntress declared her self-sufficiency and pro- tected her virginity. She and her followers would go to any lengths to keep from being possessed by a man or from being ruled by a government of men. Her worshippers may have represented a reaction to the appearance of the Zeus religion that was brought in by the Indo-European invaders, the Dori- ans. Artemis is antithetical to the patriarchal spirit of the invaders who over- came the native population and set themselves up as rulers. The mythologem of the Amazon, as female archer who has burned away her right breast to accommodate the bow, speaks to a symbolic renunciation of the purely femi- nine nature of woman as exemplified by Demeter, and to the adoption of a masculine component as dominating element in her way of being. The Artemis-Amazon type of woman is a phenomenon that often comes to the fore in a period of transition between two cultural epochs. Rejecting the to- tally feminine as her ruling element, she also sets herself against the invading masculine power by attempting to be even more powerful. She is the proto- type of the radical feminist who has little interest in relating to man. In an- cient art and artifacts her martial aspects are symbolized by her hunter's garb or by her theriomorphic appearance as a horned bitch.[2]

The Amazon woman is not the same as the androgyne, although she may serve as a preform for the androgyne. The Amazon is a woman who has tak- en on characteristics that are generally associated with the masculine disposi- tion but, rather than integrating the "masculine" aspects that could make her strong, *as woman,* she identifies with the power aspect of the "masculine." At the same time, she renounces the capacity to relate lovingly, a quality that has been traditionally associated with the feminine. Whether these qualities are, actually, feminine or masculine will be discussed at length later, but it seems clear enough that these qualities are opposite in nature—so that the Amazon woman who takes on the power as she negates the capacity to relate lovingly to other human beings, becomes one-sided, and consequently, she is the victim of the very attribute she had tried to overwhelm.

Determined, aggressive, fearsome and one-sided as the Amazon is, she nevertheless paves the way for the emergence of the woman of androgynous nature. Had the Amazon type never broken the stereotype of "femininity," the independent woman of self-esteem would never have found the courage to make her voice heard. It is, as it always was, the extremists of the world who initiate changes that the moderates only later make palatable to the broader ranges of society.

This transitional female element appears in the form of Hippolyte, Queen of the Amazons. According to one legend she is the daughter of Aphrodite and Ares. Another has it that the progenitors of the race of Amazons sprang from that union, and that Hippolyte was one of the later queens. At any rate, she ruled a tribe that reckoned descent only through the mother. Her predecessor, Lysippe, had laid it down that the men must perform all the household tasks while the women fought and governed. Some say that the arms and legs of the baby boys were broken to incapacitate them from war or travel. Others relate that the boys were sent back to the land of their fathers, on whose borders they had been conceived during an annual month of ritual sacrifice and promiscuous intercourse. It was also reported that the Amazons had captured Troy on one expedition, while King Priam was yet a child.

As daughter or descendant of Aphrodite and Ares, Hippolyte carries within her nature on one side, everything that is beautiful and charming and feminine; and on the other, the striving, ruthless warring nature of Ares. Were she united within herself, she could be the androgyne to perfection, but she is not. Her father, Ares, had given his daughter his own girdle, and this she *wears* as evidence of chastity, or psychologically, of her unwillingness to bring together the feminine and masculine elements of her nature. Hera, the guardian of fertility and marriage, true to form as Mother Goddess, sends her son, Heracles, to capture the girdle of Hippolyte as the ninth of his labors in his mother's service. At the same time, Hera prevents him from getting it. The girdle symbolizes the bond between daughter and father, a bond from which the daughter cannot free herself. Hippolyte has seen Heracles, and has found herself attracted to him. She would have removed the girdle and given it to him, but according to one version of the tale, Hera goes about disguised as one of the Amazons and spreads rumors that a stranger is plotting to kill Hippolyte. The Amazons, hearing this, attack the ship of Heracles; and Heracles, suspecting treachery, kills Hippolyte. In another version of the myth, Hippolyte refuses to give up the girdle and is killed in the struggle that ensues as Heracles attempts to fulfill the wishes of his mother. The power of

Hera, which is supposed to be directed toward supporting the institution of marriage, also undermines the development of the love between man and woman by holding fast to her son and preventing his union with Hippolyte. The Amazon queen is caught in the classic conflict between a matriarchal society, which seeks control of the male children, and a patriarchal society, which seeks control of the females. The resolution must be a one-sided one, because a peaceful union cannot take place. Any real solution would have to be androgynous; Hippolyte approaches, but cannot achieve, this ideal. Yet she remains the prototype for those women who seek to be defined in their own terms, rather than in terms either of convention, or of revolution.

Myths tell also of another sort of woman, the roving bands of Maenads, who left their staid lives in the Grecian community to wander in the Thracian wilds following Dionysus, the god of wine and madness. As the Amazons, with whom there is some association, have a relationship with only one god, their father Ares; so the Maenads have a relationship with only one god, Dionysus. This relationship, like the former, is extremely problematic. Dionysus is the son of only one parent, Zeus. He was originally conceived out of Zeus' union with the mortal, Semele. Semele had boasted to her friends that she was carrying the child of the greatest of gods, and they had taunted her to make him reveal himself visibly to her. Zeus had warned her that no one might look upon him and live; nevertheless Semele insisted until she gained her demand, and in her encounter with Zeus in his full blinding immediacy, she was struck dead. Zeus took the unborn child from her womb and sewed him into a hollow place in his own thigh until he was ready to be born. Hera, the jealous wife, again plays a role in setting the legalism of marriage against the free enjoyment of love. She orders the Titans to tear the new-born into shreds and then boil him in a cauldron, which they do. Nevertheless, he is reconstituted by his grandmother Rhea, and entrusted by Zeus to Persephone for his safety. Persephone, who is alternately enchained by female power in the form of Demeter and by male power in the form of Hades, places the infant Dionysus with King Athamas and his wife Ino. Dionysus is kept in the women's quarters and disguised as a girl in order to keep him from being discovered by Hera. He is treated and educated like a girl and he grows up to be effeminate. Unable to differentiate feminine from masculine functioning in himself, he scarcely knows who he is. Like an eternal youth he wanders over the world, changing shape, going mad, drinking himself into insensibility, living the abandonment of total nature and, like nature, experiencing the cycles of death and rebirth.

Dionysus is not the true androgyne any more than Hippolyte was, for he has not come to peace with his feminine side. His masculine and feminine aspects are not fused, they are merely confused. The women who follow him, and whose tale is dramatically presented in Euripides' *The Bacchae*, are equally confused—between their wine and their madness. They have deserted their own feminine natures, and they have not, therefore, been able to experience the strong masculine element which functions in a complementary relationship to the feminine. Wholeness is not achieved, for frenzy is not freedom. This sorry state of affairs is an outcome of the never-ending struggles for power carried on by the masculine and feminine principles, as mythologically incarnated in the figures of Zeus and Hera.

The Mother, first as the divine Earth herself, then in her many forms as Great Goddess, Mother Goddess, and also in her ruling role as human representative or queen ruling by authority of the Goddess, had held the human race in thralldom until the dawn of historical time. So it was, according to ancient traditions of many lands. Then in one place and then in another, men outgrew the childhood of the race and developed into rebellious adolescents, determined to assert their own wills and to exercise their capacity for active aggression. On the transpersonal level, father gods wrested power from the Great Mother Goddess and her company; and politically, the new patriarchies displaced the matriarchies of old.

In the process, it was necessary to establish the incest prohibition, whereby the son's defiance of the mother, despite his longing for her, might be supported. Only by leaving the world of the mother and becoming initiated into the society of men, from which women were in certain respects ritually excluded, could men band together and establish their solidarity and strength. The feminine had to be suppressed in the world; that is, relegated to a lesser position in society. And within himself, man had to repress his own feminine nature lest it betray him with its softness, its impetuosity, and its tendency to submit to the demands of passion and of nature.

# Chapter 7

## Monotheism in a Patriarchal System:
## Its Disintegration into Polytheism

During the Late Bronze Age, the time of Homer's Achaeans—the heroes of Troy—Aries, the age of the Ram, was ushered in. The name Aries was associated with the sheepherding nomads who entered Greece from Anatolia in Asia Minor, and who perhaps in the more distant past had traveled further eastward into India. One of these may have been Rama, the dissident Aryan who converted India from gynarchy and goddess worship to patriarchy and the worship of gods about five thousand years ago.[1] Rama was India's first patriarchal hero. Before Rama, women in India were regarded as divine beings and were entrusted with law and justice, philosophy and the arts. Rama, who was unable to overthrow the rule of the feminine in his own country, may have departed for India in search of power, or he may have been expelled. This would explain the existence of the Rama myth in both Europe and India.

After two thousand years of matriarchal cultures under the astrological sign of Taurus, the bull, the next two-thousand-year period preceding the birth of Jesus was known as the Age of the Ram. Around 2000 B.C., Aries began to replace Taurus as a cultural dominant. Patriarchy began to lay claim to a position of power, a claim that it has not relinquished to this day. The aggressive, intrusive Ram was not deterred once he discovered his potency. Unsuccessful in Asia Minor, he traveled into the wilds of northern Greece, where he gathered strength and power.

By the time the Dorians swept down from Europe through Thrace, around 1000 B.C., bringing the dark ages to Greece, the world Hesiod had described had been relegated to vague remembrance and traces of oral tradition—that world "with its dominant mother lavishing eternal loving care on an ever-dependent son who, growing more physically than spiritually, lived beside his mother to a ripe old age, enjoying the peace and abundance of an agricultural life."[2] Passing also, were the fading memories of the age of which Erich Newmann wrote so comprehensively, the early history of consciousness when the male sex, far from living in peace and bliss under the aegis of an ever-loving mother, had also to fear the terrible and deadly mother, the goddess who was

51

both mother and virgin, and the hetaera who belonged to no man but stood impersonal, ready for anyone who, like herself, was in the service of fertility.[3]

The Iron Age began in Greece when the Dorians brought with them their own new god, Zeus. Goddess worship was virtually abolished as the Dorians set up shrines to Zeus and his family throughout the land. Myth again confounds history, as when Euhemerus tells us that at the time of the patriarchal Zeus revolution the people of the Golden Age became the minor gods and goddesses and ascended into an upper world, while the people of the Silver and Bronze ages were consigned by the Dorians to Hades because of their refusal to pay due honor to Zeus and the Olympians.[4]

This cataclysmic separation of the masculine and feminine can be understood psychologically as the creation of a duality that was the inevitable though long-delayed consequence of the disintegration of the primordial androgyny. The gods and goddesses, representing the principle of immortally or of spirit, were separated from earth and elevated to a higher level of existence. Those men and women who did not recognize the gods were punished by being relegated to a lower state, a state characterized by earth, by the body and its mortality, and by the animal nature of humanity. The world of spirit from that time on was placed over and against the world of human men and women. More and more the gods and goddesses were worshipped from afar, and less and less did they make excursions down to earth to take their pleasures with mortal beings.

In the land of Canaan, also, Aries began making its presence felt at the beginning of the Iron Age. A shepherd people migrated into an agricultural land where nature goddesses were being worshipped to ensure their power for the fertility of the earth. Abraham, the first of the Hebrew patriarchs, was established in his patrimony over his descendants by the appearance in the thicket of the Ram that was to be substituted for the sacrifice of Isaac. It was with Abraham that the covenant was made — to bind the people of Israel to the Father God through the sign of circumcision, the phallic identification of Yahweh's people.

Nor is it by chance that the shepherd analogy abounds in the Old Testament, nor that the golden calf was the object of anathema to the prophets of Israel. Seeking to gain favor with their Father in heaven, the prophets abjured the adoration of things made of wood and stone, the icons of the idolatrous neighbors of the Israelites, and they even inveighed against the Israelites who had become "uncircumcised in heart."

Aries held sway for two thousand years before the birth of Christ, and shaped the world into which Jesus would be born as the first fish of the Pisces era, and would be doomed to die as the last ram (or lamb) of the declining Aries era.[5] The rigorously monotheistic Judaic background of the Christian era left its imprint on the collective psyche of mankind. Its myths have not been eliminated; in fact, they have become even more potent as they have been repressed and concealed under a more liberal contemporary facade. The history of the Aries era provides a background for the myth of male superiority in the countless legends of the patriarchy of men under the fatherhood of God.

*Bereshith*, "in the beginning," is the time-honored phrase that starts the Hebrew culture myth. It is the same as "once upon a time," or "there was a time long, long ago," or *"in illo tempore."* All these expressions mean that what is about to follow pertains to a mythical time that has its beginning and end in the human psyche, that spinner of never-ending tales about itself. In that time that never was, we discover the time that always is, for Creation is a never-beginning and never-ending process, as far as we can understand it. Everyone, no matter how simple or naive, how sophisticated and learned, addresses himself or herself to the questions, "Where did I come from" "Where am I?" and "Where do I go from here?" All that we can truly experience and know is the present, the "eternal now," yet all of the past is embedded in it, and all of what is to come springs forth from this moment in time. Therefore it is necessary to pay attention to our mythological past although it has faded from view, for the past is also present within the collective psyche, unceasingly creating the conditions that affect our every thought and movement.

Because, as Pope John said in speaking of the Western world, "spiritually we are all Semites," we turn to the Hebrew Bible as repository of the myth of the Hebrew people and the *Urgrund* of her daughter religions, Christianity and Islam. The first chapter of Genesis reads, "In the beginning, God. . ." Who is this "God"? His name is unknown, or if known, it must not be uttered. The name of God is the great mystery, for the naming of anything implied that the one who named it would have a certain power over it. A most significant element of the Hebrew faith was that all power resided in the Lord of Hosts and was derivative from Him. Therefore, no one could presume to gain any power over Him through the utterance of His name. Yet there were names that referred to Him, by which He was approached, in the limited way in which the human being could approach the awesome mystery of the universe, the One in all.

The name *El* was used as an approximation. El was originally the patron god of the shepherds of Palestine, and the bringer of thunderstorms, much like Jupiter or Janus or Bel or Marduk.[6] His nature power was not forgotten by the psalmist:

> O God, when thou didst go forth before thy people,
> when thou didst march through the wilderness,
> the earth quaked, the heavens poured down rain,
> at the presence of God;
> yet Sinai quaked at the presence of God,
> the God of Israel.
>    Rain in abundance, O God, thou didst shed abroad;
> thou didst restore thy heritage as it languished;
> thy flock found a dwelling in it;
> in thy goodness, O God, thou didst provide for the needy.
>                                        (Psalm 68:7-10 RSV)

Here the Hebrew God seems to have been identified with the young male gods in many places in the Near East who were usurping powers that had previously been maintained jealously by the Great Mother and all her divine female offspring. Yet the ancient memory of the Mother Goddess remained, according to Robert Graves, for the people of Palestine associated El with the terebinth, sacred to the Cretan Dove Goddess of Cyprus, and his title Ia-hu ("Jehovah"), meaning "Exalted Dove," seems to have been borrowed from Iahu, or Bahu, the Dove Goddess. But he eventually came to be identified with several local deities, among them a moon god, a sun god, a smith god, a war god, a wine god and a corn god.[7] Iahu, "Exalted Dove," may have been a preform of the Holy Ghost in the form of a dove in the still later Christian tradition.

By the time that the book of Genesis was codified and canonized during and after the Babylonian exile in the sixth century B.C., the Hebrews had become conscious of themselves as a unique people whose God was not to be confused with any of the gods or goddesses who had been worshipped in the places where the Hebrews had traveled in their wanderings. Forgotten or expunged from the corpus of legend was the myth of Eurynome and her dance that inflamed the serpent whom she allowed to coil about her body and to know her. They did not remember that in the process of time the *Mother* took the form of a *dove*, and brooded on the face of the water, and was delivered of a great egg; which the serpent coiled about to hatch, so that it split open and all things were created.[8] Yet in Genesis, *the spirit of God* hovers over the face of the waters. The masculine principle, it would appear, has assimilated the feminine.

The waters tell a different story, but the end of it may be androgynous also. The primordial watery chaos is a feature found in the cosmogonies of Egypt and Phoenicia and in Vedic literature. The accounts of Creation in both the Babylonian cosmogonic myth, *Enûmah elish,* and in Genesis present an etymological equivalence in the names by which this watery mass is designated. In *Enûmah elish* the word is *Ti'âmat;* in Genesis, *tehôm,* which occurs in 1:2 and is usually translated as "the deep." Though coming from the same root, these words do not denote the same thing. Ti'âmat is a mythic personality, the great chthonic Mother Goddess who gives birth to all creation.[9] The first tablet of *Enûmah elish* begins:

1. When above the heavens had not (yet) been named,
2. (And) below the earth had not (yet) been called by a name;
3. (When) Apsu primeval, their begetter,
4. Mummu, (and) *Ti'âmat she who gave birth to them all* [Italics mine.]
5. (Still) mingled their waters together,
6. And no pasture land had been formed (and) not even a reed marsh was to be seen;
7. When none of the other gods had been brought into being,
8. When they had not (yet) been called by (their) name(s), and (their) destinies had not (yet) been fixed,
9. (At that time) were the gods created within them, [Within Ti'âmat and Apsû.][10]

*Enûmah elish* refers to the mingling of Ti'âmat (the bitter waters ) and Apsû (the sweet waters) in the divine androgynous matrix. Mummu, who is also present in the moment of creation, probably represented the mist rising from the two bodies of water and hovering over them.[11] Compare Genesis 1:6 where we read, "And God said, 'Let there be a firmament in the midst of the waters, and let it separate the waters from the waters.'"

Thus *Enûmah elish* conceives of the primordial chaos as *living* matter and as being made up in its integral parts of the first two principles, Apsû and Ti'âmat, in whom all the elements of the future universe were commingled. According to Genesis, *tehôm* is nothing but a mass of inanimate matter, the vast amount of water from which the waters above the firmament were separated from the waters below the firmament and out of which dry land emerged. While *tehôm* stands for the entire body of water, *Ti'âmat* represents only one *part* of it, the other being represented by Apsû, who has no parallel in the biblical creation story.

It seems that the Hebrew scribes, in setting down their own sacred document, eliminated anything that would undermine the belief in the Father God, the One-God who was the deity of Israel. Thus anything in their own tradition that resembled the two aspects of the Babylonian myth had to be excluded in order to retain the purity of the Hebrew conception. They expunged all references to creation as the product of an androgynous god-goddess and to the offspring of that mingled pair, namely a company of gods and goddesses that would require a polytheistic religion to serve them.

One cannot help but wonder if more traces of what was suppressed remain in the Genesis creation narrative. Interpreters and commentators of the Bible assert that there is evidence to support a positive conclusion.

It is easy enough to understand why the Hebrews, having returned to the Land of Israel after many wanderings throughout the Egyptian and Syrian deserts and the wilderness of Sinai, should insist upon the supremacy of their own tribal deity, the male god Yahweh. Battles between tribal nations were imagined as a conflict between tribal gods, and each side called upon its deity to show superior power by allowing the people who served him or her to be victorious in the fight. Since earth-mother-fertility goddesses were being worshipped in the agricultural societies into which the Hebrew nomads came, it became necessary that the patriarchal principle challenge the matriarchal authority. As long as Yahweh remained a tribal god of a particularistic people, there was not very much difference in the basic nature of the struggles that ensued in the land of Israel from those that occurred when the Dorians brought Zeus to challenge the hegemony of the older goddesses in Crete and Mycenae, or when Marduk destroyed Ti'âmat in Babylonia. The Hebrews' god was a self-proclaimed "jealous god," warning his people, "Thou shalt have no other god before me." This was clearly an acknowledgment that though other gods or goddesses might exist, they were not to be worshipped by the people of Yahweh. Although the Hebrews claimed to be a monotheistic people, there was in them a tacit acceptance of polytheism, else how would their

god be provoked into contesting for recognition against the worshippers of
Baal?

Yet then, as now, there were always those individuals who stood against
the collective fervor and the collective fury, to touch the core of things and
attest to the unity of all that is. Among the Hebrews, these individuals were
the prophets, those who envisioned the many names of the Holy and all the
manifestations of power in nature as multiple attributes of One Totality. While
others went about worshipping their tribal gods and shrugging at foreign nations who were worshipping their own tribal gods, whether a single god or
a great company of gods and goddesses and nymphs and nixies, the prophets
comprehended that all these were merely images, fragmented images of parts
of the great Whole. Even the image of the masculine and the image of the
feminine were contained in that Whole, as the prophets saw it, for God was
incomplete without his people, Israel. Nor, in the prophetic view, did the term
"Israel" refer only to a limited group of individuals who resided in Canaan
or who were exiled from the land of their fathers. Israel was to be a servant
of God, that is, the *means* by which His *power* was to work in the world. For
*power*, as we have seen and will continue to see, is used consistently as a metaphor for the energy that moves matter; and matter, or the material world,
is understood as the vehicle through which energy can transform itself. What
the prophets knew—and what Einstein discovered about the unity and interdependence of energy and matter—is the essential fact concerning that Wholeness which is divine, yet which needs humanity for its realization. The
parochial god of Israel, through the prophetic revelation, became a God of
all peoples:

> It is too light a thing that you should be my servant
> to raise up the tribes of Jacob
> and to restore the preserved of Israel;
> I will give you as a light to the nations,
> that my salvation may reach to the ends of the earth.
>
> (Isaiah 49:6)

Challenges to the faithful such as these occur throughout the prophetic writings. They are interspersed between frequent diatribes against sinning Israelites who have strayed from the worship of the God of Israel, having become
disaffected or enticed by exotic gods. Only in the period of the Babylonian
Exile were the Hebrew people put to the acid test. No longer in their beloved
land, the prophets feared that their people, as so many other nations had done
before, would either merge their gods with those of their captors or add the
rituals and sacraments of the foreign gods to their own. There were some few
apostates who abandoned Yahweh altogether as they succumbed to the charms
of an idolatrous fantasia. The great test of the Hebrew people came when
they had to make the choice between a pseudo monotheism—which masked
a polytheism by proclaiming that their god was the greatest of all gods—and

a true monotheism — which recognized only one Absolute and Unknowable Majesty, who proclaimed loudly for all nations. "Hear O Israel, the Lord our God, the Lord is One!" The people of Israel often stumbled and fell between the two alternatives, and always there were the particularistic followers of Yahweh who isolated themselves, out of a sense of superiority and from fear of contamination. But there were also those who were careful to maintain the purity of their faith without forgetting its essentially universalistic nature. The two traditions have come down in Judaism, and through Judaism into the Judeo-Christian tradition — out of which our Western culture images of the masculine principle and the feminine principle have been derived.[12] The idea of a Universal God remains somewhat obscured in both faiths; today it shines but dimly through the traditional pseudo-monotheism with their parochial and patriarchal god-images.

The long historical tradition of the so-called inferiority of women is evident in our Judeo-Christian culture myth as soon as we read the creation myth in the second chapter of Genesis (18-22). There we are told that God has fashioned man, that is Adam (*Adamah*, meaning "earth man" because he is made of earth) in His own image. Eve is fashioned only secondarily, and from Adam's rib, to be a helpmate for Adam. In an essay "On Psychological Femininity," James Hillman points out that the primacy of the male in our culture is established in the "first-Adam-then-Eve" narrative in the second chapter of Genesis.[13] He summarizes a great many purportedly "scientific" statements which, over the centuries, have given rise to the conventional view that the female is weak, impure, unripe, imperfect and incomplete. "The male was the prototype, the female the analogue.... The ovaries are inferior testes; female seed is inferior to male.... The male is the realized, perfect, actualized. The female remains in nuce, within the perineum, not yet ripe."[14] So proceeded the old and endless arguments from Aristotle and Galen all the way to Freud.

The myth of female inferiority had been consistently upheld by scientists who, viewing the morphological differences between males and females, preferred the male for their own psychological reasons. The "scientific mind" has been called "Apollonic," emphasizing as it does the characteristics that are associated with the masculine; that is, with itself. These qualities are: consciousness above the unconscious, clarity above mystery, light above darkness, pursuit above receptivity, order above chaos, and discrimination above acceptance. The Apollonic-scientific view values objectivity; thus it must keep its distance from the material under consideration. This view requires the apposition of the feminine or material aspect of nature; but it needs the feminine to be in her "proper" place, namely, the inferior position. Therefore in the Apollonic construct, the relations between the masculine and the feminine are out of balance. This is true both in reference to relationships between men and women and in reference to the masculine/feminine qualities within a man himself. As for woman, this view has little to say about her psychology, as she is regarded nearly as a non-person, finding her identity only through her relationship to a man; as daughter, mother, wife, lover, sister, friend or enemy. Even the old nineteenth-century physiological view, which is in essence reiterated by Freud: "Ideally every child should be a boy,"[15] restates the myth of female inferiority.

One solution that has been suggested for this problem is to invoke the bisexual god, Dionysus, in whom the masculine and the feminine opposites are united. In marked contrast to Apollo, Dionysus — as god of madness, ecstasy, drunkenness and frenzy—was given to wild outbursts of excitement, performed preferably before an audience. The first-Adam-then-Eve view of the psyche required an Apollonic interpretation represented as "light." This would be replaced by a Dionysian view, where the light of spirit would mingle with the darkness of matter and materiality, and where madness would be seen not as insanity but as ritualized religious enthusiasm. If this point of view were carried further, the image of the psyche, here split into two god-images, could be fragmented still further. Every aspect of the psyche, each archetype, each human complex and neurosis, could be identified with another god or goddess: unbridled passion with Aphrodite, jealousy with Hera, combativeness with Ares, and so on down the Olympian pantheon.

The new polytheists' viewpoint may represent a reaction to a desacralization of society that followed the disillusion with too much parochialism. A few years ago the patriarchal god-image began to be challenged in the Western world by the rise of the feminine consciousness on one hand, and the increasing dissemination of Eastern religion and philosophy on the other. Inevitably, the old Nietzschean proclamation was heard again, "God is dead!" In the wake of the Death of God theology, a new polytheism, along with all sorts of other cults and creeds and psychological panaceas, came on the scene. Having let got of the grandeur implicit in a holistic conception of universe and mind, the popular "soul makers" picked up the shattered pieces of many ancient faiths. Like archaeologists, they took each shard in hand and extrapolated from it until it became a living thing full of drama and mystery; and then they offered it to an eager populace. The new heterodoxies were accepted by those who had lost sight of the universal aspect of the Judaism and Christianity and had become disenchanted with their narrow sectarian aspects.

If the old monotheism no longer serves, it seems to me that this is because its patriarchal thrust has been rejected as a failing of an outworn authoritarian religion. What has been overlooked is that the *idea* of monotheism is a purely human fabrication, as are all ideas, and consequently it is subject to all the shortcomings implied by the human condition. But this God, or whatever designation we choose to use in speaking about the Ultimate Mystery, is not a product of the human imagination. This God is Self-created, encompassing all. The old patriarchal monotheism tended to lock people into the idea that monotheism means allegiance to a god who is higher than all the others; and it required of its adherents a rejection of all other gods. The consequence of this belief was a superior attitude toward other human beings who happen to worship "other gods." Therefore it is more accurate to call such a belief structure a "pseudo-monotheism" rather than a true monotheism. This pseudo-monotheism is no better as a solution than the alternatives — the heterodoxies in which the would-be-gurus and their childlike followers are continually contesting with each other. In the popular cults, a great deal of energy goes into the competition among the children; and God is seen only as the Father who, in the Freudian sense, must be deposed.

Androgynous monotheism, it seems to me, is a better religious alternative in the Western context. Androgynous monotheism is the recognition of One God, in whom are contained the World Parents. Were God imaged as a pervasive Divine Essence containing the World Parents, the Two in the One, then a new culture-myth would come into being. The motif of *loving* (union) would characterize the prevailing myth; instead of the more typically experienced motif of *strife* (separation), which produces so much of the degeneration and fragmentation we see all around us.

It is to the great credit of C. G. Jung that he clarified the difference between the *psychological* fact of man's *belief* in a God, or gods, and the possibility of God's existence.[16] Man's belief in a God or in the gods is taught to him by the religious authority of his cultural group. Theologians (and recently more and more psychologists have joined with them) are in the business of studying the cultural symbol systems and the suggested periodic revisions of religious integration that correspond more exactly with the actual practices of people. Thus when the Protestant theologian Richard Niebuhr defines "gods" as "value centers,"[17] "the principle of being and value,"[18] and the "center of worth,"[19] many people, especially younger ones reared in a visually oriented media world, find that religion as ordinarily preached from the church pulpit has lost its luster. They are seeking an expression of their sense of the spiritual more in experience than in precept, and they find their whole beings entranced by the possibility of active awareness of their participation with the cosmic forces. For some, the sense of magnitude comes through the revival of astrology, which currently is a fad of the pop culture. Others practice yoga or meditation in other forms or techniques for integrating the various parts and functions of the human organism. Still others investigate comparative mythology, becoming acquainted with one or another pantheon of gods and guiding daimons.

Some theologians were quick enough to see these developments as evidence of the fall of the old God-image. A new polytheism would be just what was needed to capture the attention of the young people born in the post-World War II period, as they were moving out of adolescence and into adulthood in the late '60s. The theologians began to name the gods (read *values*) that would preside over what people were doing anyway.

Psychologists were discovering, or rediscovering in the old-new mythology, a play ethic that could cheerfully replace the work ethic. The joy of sex could replace the passionate commitment of love; and the divisive images — Dionysus the dismembered one, Siva the destroyer, and Aphrodite and Hera with their jealousies — could be given priority over the opposing tendency of the psyche to pull together its disparate aspects in service of a monotheistic ideal of wholeness. It became fashionable in this milieu to bring chaos out of order.

Meanwhile the universe remains much as it was before the "Death of God," and also as it was before his rebirth into multiplicity. The stars look down, unconcerned as ever as to whether they are individual worlds or integral parts of an unimaginably wide cosmos.

# Chapter 8

## Eden Revisited:
## The Divine "Us" Who Created Persons

I have not finished yet with the Judeo-Christian culture myth of Adam and Eve. If the conquest of the Mother-Goddess-Sphinx by Oedipus, the youth winning his manhood, was the basic archetypal myth of a patriarchal psychology (as in Freud), then the story of Adam and Eve is the archetypal myth of the new androgynous psychology.

I am not using the biblical story to establish the nature of the androgynous psyche. Nor am I using the concept of an androgynous psychology to explain the elements in the Genesis myth. I am not attempting to produce a polemic for the virtues of androgyny, but rather to conduct an investigation into the numerous appearances of androgynous images in various cultures, and into the peculiar tendency in our own culture to suppress these androgynous images. I noted that when such images do appear, they show themselves not so much as true androgynes, with their compensatory masculine/feminine aspects working in harmonious relationship, but rather as the imperfect, incomplete, distorted image of the hermaphrodite. Such an image is the double-sexed Dionysus, whose borderline nature makes it impossible to tell whether he is "mad or sane, wild or somber, sexual or psychic, male or female, conscious or unconscious."[1] So, also, is the hermaphroditic Adam of the second chapter of Genesis, who is born of no woman, but himself has an ectopic pregnancy, by which a woman-child or child-woman is born of him. It is this Adam who is the source of the "male-superior" version which has characterized the wider cultural view of the male-female relationship that has prevailed for several millennia in the Western world. Or, put another way, it was the cultural norm which created the Adam in whom Eve slumbered, unrecognized, unvalued, until she was needed to help the man and to sweeten him out of his loneliness.

This Adam was a reflection of the God of Genesis, who was also lonely, being a patriarchal God who had no partner in Creation. God's loneliness suggests the reason for his embarkation on the entire project of creation: "It is not good that the man should be alone; I will make him a helper fit for him." (Genesis 2:1) This God's loneliness is like that of Eurynome, like Earth-

61

maker of the Winnebago creation myth, like Purusha of Hindu lore, and a myriad of other creator goddesses and gods. Each desired to create something to which he could relate, because he felt incomplete in himself. Out of agony or tears or words, or even the dismemberment of bodies, the worlds were made.[2]

So the loneliness of an incomplete god, a Father God or Mother Goddess without a mate, must be an expression of the human need for that which is unknown to him or her, the unconscious element in the psyche that carries the potentiality for creation.

All that a person experiences directly, he experiences through the psyche, that indefinable apparatus through which perception takes place and by which perception is transformed into knowing. Myth is the speech and the imaginings of the psyche, it is our way of expressing ourselves from the inside out. Myths speak to every disposition and to every point of view. Therefore we may learn much about a society through a study of the myths it enunciates but, and more importantly, we may learn even more through a study of the myths that it hides away. The myth-making process is always going on; it consists primarily in sifting through the old myths and elaborating some of them while casting others aside. The new androgyny may be involved in just such a myth-making process. We need to let our imaginations associate with it and, like the gods, create with it, realizing that although the new androgyny is rooted in antiquity it contains a powerful message for our own time.

Returning again to the Beginning, we see that the Creation story has several features that bear importantly upon our theme. For one thing, there is not one Creation story in Genesis, but at least two, with fragments that may come from still more sources. In the first chapter's version, Creation began in a state of confusion when the spirit of God moved on the waters. The Pelasgian myth began also with the spirit — here feminine — dancing upon the waters. In the latter tale the serpent is there at the beginning, while in Genesis he is present when needed, although just when he first appears is not clear. It is one of the questions the rabbis argued about in the days when every verse of Scripture was turned inside out and examined for hidden meanings and clues to the unfathomable nature of Nature. The seven days of Creation, including the seventh day set aside for sanctification and rest, correspond to a mystical number that pervades esoteric literature. The week is composed of seven days for no particular logical *reason,* but in conformity with the number of the sun, moon and planets known to the ancient Greeks, Egyptians and Chaldeans. True, the twenty-eight-day cycle of the man divides easily into four seven-day periods, but it also divides into periods of two or four or fourteen days. But seven days it was, each named after one of the heavenly bodies, or after the god or goddess whose attributes were associated with the planet, sun or moon. The Hebrews were as cognizant as the rest of the ancient world that there existed a relationship between human life and the life of the cosmos; it is only their explanations of the relationship and their ways of responding to that relationship that differed radically from their neighbors'.

With the first act of separation of the androgynous chaos that preceded it, Creation began. On the first day, light was separated from darkness, and day from night. On the second day the vault which is called firmament was created, separating "above" from "below." This is crucial because out of the interpretation of this act came the dictum so familiar in alchemical literature, "as above, so below," from which stemmed the concept of *microcosmic man* as a minute reconstruction of the macrocosm. On the third day came still another separation: the dry land from the waters; bringing into being the earth and the seas.

From here on the polarization of the One into the succession of twos gives way to the creation of myriads of entities, all vegetative; plants and trees, each categorized according to its particular nature and producing seeds of its own kind. The Genesis sequence differs from that of similar myths of antiquity in that the creation of the pastures here precedes that of the heavenly bodies; perhaps a consequence of the fact that the Hebrews were a nomadic people, concerned more for the welfare of their flocks than, for example, were the Babylonians, who watched the skies for signs that would affect their agricultural civilization. On the fourth day the sun and the moon are placed in the heavens, the sun to have dominion over the day, and the moon over the night, and the stars are also created. The sun is the greater of the lights and is associated with the masculine, and the moon is the lesser, and associated with the feminine This does not imply that male superiority is the hidden message, for there is another element which acts as a balance — each day is conceived of as first evening and then morning, one day. As creation began in darkness, which is associated with the female, so each day springs forth out of the womb of evening.

On the fifth day all creatures are created, and it is made very clear that each kind was separate from every other kind, and swarmed or swam with it own kind. The proliferation of the One continues.

On the sixth day the following happens:

> Then God said, *"Let us* make man *in our image, after our likeness;* and let *them* have dominion over the fish of the sea . . . and over all the earth, and over every creeping thing that creeps upon the earth." So God created man in his own image, in the image of God he created him; *male and female* he created *them.* And God blessed *them* and God said to *them*, "Be fruitful and multiply, and fill the earth and subdue it..."
>
> (Genesis 1:26-28.) [Italics mine.]

This version, while not corresponding with the first Adam-then-Eve tale, seems better suited to the psychological needs of the Hebrew people. The curiosity of some has been provoked by the peculiar wording of the text, especially the parts italicized above. S. L. MacGregor Mathers, who translated from Latin to English the classical studies of the Christian Kabbalist, Knorr von Rosenroth, observes in his Introduction to *The Kabbalah Unveiled,* that for some reason best known to themselves, the translators of the Bible have carefully

crowded out of existence and smothered every reference to the fact that the
Deity is both masculine and feminine.

> They have translated *a feminine plural* by *a masculine singular* in the case of the word
> Elohim. They have, however, left an inadvertent admission of their knowledge
> that it was plural in Gen. iv.26; "And Elohim said: Let Us make man." Again (v.27),
> how could Adam be made in the image of Elohim, male and female, unless the
> Elohim were male and female also? The word Elohim is plural formed from the
> feminine singular *Eloh*, by adding IM to the word. But inasmuch as IM is usually
> the termination of the masculine plural, and is here added to a feminine noun,
> it gives to the word Elohim the sense of a female potency united to a masculine
> idea, and thereby capable of producing an offspring. Now we hear much of the
> Father and the Son, but we hear nothing of the Mother in the ordinary religions
> of the day. But in the Qabalah we find that the Ancient of Days conforms Him-
> self simultaneously into the Father and the Mother, and thus begets the Son. Now
> this Mother is Elohim. Again, we are usually told that the Holy Spirit is mascu-
> line. But the word *Ruach*, Spirit, is feminine, as appears from the following passage.
> . "*Achath (feminine, not Achad, masculine) Ruach Elohim Chiim*: One is *She* the Spirit of
> the Elohim of Life." Now, we find that before the Deity conformed Himself thus —
> i.e., as male and female — that the worlds of the universe could not subsist, or,
> in the words of Genesis, "The earth was formless and void."[3]

Reading the above passage had a profound effect upon me, for more than
one reason. Having meditated much upon the Adamic myth of male superiority which occurs in the *second* chapter of Genesis, I found it puzzling that
scholars and psychologists should have overlooked the tale of the simultaneous creation of man and woman that appears in the first chapter. I failed to
understand the juxtaposition of singulars and plurals in the *first* chapter version, but not being sufficiently versed in the knowledge of the language to
trust my own reading, I let the matter rest. I had always hesitated to look
at the Bible critically, since years of being married to a rabbi who did so with
competence had made me all too conscious of my inadequacy in this complex
and convoluted area. So it was without any intent on my part to pursue the
questions, that one quiet Sunday afternoon my hand fell upon a volume in
my husband's library of Judaica which I had for some unknown reason retained after his death. I drew *The Kabbalah Unveiled* from the shelf — it was a
book I had never noticed before — and immediately it fell open to the passage
that is quoted above. I was amazed, in the true sense of the word: plunged
into a strange labyrinth and enchanted, held fast, by some power that had
me in its grasp.

Somehow I knew that the Kabbalah held the key to the lost, suppressed
and hidden material that completed the traditional material that appeared
in the Bible. But I knew nothing of Kabbalah: only that it was a body of mystical writings which were not meant for everyone, but only for those who were
called to its study; that it was vast and that it was cryptic, and that it involved
an extensive knowledge of the Hebrew language, not to mention some ac-

quaintance with numerology, magic, astrology and intricate
and symbols and words all intertwined. I further knew that o
not to undertake the study of the Kabbalah until one was at ...
years old. By then, one should have solved most of life's practical prob...
and have an inclination and some time to devote to speculation. Well, I had
at least one qualification!

On the dusty shelves containing the books I had kept but never opened
was a five-volume translation of the *Zohar*, the fundamental book of Jewish
Kabbalism. I now knew why I had saved those books for ten years, and why
I was now to look into them for the first time. Strangely, I discovered as I
read, that several passages directly relevant to my quest had been pencil-
marked in the margins. I write this, instead of keeping it for myself, because
I need to state that a study of mine is not purely an exercise of the mind,
but a seeking on the part of a whole person, involving not only thought, but
also emotion, and feeling, and the reflective value of having lived through
both an experience of religion and a religious experience.

The *Zohar* contains a series of discourses in which the Kabbalistic rabbis
shared their inspirations and insights into the hidden meanings of the text
of the Torah. This material makes up a portion of the Simon and Sperling
English translation. More will be said about the Kabbalah later on, but I would
like to summarize here a discussion among the rabbis which is reported to
have taken place concerning the statement: "And God said, Let us make man."

The discussion begins with the statement, "It is written, 'The secret of the
Lord is to them that fear him.'(Psalm 25:14)"

Then a most unusual thing happens. The reverend Elder opens an exposition
of the verse by saying, "Simeon, Simeon, who is it that said 'Let us make man?'
Who is this Elohim?" With these words the most reverend Elder vanished before anyone saw him. R. Simeon was struck with awe, for the Elder had not
addressed him as Rabbi Simeon, as was the custom, but had called him plain
Simeon. The rabbi understood this to signify that the Elder was none other
than the Holy One, blessed be He, and that His appearance marked the time
to expound the mystery which hitherto it was not permitted to divulge. Now
it was perceived that permission was given. (I, myself, could read this as a
sign to proceed.)

Rabbi Simeon then goes on to tell a parable in which there is a king who
wants several buildings to be erected and who has an architect in his service
who does nothing without his consent. The king is the supernal Wisdom above,
and the Central Column of the building below. *Elohim*, being the supernal
Mother, is the architect above; *Elohim* is also the architect below, being the
Divine Presence (*Shekhinah*) in the lower world. In the process of emanation
through which the upper world comes into being, the Father says to the Mother,
"Let it be so and so," and straightway it is so, as it is written, "And he said
to *Elohim*, let there be light": the master of the building gave the order and
the architect carried it out immediately. When it came to the lower world,
the world of separation, which is the sphere of individual beings, the archi-

tect said to the master of the building "Let us make man in our image, after our likeness." But the Father said that one day the man would sin before his mother, because he is foolish, as it is written, "A wise son rejoiceth his father and a foolish son is a heaviness to his mother." The wise son is Man (that is, Primal Man), formed by emanation of the Father, and the foolish son is man (that is Adam of the Garden of Eden) formed by creation of the Mother.

The colleagues of Rabbi Simeon here interrupted the parable and clamored "Is there such a division between Father and Mother that Father has formed Man through emanation and Mother has formed him through creation?" He replied "It is not so, for the Man of emanation was *both male and female from the side of both Father and Mother*, for he was all of light, that came into being through the order of the Father and the execution of the order by the Mother. But this pre-Edenic Primal Man had no image and no likeness, for there can be no image nor likeness when there is only light. Light was the supernal garment that God stored away for the righteous on the first day when he had created it, but the darkness which had also been created on the first day was stored away for the wicked. On account of the darkness, which was destined to sin against the light, the Father was not willing to share in the creation of Edenic man, therefore the Mother (Elohim ) said, "Let us make man in our image, after our likeness." "In our image" was said to correspond to light, while "after our likeness" was said to correspond to darkness, both being necessary in order for anything to be visible or palpable at all. "Thus," said Rabbi Simeon, "darkness is a vestment to light in the same way that the body is a vestment to the soul, as it is written, 'Thou didst clothe me with skin and flesh.'" Then did his colleagues rejoice and say, "Happy is our lot that we have been privileged to hear things which were never disclosed until now."

This exposition in the *Zohar* brings meaning to the duality of the creation stories of Genesis. The first version, in which Man is created, male and female, refers to the archetypal androgyne. He is also known by the term Primal Man, being so-called because his existence is hypothetical, as a sort of prototype in a world preceding Creation which is to provide a pattern for the man who will later be created in the world of flesh. This Man is known as Adam Kadmon in the Kabbalistic literature. He is light, he is energy, and in the Platonic sense, he is "Idea." He is the basis for our psychic image of the Divine Androgyne, through which — after a long series of transformations in myth and literature and human experience — we come to know our own androgyny.[4]

The theme of androgyny finds its way into the *Midrash*. Mircea Eliade, in his study of "Mephistopheles and the Androgyne," reminds us that Adam is represented several times in that early rabbinic commentary on the Bible as having been androgynous.

According to the *Bereshit rabba*, "Adam and Eve were made back to back, joined at the shoulders; then God divided them with an axe stroke, cutting them in two." Others hold otherwise, that "the first man (Adam) was a man on the left side, a woman on the right, but God split him in two halves." . . .Terrestrial Adam was no more than image of the celestial archetype; he too, therefore, was an androgyne. By the fact that the human race descends from Adam, the [male-female] exists virtually in every man, and spiritual perfection consists precisely in rediscovering within oneself this androgynous nature.[5]

All that we think of as divine, supernal or sacred has a quality that is beyond linear time; it is of another dimension of reality. We cannot speak about it in the terms in which we speak of everyday experience with one eye on the clock and the other on the calendar. The common everyday experience of living is incomplete and imperfect, and sometimes it is downright miserable. That is because the human condition, in contrast to our "idea" of the Divine, is incomplete and imperfect and sometimes miserable. It is to this image of the temporal human condition that the myth of Edenic Adam corresponds. Far from being made of light, he is the child of dust. The Adam from whose rib Eve is taken is the hermaphroditic Adam. He fulfills the definition of the hermaphrodite as one who is imperfectly formed as to sexuality, with the characteristics of the opposite sex anatomically present but in a distorted, incomplete and inferior form. From here comes the tradition that the hermaphrodite is a distortion of the natural man. Like Dionysus, the Edenic Adam is man-woman, and as hermaphrodite he is basically asexual. This is because the feminine is present within him but he is unconscious of her being there; hence he cannot relate to her, nor, by the same token, can she relate to him. This asymmetrical relationship, which is also unconscious, is necessarily impotent and passive. Nothing dynamic can come of it until the male is first separated from the female.

Charles Poncé, who has written much on Kabbalah and other esoteric traditions, has taken up the problem of hermaphroditism in the Garden of Eden. In his "An Alchemical Allegory: Notes Toward an Understanding of Genesis," he recognizes that the hermaphroditic human figure who awakens in Eden may be modeled after the God of Genesis, but somehow the image has misfired:

> The admonition given this newborn creature not to eat of the Tree of Knowledge of Good and Evil implies that he is not a true image. At the most, the creature's awareness is limited to a process of naming (". . .and whatever the man called every living creature, that was its name." Genesis 2:19) similar to that encountered in a young infant.
> The radical alteration of God's image by His own hand that occurs when God extracts Eve from the body of Adam represents the first act of differentiation that occurs within the infantile psyche. Here, the first step away from the unconscious hermaphrodite is taken with the appearance of two distinct units of opposites. But with this first act of differentiation a strange event occurs. The division of the figures yields a type of creature God had not anticipated. Here for the first time the *possibility* of consciousness occurs. . .Suddenly, for the first time since their separation out of the original hermaphroditic mold modeled after their Maker the two perceive one another. They look at each other and see each other in their nakedness; they have feeling for one another.[6]

If this is the beginning of consciousness, it is also the beginning of Death, for man's first disobedience results in the loss of Paradise. Before the serpent induces Eve to eat of the Tree of Knowledge and Eve convinces Adam to do likewise, the innocent couple is permitted to eat any of the fruits of the Garden, except only that fruit. So they were allowed to eat of the other great tree, the Tree of Life. But after they had gotten the beginnings of consciousness, a beginning that has no ending while man yet lives, the two were banished from Eden before they could again eat of the Tree of Life and so be immortal. For with both Knowledge and Eternal Life, they would have been like gods.

Consciousness, then, implies man's awareness of his own mortality, over and against a cosmos that appears to him timeless and of another order. Gradually in the process of acquiring consciousness he becomes aware of all of the other pairs of opposites, the male-female pair being among the most important, for this pair can be seen as a metaphor for nearly all the others. All the events comprising a consciousness-seeking way of life present themselves in the form of pairs of opposites. The hermaphroditic mode is the mode of imbalance, ambiguity, confusion. The hermaphroditic union of the opposites is not a true union but merging of undifferentiated aspects. It is cloudy, chaotic, and yet it is a fertile space. Much can grow there as consciousness enters in, nurturing and ordering. We need not, however, revert to a pagan polytheism that rejects values and ethics, in order to realize the infinite variety of our natural potentialities. In the differentiation of the hermaphroditic anomaly, the way is opened for the recognition and ultimately for the marriage of the pairs of opposites. In this lies the promise of the return to the ideal of the true androgyny, in which the masculine elements and the feminine elements in the human psyche are fused, and not confused. The guiding metaphor for this is still monotheism, but it is not the monotheism of the God of Genesis. The Kabbalists were aware that there is One, beyond Jehovah, beyond Elohim, beyond all knowing, whose nature may be contemplated but never grasped. So also have other mystical theologies perceived the *One* which lies behind the *Two* and the many. When we begin to seek out the motif of the *Two* in the One, we find it in more places than we have ever dreamed of.

# Chapter 9

## Zodiacal Man as Macrocosm:
## The Astrological Model for the Psyche

### THE KING WHO DIVINED HIS FUTURE

A king who was also an astrologer read his stars that on a certain day and at a particular hour a calamity would overtake him.

He therefore built a house of solid rock and posted numerous guards outside.

One day, when he was within, he realized that he could still see daylight. He found an opening which he filled up, to prevent a misfortune from entering. In blocking this door, he made himself a prisoner with his own hands.

And because of this the king died.

from Idries Shah's *The Way of the Sufi* [1]

Astrology was one area of esoteric lore I did not place on my map for those flying excursions in search of androgyny, which were to touch me down on Alchemy and Gnosticism, the Kabbalah, the Tao, Tibetan Tantrism and Kundalini Yoga. There was always good reason. For one thing, I told myself, astrology had always offended my natural predilection toward common sense. The idea that my life pattern could be determined by the arrangements of the constellations at the moment of my birth, and an inaccurate knowledge of the constellations' movements at that, seemed ridiculous to me. Even more so was the idea that astrology could have any predictive value for individuals or nations.

In my excursions, however, I could not help being struck by the fact that many people do observe and study the heavenly bodies, not so much from a naturalistic position but from an interest in their role in the functioning of that subtle essence called *psyche* of which all the esoteric disciples take notice, regardless of the name they give to it. I had allowed myself the freedom to follow my curiosity in all these other fields, telling myself, perhaps, that each had a certain legitimacy either as a recognized religious tradition though not necessarily orthodox or, as in the case of alchemy, historically important as the forerunner of an exact science. Astrology might have fit into the latter category, but for some reason I felt an inner resistance. Nevertheless, in my pursuit of the Androgyne, astrological references kept turning up.

The only place in my inquiries where I did not come upon astrology was in my consideration of Genesis. In the creation story, God sets the stars in the heavens to mark off the times and the seasons, but there is no evidence that they are to have any more real *influence* over people than does an ordinary calendar. He also set the sun "to rule over the day" and the moon "to rule over the night," but there is no sense that this means to *govern* in any way, but simply for the sun and the moon to determine which is day and which is night. I had the intuition that this was no happenstance, that very likely the early Hebrews purposely avoided the idea of astrology much as they had avoided the recognition of the androgynous nature of the Godhead. There is little in the Bible that just "happens" to be there.

Pursuing this, my research led me to discover that this separatistic God of the Hebrews had expressly forbidden his people to traffic with astrologers, for these were the soothsayers and sorcerers of the pagan countries. Especially in Egypt and Chaldea, the planets and stars were linked with the gods and goddesses of the polytheistic horde; the heavens were looked to for advice on every subject, and their indications, as interpreted by the "wise men," were guides to the people who believed in them. But the God of Israel demanded that his people not look to false gods for truth or understanding, only to the One God who ruled over all.

In some rabbinic legends it is told that Abraham, the Chaldean, bore on his breast a large astrological tablet on which the fate of every man might be read. It is to this tablet that the words, "the Lord had blessed Abraham in all things" (Genesis 24:1) are said to allude. Abraham himself saw that he would have no second son, but God said to him, "Away with your astrology; for Israel there is no planet." Elsewhere it is stated that Abraham was no astrologer at all, but a prophet, inasmuch as "only those beneath the stars could be subject to the influence, but Abraham was above them."[2] It is clear to see that although in actuality the practice of astrology was strictly proscribed in the Hebrew Bible, by the time the rabbis came to discussing the texts, a certain ambivalence had developed.

According to the biblical legends, the Hebrews were subject to the influences of traditions that had a strong astrological flavor, though they were commanded to pay no attention to the lore of the stars. Assyrio-Babylonian monarchs received from their astrologers a monthly forecast of events, and they made no important moves without consulting men learned in the art. The Roman Empire had a complete set of Chaldo-Greek literature on the subject, which was cultivated by pseudo prophets for rich financial reward. We read that astrologers called into question Pharaoh's selection of Joseph as vice-regent. Pharaoh's astrologers also predicted the birth of the future redeemer of Israel, Moses. Haman, in the Book of Esther, determined the time for the extinction of the Jews by means of astrological calculations. And there is the typical kind of tale: astrologers predicted that Jews would shed a barber's blood. Terrified, the barber murdered eighty or three hundred of them. But he erred—his blood was shed on the occasion of his circumcision as he converted to Judaism.

There were probably no Jewish astrologers either in the Holy Land or in Babylonia during the Exile; and the art, together with those who practiced it, was condemned, although astrology's reliability was as little questioned then as it was by the rest of the world up to the seventeenth century. It was indeed considered to be of celestial origin and as having been revealed to mankind by rebellious angels. Talmudists resisted the "Wisdom of the Orient" except for one, Samuel of Babylonia, who became an adept in astrology; and even he, quoting the words "It [the law] is not in the heavens," says, "Torah cannot go together with the art that studies the heavens."[3]

The question of astrology had come up also in the Book of Daniel. After King Nebuchadnezzar's wise men have been unable to reveal to their master the dream which he has had and its interpretation, Daniel is called in and asked if he can make the matter known to the king. Daniel replies, "No wise men, enchanters, magicians or astrologers can show the king the mystery which the king has asked, but there is a God in heaven who reveals mysteries." (Daniel 2:28.) Joseph, also, was able to interpret the dreams of Pharaoh when the astrologers had failed, and Joseph did not base his authority upon the stars.

All this together showed me that there could be an unconscious basis within myself for my resistance to exploring astrology, whatever logical reasons I might propose for it. Either forgotten, repressed or not yet made conscious, the prohibition of astrology, with the polytheistic heresy that must follow in its wake, was the unconscious factor that had interposed itself because my supposedly objective studies and my manner of pursuing them. I was personally experiencing a conflict of opposites in my own psyche, that of the monotheism to which I was heir and the separation into dualism and then the fragmentation into polytheism that is of essence in the consideration of the whole problem of androgyny. Having once understood this, and made the matter conscious, I was able to consider my *conscious* objections to the study of astrology.

My first objection had to do with the fact that the entire system of astrology was based on ancient and now obsolete observations of earth and sky and their relationship. As early as 3000 B.C. the Sumerians had formalized their idea of the universe into a total world picture. They saw mankind as ruled by the gods who resided in the heavens and operated through their agencies, the celestial bodies and elements. Their theories underwent various modifications at the hands of the rational Greeks, and by the time of the Alexandrian astronomer Ptolemy, in the second century, A.D., the various world models had crystallized into a geocentric system which came to be called the Ptolemaic world view. The earth was the center, surrounded by the elements of water, air and fire. Circling around this was the crystalline sphere of the moon, which revolved below those of the sun and the five planets, Mercury, Venus, Mars, Jupiter and Saturn. This "cosmic onion" was enclosed by the sphere of the fixed stars, and the sphere of the "Prime Mover" enveloped all of these. Beyond lay heaven, the home of the gods.

When the Greeks improved on the measurements of the Oriental astrologers, they found that there were discrepancies in the Ptolemaic system, and that certain stars had shifted in their positions over the years in relation to the first degree of Aries. This meant that there were two zodiacs, one oriented to the sun, and the other to the constellations. As can be imagined, other problems arose in the process of attempting to justify the many discrepancies that kept appearing as new knowledge came to light that did not correspond with the classical Ptolemaic view.[4] The modern mind laughs at the quaint idea that the earth is the center of the universe. Nevertheless we must remember that for all practical purposes the old calculations worked.[5] As Charles Poncé points out, Columbus and Magellan plotted their courses by it![6]

I was aware that what made astrology so seductive was the ambitious scale of its intellectual pretensions. It offered a systematic explanation for all the vagaries of human behavior and natural events and there was scarcely a principle it did not account for, or a question it could not answer. A medieval authority wrote, "Who that knew well astronomy, there is nothing in the world of which he could inquire by reason but he should have knowledge thereof." In the Middle Ages, astronomy was synonymous with astrology. It was not until the astronomical revolution initiated by Copernicus and consummated by Newton that the intellectual pretensions of astrological theory were shattered, and astronomy went its separate and scientific course—leaving astrology to those who still held to the Aristotelian distinction between terrestrial and celestial bodies. Galileo's discovery of the four satellites of Jupiter made people aware that the heavens were full of unseen stars whose influence could not be accounted for. The assumption that the heavens were immutable was upset by the appearance of previously unobserved nebulae, uncovered by the telescope. With the confirmation of a plurality of worlds, the geocentered universe of Ptolemy was no more. Yet even the revelation that the heavens were immutable did not make astrology impossible, although it made the calculations of astrology considerably more difficult. Heliocentrism was not inconsistent with astrology, but it would require a whole new system to be worked out. Sir Christopher Heydon declared in 1603, "Whether (as Copernicus saith) the sun be the centre of the world, the astrologer careth not."

I knew that what had really destroyed the possibility of a scientific astrology were the discoveries of Galileo and Kepler and those who followed them, which proved that the opposition between things terrestrial and things celestial was no longer tenable. Once this had been abandoned, it became impossible to define the nature of that one-way astrological influence which the stars were supposed to exert upon the earth and its people. Earth and heaven could no longer be viewed as a compact, interlocking mechanism. Earth and heaven now belonged to an infinite system from which hierarchial subordination of one to the other had irretrievably disappeared.[7]

Nevertheless, because it filled a clearly felt psychological need, astrology was able to make its claims, and in our time again to build these claims into a profitable industry. I saw astrology exploiting the gullibility of naive individuals who were impressed by "statistical" data, and who never bothered to consider whether the *premises* on which the statistics were based were valid. It was of no concern to them that astrology lacked the essential quality of a science — the capacity for demonstration.

I constantly observe in my practice of psychotherapy that people will believe with remarkable ease any nonsense that will enable them to avoid responsibility for their own actions. Astrology, by defining personality qualities and limitations in terms of celestial constellations, provides excellent rationales for people who want reasons outside of themselves to account for their problems or to assure them of good fortune.

I see astrology used frequently as a vehicle for preying on the suggestibility of people, for responding to clues given out by the unwary, and for establishing "prophecies" that may turn out to be self-fulfilling.

And finally, I have never seen any astrological data from an experiment that has been carried out in a scientifically objective manner utilizing modern research procedures, including safeguards against bias, that really proved anything. (This is notwithstanding my awareness that C.G. Jung in his essay on "Syncronicity: An Acausal Connecting Principle" describes in detail how he carried out an experiment based on a hypothesis that the horoscopes of married couples would show a correspondence beyond that which could be accounted for by chance. After a great deal of investigation, Jung had to admit, "There is little hope of proving that astrological correspondence is something that conforms to law."[8])

Nevertheless, despite all these objections, I have still been unable to dismiss the matter of astrology entirely, for several reasons. Despite the progress of science, astrological thinking and doctrine has survived since many centuries before the birth of Christ. Any holistic theory that sees man as microcosm in a macrocosmic universe, that sees human beings as part of and in correspondence with the entire universe, cannot discredit the view that there is a relationship between all natural phenomena — from man and all other living creatures, to plants and rocks and stones and stars, and all other apparently non-living things. The relationship, however, is not one way, but is mutual and reciprocal.

One cannot help recognizing that the oldest of sciences, astrology, existed at the beginning of man's efforts to understand the laws that governed his relationship with the universe in which he found himself. All pure science is a continuation of these efforts. Nuclear physicists and molecular biologists alike admit that although our methods are far more sophisticated today than they have ever been and our data more convincing, and although we have been to the moon several times and back, we are still in the cosmic woods when it comes to understanding the vast mysteries of our relationship to the universe.

I could not help reflecting on the fact that although he may never have proved the validity of it, Jung always had more than a passing interest in astrology. That is not to say he believed the assertions that were made by astrologers, but if not that, then what was the basis of his interest in the subject? I had often suspected that there was a "trickster" element in Jung's dealing with it at all. Was he using the horoscope as a sort of projective technique with certain patients who had faith in it; a Rorschach-like device to get them to expose their unconscious ideas in the process of talking about such ambiguous figures as astrological signs? Was he interested in the subject in connection with some research of his own? Was he using it purely intuitively, to see what might come up out of discussing these matters with his patients?

I began to suspect that one reason why Jung was so intrigued with the subject of astrology was that he may have seen in its lore an opportunity to examine manifestations of the celestial archetype. In a book on astrology, I discovered an image that substantiated my theory. It is a beautiful picture of an androgynous figure who appears as two bodies joined back-to-back, standing against an azure vault filled with layers of golden clouds. The image is Zodiacal Man, and this is a frequent theme in medieval manuscripts. The signs of the zodiac are associated with principles corresponding to the functions of the soul. These signs are superimposed upon the body so as to show Man, the most perfect creature in the world, as the microcosmic image of the heavens.[9]

This Heavenly Figure, the model for the eventual creation of man on earth, was the inspiration for the Roman astrologer, Manilius, who wrote:

> Now learn what signs the several Limbs obey,
> whose Powers they feel, and where Obedience pay.
> The *Ram* defends the *Head*, the *Neck* the *Bull*,
> The *Arms*, bright *Twins*, are subject to your Rule:
> in the *Shoulders Leo*, and the *Crab's* obeyed
> In the *Breast*, and in the *Guts* the modest *Maid*:
> In the *Buttocks Libra*, *Scorpio* warms Desires
> In *Secret Parts*, and spreads unruly Fire:
> The *Thighs* the *Centaur*, and the *Goat* commands
> The *Knees*, and binds them up in double Bands.
> The parted *Legs* in moist *Aquarius* meet,
> And *Pisces* gives Protection to the *Feet*.[10]

The image is the central figure of a great cosmic diagram that purports to contain within it the scheme of all the operations of the celestial spheres that transpire at the cosmic level. The earth is shown as part of this same cosmos and therefore a microcosm following in principle the operations of the macrocosm. The assumption was that *if* we could discover the laws of the macrocosm, we would then be able to infer the laws governing the microcosm, even down to the details of human personality and human destiny. This would require, of course, a human intellect capable of understanding the entire cosmic order. Where the astrologers parted company with the astronomers was that the astrologers claimed that they understood the workings of the cosmic order sufficiently to be able to draw conclusions from it concerning the personality characteristics and the destiny of the individual, while the astronomers were not prepared to apply what they knew of the cosmos to the individual human's fate. Astronomers were not interested in establishing correspondences, but were committed instead to discovering more about the natural order of the universe and its laws.

The very inconsistency between the Ptolemaic calculations and the sidereal calculations that had troubled me now provided the sought-for clue to the meaning of astrology for our times and, more specifically, in relation to the human psyche. The idea of ourselves and the world we live in as microcosmic, reiterating in an imperfect way the perfection of the all-encompassing macrocosm, may seem like pure philosophical speculation and of little practical use. But if we consider the question from the point of view of the *experience* of the human psyche, as I believe Jung attempted to do, we find a map, a pattern, a model, that helps us to understand our place in the entire scheme of things. We begin, as Blake put it:

> To see a World in a Grain of Sand
> And a heaven in a Wild Flower,
> Hold Infinity in the palm of your hand
> And Eternity in an hour.[11]

This means that we exist in both dimensions at the same time. The concept is non-dual. It simply points out that we view our existence from more than one perspective. We exist on this earth and we have to deal practically with the problems of the world in its own temporal terms, cognizant of the linear pattern of the individual life which commences at conception and concludes with organic death. We also live in eternity and are concerned with problems that go beyond the practical and the temporal (else I would not be writing and you would not be reading these words). To the extent that we think in practical everyday terms, we are in touch with the "Edenic Adam," in ourselves, but to the extent that we reflect upon the cosmic scheme, we are in touch with the Archetypal Man, Primal Man, Celestial Man, Zodiacal Man, the Man of many names whose nature is pure existence and who has no manifest form. We are, according to my understanding, both of these.

As Edenic Adam, we are men or we are women aware of ourselves primarily as "ego personality," which is to say that we are basically unconscious of the contrasexual psyche or soul element that lies asleep within us. We spend the greater part of our lives concerned with attaining our own security and our well-being, with establishing human relationships and, if we are socially minded, with improving conditions of living for others as well as for ourselves. We see ourselves in terms of what we do and also in terms of how other people respond to us. In this sense we are, each of us, the centerpoint of the universe.

In another sense we know that we are, each of us, but a grain of dust whirling on one small planet that is set in the universe on a predictable course. This would be quite a miraculous happening if we were to think of the universe as a sort of chancy space presided over by a pantheon of gods who are always quarreling with each other and competing with each other. The human psyche, as the playground of these gods, would be a scene of pure madness! Perhaps this is what it is; as the contemporary polytheists believe, that our lives are subject to autonomous, capricious forces—stars, childhood traumas, or characterological traits about which we can do nothing. I find myself however, with those who subscribe to the principle that there *is* an overriding order; although I recognize that as human beings our capacity to come to an understanding and appreciation of that order must be limited. So I do not see life as abounding in miracles, unless Nature is herself miraculous. I see it as natural that human beings function according to universal laws, inasmuch as we are specks of the same atomic "dust" of which the universe is composed. We are of the universal stuff and inseparable from it. I should like to add that this is an idea on which I like to reflect before I fall asleep at night, for it is a certain antidote for insomnia. When I understand myself and feel myself as a mere speck of dust in a dusty universe or as a drop of water in an endless ocean, all troubles fall away because there is nothing to push against. And in the morning after a refreshing night I can get up and face my temporal world, the world in which I, as Edenic Adam (and Eve) am, of course, the very center. We live in the two dimensions at the same time.

The ego, the part of ourselves with which we consciously identify, is only one element in the psyche. The psyche, and more specifically the center of the totality of the psyche, which Jung has called the *Self*, is indeed "bigger than big and smaller than small." I am my ego. I am the Self. I am the traveler, the world is a my terrain. I am a pilgrim taking tiny faltering steps on the road that stretches backward into infinity and forward into infinity. Which am I? Or am I both?

I cannot choose between the one and the other. Were I to choose and say, "I am right and the others are wrong," there would always be someone to say, "No you are wrong, I am the one who is right." As Jung often said, must it be "either or"? Can it not as well be "both and"?

This brings me to the possibility that the apparent dichotomy that seemed to invalidate astrology as an objective science may be, in fact, the principle that makes of astrology a credible mirror of the human psyche. The Ptolemaic system corresponds to a view of each human being as the central point upon whom the influence of the whole universe converges. The idea that we are, each of us, the recipients of the effects of universal processes corresponds on a personal basis to the astrological formula that the earth is the center of the universe, and if we venture too close to the edge of the earth, we are liable to fall off and tumble into the abyss. The Ptolemaic system corresponds psychologically to an ego-centered system: if we lose our sense of ego, if we forget for too long who we are and where our physical and psychological boundaries are, there is a good chance that we may drop off into the abyss of psychosis. Of course we do forget our identities and our boundaries for short spans of time, as in sleep, or in flights of fantasy, or under the influence of mind-altering drugs, or in the rapture of orgasm, but we return soon enough to ego and to earth.

An exception to this is found in those "highly realized persons" who are able to exist out of this world, so to speak, and out of the ego state, for long periods of time. But, I submit, they would find it difficult to do this in a contemporary city. Perhaps a Thomas Merton in his monastery or a hermit on a Himalayan mountainside can be at one with nature and with the universe, forgetting even his own name. For it is the practice of those who move into the state called Enlightenment to give up the names their mothers attached to them, even as they give up their sense of being entrapped in that ego-personality that began to develop as soon as they emerged from the womb.

The Ptolemaic system is a geocentric system, corresponding to an individual's ego-centered approach to life. In relation to sexuality, the psychological approach for which this system is a metaphor would be characterized by the conscious perception of ourselves as men and women, relating to other men and women largely on the basis of their sex and gender roles. This egocentric system would cover the practical kinds of relationships that are focused upon interpersonal consideration and independence-dependency needs. Beyond that, this system would be focused on the needs of society to break free of parental authority, to establish support networks such as family and community, and to establish institutions, such as marriage, to solidify the support system. Then, possibly, as one either achieves fulfillment in sexual relationship or as one grows beyond the pressing need for such fulfillment, the system centered on ego may actually propel an individual into another dimension in which a Self-centered system can come into awareness. Note that this is exactly the opposite of the common expression "self-centeredness."

The sidereal system, then, is the "star-centered" or universe-centered, or cosmic-centered system. In its psychological analogue the system is centered on what Jung called the *Self*, rather than on what Jung called the *ego*. It is in the vast realm of the Self that we seek correspondences between the specks of dust we are as individuals, and the immeasurable mystery of which we are an integral part.

The Ptolemaic system speaks to the relationship of the individual to the stars or to the universe; it speaks of ego and Other. The sidereal system speaks to the individual as a minute and microcosmic manifestation of the universe, of one in All. The Hindus understood this and had expressions for it. Considering the ego-centeredness of the Ptolemaic system and all the false perceptions and conceptions of the Self stemming from it, they would say *Neti, neti* (*not this and not that*). Of the sidereal system, they would say *Tat Tvam asi* (*Thou art that*).

Now how does all this relate to the sexes, to sexuality, and to the problem of Androgyny? It is necessary to consider one core idea that was commonly accepted in astrological circles until the appearance in 1661 of a work by Robert Boyle entitled *The Sceptical Chymist*, which called the Aristotelian illusion into question. The view, according to Aristotelian science and elaborated in the Ptolemaic world view, held that matter was composed of four elements: fire, earth, air and water. This idea was crucial to astrology because it was believed that man himself was composed of a combination of these elements in varying degrees. The concept dates back to Empedocles in the fifth pre-Christian century, who stated that the four elements do not change into another but are, instead, four unchangeable kinds of matter that, through combination, make up all the objects of the world.[12]

> [Empedocles] makes the material elements four in number, fire, air, water and earth, all eternal, but changing its bulk and scarcity through mixture and separation; but his real first principles, which impart motion to these, are Love and Strife. The elements are continually subject to an alternate change, at one time mixed together by Love, at another separated by Strife.[13]

Aristotle contributed to this theory the idea that the elements were distinguished by four qualities: hot and cold, and wet and dry. Fire was hot and dry; earth was cold and dry; water was wet and cold; and air was hot and wet. His theoretical position was that each element combined within itself these two qualities. What is particularly important is the further idea, credited to Anaximander, that the universe came into being through separating out the qualities of hot and cold from the original substance of the universe. This introduced the idea of polar opposites to cosmological theory and perhaps even provided the germ of a way of thinking that has led to the kind of multiple polarizations characterizing Western thought today. Almost immediately these hot and cold qualities, along with dryness and moisture, became identified with the sexes: heat and dryness with the masculine, and cold and moisture with the feminine. In astrology, half the signs of the zodiac are called "masculine" and the other half "feminine."

The ancient astrological design was a preform of modern science in that it attempted first and foremost to categorize and arrange its observed data, and especially to assign numerical descriptions wherever possible. Diagrams, charts, angles and degrees were of the essence; and the horoscope, that chart of the heavens as seen at a particular moment in time and from a specific place on earth, provided a schema to which earthly events would correspond. The study of these astrological charts was supposed to be a foundation for the comprehension of Nature's laws. Over the centuries the "science" of astrology expanded in scope and influence, reaching its tentacles into every area of investigation and speculation where universal principles were sought. From magic to medicine, from alchemy to chiromancy, from dream interpretation to crop planning, from government to love-making, there was no area of human relations for which people did not at some time or other turn to astrology for guidance.

However limited, inaccurate and primitive some of the conceptions of the

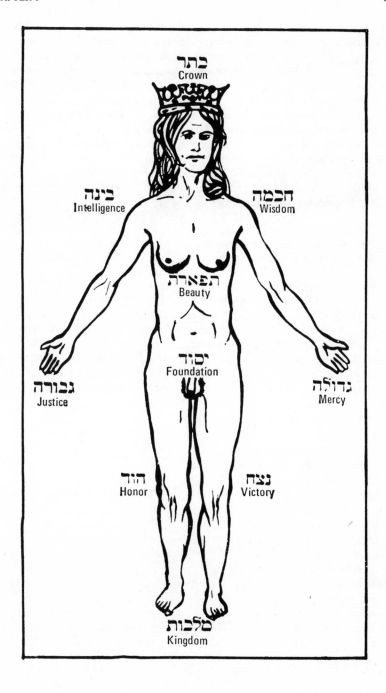

astrologers were and are, there is one point that must be emphasized. Astrology must have supplied a psychological need, else it would not have survived. The appeal of astrology was in the way it accommodated an intuitive recognition that is familiar to many people even if they do not put it into words. It is that when a person functions in a way that seems to him to be in harmony with a broader system of which he is a part, he experiences a sense of well-being, of order and of relatedness. When he has no schema, on the other hand, he tends to feel disarrayed and isolated. Highly attractive, therefore, is the idea that one can get information for oneself about a broader system from that cosmic diagram, the horoscope, which purports to describe those operations that manifest themselves in the heavens before manifesting themselves on earth. Those who feel that this idea is limited today only to those who believe in astrology, are reminded of the words:

> Our Father who art in Heaven, hallowed be thy name
> Thy kingdom come, thy will be done,
> On earth as it is in Heaven...

We are enjoined to put ourselves into a relationship with the cosmic order and, if we do this, a life of peace and harmony is promised to us. This sense of the reciprocity of the individual and the universe underlies much of what is in religion and philosophy, and especially in those esoteric doctrines that have been hidden away from the collective consciousness. Today these doctrines remain as part of the heritage of the collective unconscious, but in many places and among more and more people the old disciplines through which they may have been realized in the past are only now emerging again into consciousness.

# Chapter 10

## Plato's Androgyne:
## Origins of Heterosexuality and Homosexuality

Today we recognize two sexes on this earth, male and female, but the image of the Androgyne is impressed on the psyche as a dominant of the collective unconscious. Its existence is proved by the fact that it emerges from time to time in a multiplicity of guises, and in every part of the world. To study all its manifestations would be an encyclopedic work, yet a few excursions into the systems where androgyny plays an important part will give us the sense of how pervasive and influential the archetype is.

Of all the schools of ancient and classical astrology, from the Chaldean to Ptolemaic, one body of mythology has come down to us that stresses the *psychological* nature of sexuality. While the purportedly "scientific" systems were concerned with establishing the relationships of human beings to the heavenly bodies, and especially with celestial influences upon people and the material world, Plato's delightfully imaginative myth stands out as an expression of the human soul without any attempt to justify itself in terms of reasonableness. Yet springing from the psyche itself, pure and unadulterated, it carries perhaps an even greater weight of truth than do the formulations that depend on a logic based on faulty premises.

In Plato's *Symposium* we find the first mention of the figure of the Androgyne in Greek philosophy. It comes out of a discussion about the peculiar nature of Love and an attempt to understand its widely varied modes of expression. Aristophanes is speaking:

> Mankind, judging by their neglect of him, have never understood the power of Love. For if they had understood him they would surely have built noble temples and altars, and offered sacrifices in his honor. . .

In describing the power of Love, he speaks of the original nature of man, and of what happened to transform him into his present state:

> [The] original human nature was not like the present, but different. The sexes

81

were not two, as they are now, but originally three in number; there was man, woman and a union of the two, having a name corresponding to this double nature, which once had a real existence, but is now lost, and the word "Androgynous" is only preserved as a term of reproach. In the second place, the primeval man was round, his back and sides forming a circle; one head with two faces looking in opposite ways, set on a round neck and precisely alike; also four ears, two privy members, and the remainder to correspond. He could walk upright as men do now, backwards or forwards as he pleased and he could also roll over and over at a great pace. . .

The man was originally the child of the Sun, and the man-woman of the Moon which is made up of sun and earth, and they were all round and moved round and round like their parents. Terrible was their might and strength, and the thoughts of their hearts were great, and they dared to scale the heavens and they made an attack on the gods.

The gods took council and Zeus discovered a way to humble their pride and improve their manners. They would continue to exist, but he cut them in two like a sorb-apple which is halved for pickling.

After the division, the two parts of man [the Androgyne], each desiring his other half, came together and throwing their arms about one another, entwined in mutual embraces, longing to grow into one; they were on the point of dying from hunger and self-neglect because they did not like to do anything apart; and when one of the halves died and the other survived the survivor sought another mate, man or woman, as we call them — being the sections of entire men or women — and clung to that.

They were being destroyed when Zeus in pity of them invented a new plan; he turned the parts of generation round to the front, for this had not always been their position, and they sowed the seed no longer as hitherto like grasshoppers the ground, but in one another; and after the transposition the male generated in the female in order that by mutual embraces of man and woman they might breed and the race might continue; or if man came to man they might be satisfied, and rest, and go their ways to the business of life: so ancient is the desire of one another which is unplanted within us, reuniting our original nature, making one of two, and healing the state of man.

Each of us, when separated, having one side only, like a flat fish, is but the indenture of a man, and is always looking for his other half. . .And when one of them meets with his other half, the actual half of himself, the pair are lost in an amazement of love and friendship and intimacy, and one will not be out of the other's sight, as I may say, even for a moment; these are the people who pass their whole lives together; yet they could not explain what they desire of one another. For the intense yearning which each of them has for the other does not appear to be the desire of lovers' intercourse, but of something else which the soul of either evidently desires and cannot tell, and of which she has only a dark and doubtful presentiment.[1]

This charming fantasy springs from the feeling side of man, and puts into words the sense of longing that lovers experience — whether for one of the other sex or for one of their own — that goes beyond any rational explanation. Plato's Androgyne seems indeed to be extinct, and only the myth remembered. But, of course, the myth never remotely referred to a species existing on earth fitting that description, but rather to that celestial world of the imagination where all the immortal prototypes for Creation have always existed. The prototypes, like so many ideas conceived in the brilliance of pure inspirations, go through successively disappointing transformations until they are brought forth as mere shadows of the original conception. So it was with the Androgyne, who arose in the collective unconscious of the human race as an archetype; that is, as a dark intimation of a potentiality, never fully to be realized.

Plato's Androgyne suggests, from a psychological point of view, why human beings seem to need each other in a way that goes beyond the demands of pure sexuality or reproduction, of companionship or of social necessity. How often do lovers say to each other, "I am lost without you, incomplete. With you I feel fulfilled. I experience a sense of union when we are together." There is that oceanic feeling that is often ascribed to orgasm, the sense of total merging both with the other person and with the entire universe. Then it is that all boundaries are lost and the one and the other forget who they are as individuals and nothing exists but the soaring harmony of the spheres. In the hope of achieving the feeling of love, this mystical joining of two beings into a primordial oneness, people will do the most ill-advised things, beyond all reason. The loss of love can drive people to murder or suicide. There is very little else on earth that has this power over the human psyche.

This kind of love is a symbiotic relationship, a mutually dependent relationship where each person fills very basic needs for the other. Each is the other half of the sorb-apple, so to speak, and one without the other is not a complete person. The archetype of the Androgyne is at the base of much of the anxiety that surrounds love. It is connected with the emotion of jealousy because it points to the fear of being torn asunder from that other person who is required to be present for the rounding out of one's own personality — who is, in fact, required for one's very existence.

Plato did not neglect to consider the homosexual lover when he spoke of the kind of need of one person for another that is experienced in a threatening and anxious way. He elaborated his myth, telling that sometimes the man and woman, separated from one another in the splitting of the Primordial Androgyne, went through a further process of fragmentation. As men were split off from other men, a race of men was created who were incomplete without fulfilling their need for attachment with another man; and likewise women were split off from women, thus creating the race of Lesbians. The myth responds to questions that people feel in their innermost beings; it answers them with archetypal images coming from a deeply buried layer of the collective unconscious. It gives us some basis for the grounded sense of knowing who we are, a "knowing" that is neither culturally determined nor even necessarily the result of imprinting at an early age. Freudian theory aside, psychosexual development proceeds in vastly different ways even among children subjected to similar primary relationships and patterns of child rearing; for example, some become homosexual, some heterosexual, some bisexual and some asexual. Much evidence comes together to suggest that these developments often have little consistency with the way the child has been reared. The child responds to events out of the particularity of his or her own nature. He is an organism designed to receive the world in certain ways, and he has his individual potentialities for reacting to it.

Unique as each of us is, there is a kind of psychological patterning that offers images from which we may deduce the structure and dynamics of the fundamental psyche. These images come to us in the form of mythological systems, and they enable us to understand psychological functioning just as much as anatomical systems enable us to understand physiological functioning. This is not to suggest that psyche and body are two separate entities, but rather that they offer different perspectives from which we may view ourselves and others.

A basic idea in the history of human consciousness became apparent as we considered the enduring nature of astrology and its myths. This fundamental idea is that the world we know and in which we live is but the latest in a series of creative endeavors. Furthermore, as we examine more mythological systems we will observe a consistent theme in which each succeeding world is of a lesser quality than that which preceded it. We saw this in the Greek system, with its progression from Golden to Silver to Bronze to Iron ages.

The mythological structures that give primacy to the principle of androgyny as essential to creation may be seen to develop through four specific stages. To present these schematically does not do justice to the complexity and beauty of the mythology, but it does help to provide a frame of reference so that the similarity of the mytho-systems will become apparent. The recognition that we live in a universe that is basically orderly, is inescapable; and correspondingly, we as human beings possess the capacity for insight into that order — at least within our human limitations. We are impelled to strive toward a better understanding of that order, which is also our own order, because we are subject to its principles, much as are the stars.

The fourfold structure of mythology goes something like this:

I. The first stage refers to an absolutely unknowable condition "before Time was." There is little that can be said about this stage because nothing existed that can be named. All was formless and void, the *tohu-v'bohu* of the Old Testament. In Taoism it is "Darker than any Mystery/the Doorway whence issued all Secret Essences."[2] In Kabbalism the unknowable could not be named but was referred to as "veils of negative existence which can only formulate hidden ideas not yet called into being."[3] Astrology speaks of the heavens before there was any sense of pattern or process. Alchemy starts in a *massa confusa*, a disordered chaos. Wherever we find it in myth, this stage refers to that which lies beyond "source" or "first cause," or even causality itself. Nothing is differentiated in this stage, yet all potentialities are present.

II. In the second stage, the indeterminate formlessness coalesces into a unified figure, the "All in All." This may be an abstract figure in which the opposites are locked together as in the familiar *t'ai chi* figure of Taoism; or it may be a God of Creation — a Jehovah emanating light or the Ancient of Days marking out the heavens and earth with his compass, or it may be that incipient stage in alchemy called the *Nigredo*, where everything is hidden in a pregnant blackness. Blake described this stage in his creation myth in *The Book of Urizen*:

> Lo, a shadow of horror is risen
> In Eternity! Unknown, unprolific,
> Self-clos'd, all-repelling... [4]

III. In the third stage something begins to stir within the chaotic mass. Something is called into shape and the nature of it is, in principle, androgynous. At first the androgynous form lies asleep, unconscious of its containing the Two within the One, and still more unconscious of its potentiality for separation and differentiation. Into this stage there comes an epoch of transition, described variously as the Fall, the banishment into the lower worlds, the transmutation of the spiritual into the material, or the degeneration of the gods into humans. *T'ai chi* is seen as Yin and Yang. The celestial principles take shape as a variety of archetypal images — Zodiacal Man was one of these. All "existence" is carried on in a proto-world that is the model for the world of Creation, which has yet to be brought into being.

IV. Creation and the created world we know and live in belong to the fourth stage. By this time the Primal Androgyne has either fallen from the supernal sphere to earth or the androgynous figure has split in two — and then perhaps into many parts — lost its immortality, and finally become human. In the created world, male and female are separated into two clearly defined entities. Each is unconscious of the traces of the categorically "other" which nevertheless remain as a hidden part, exerting a tension or pull that is experienced as a longing for reunification. Yet there is also a movement toward a further development in which the hoped-for, longed-for reunification awakens to consciousness as a real possibility.

This fourfold succession of stages forms the basis of a panoply of myths. The classical tales of Greece and the Near East proceed from the One to the Primal Couple, and thence to a multiplicity of deities. When women and men come into being, the goddesses and gods serve as models for human characterological types and ways of functioning.

In the Judeo-Christian culture myth, the androgynous aspects of the Creator are repressed in favor of a monotheistic, patriarchal God. In the world of Creation, man is made in the image of this patriarchal God — and woman is also repressed or relegated to a secondary position.

Astrology reiterates the fourfold schema: the worlds begin with an unfathomable creative principle; then comes the fragmentation of its light-giving and life-giving powers into all the heavenly bodies; the emergence of Zodiacal Man follows as the prototype of the human being; and then there is the final step, in which — in human beings — the sexes are finally separated. Then comes the Platonic recapitulation of some of these ideas in terms that will be recognized as being in the nature of psychological symbolism.

We will touch upon still other systems and themes in order to see how the fundamental stages in the development of human consciousness are expressed in symbolic terms. And, finally, we will explore our contemporary human experiences in the development of our own consciousness, an exploration that may lead us toward a clearer understanding of what our essential nature is and of where we are in the process of personal unfolding. We will see how the process also doubles back upon itself into regressive recapitulations of earlier stages that are never quite the same as they were when first experienced, but richer with meaning and more readily comprehensible.

For those who are committed to an exploration of the future of human consciousness, the questions must arise: what lies in store as we move toward the longed-for conjunction of opposites? What will be the next development in human consciousness? What if we begin to read these stories of how the gods created man from the "infernal" point of view, and realize how people created gods, and moreover how they continue to create them? Can the human psyche realize its own creative potential through building its own cosmology and supplying it with its own gods? Are we not, in fact, already doing it; and would we not be wise to look carefully at the blueprints, our myths, before we make too many unnecessary mistakes?

# Chapter 11

## Monad, Jot and Tittle:
## The Gnostic Vision of the Fall

A Star shone in the heavens. The Wise Men of the East, three kings, astrologers all, left their kingdoms. Each bore a gift in his hands as he followed the auguries of the New Age, the Age of Pisces.

> This day has given the earth an entirely new aspect. The world would have gone to destruction had there not streamed forth from him who is now born a common blessing.
> Rightly does he judge who recognizes in the birthday the beginning of new life and of all the powers of life; now that time is ended when men pitied themselves for being born...
> The Providence which rules over all has filled this man with such gifts for the Salvation of the world as will designate him as Saviour for us and for the coming generations; of wars he will make an end, and establish all things worthily.
> By his appearing are the hopes of our forefathers fulfilled; not only has he surpassed the good deeds of earlier time, but it is impossible that a greater one than he can ever appear...
> From his birth-day a new era begins.

So reads the most complete inscription from manuscripts recently found in Asia Minor that had been set up to commemorate the introduction of the Julian Calendar by the Emperor Augustus.[1]

Contemplating the image of Zodiacal Man, we see that he appears to be standing upon two fishes — and we recall Manilius' line, "And Pisces gives protection to the Feet." The prophecy of the astrologers had come to pass. In the city of Jerusalem, the Hebrews, who had been taught to close their ears to the prognostications of soothsayers and magicians, turned their heads away while the men from the east made their way to the manger. The Wise Men now stopped looking to the heavens, for they saw that the light and the glory had come to earth and was shining forth from the head of the infant who lay half-hidden in the straw.

Although born in the Land of Israel, and tracing his ancestry through a

87

long Hebrew lineage back to King David, the child had entered a pagan and polytheistic world filled with all sorts of "beings" whose magical powers were feared and whose forces had to be confronted. The beings, all manner of archangels, angels, demons and archdevils, were not part of the orthodox Jewish tradition, yet they were not altogether absent from that tradition either. They belonged to the part of the lore that had been suppressed or eliminated from the canon, probably because the doctrines bore too much resemblance to those of the worshippers of "false gods" from which the Hebrews had so decisively separated themselves. The "false gods" were associated with the shared worship of female and male principles; consequently even the hint of their presence unnerved those who were committed to the primacy of the patriarchal "Lord our God, King of the Universe."

Yet that presence made itself known in the secret books of the Egyptian Gnostics that were uncovered in the archeological finds recently made at Chenoboskion in Upper Egypt. The following *Hymn of the Soul* came to light in one of the forty-four third-century manuscripts discovered in a cave:

> "See, Father," said Jesus, "how pursued by evil (the soul) is wandering far from thy spirit over the earth. She tries to flee from hateful chaos; she knows not how to emerge from it. To that end, Father, send me! I will descend, bearing the seals. I will pass through all the aeons; I will unveil every mystery; I will denounce the appearances of the gods and, under the name of Gnosis, I will transmit the secret of the holy way."[2]

During the first two centuries of the Christian era, many sects arose and created the strange and heretical theology called Gnosticism. Their mythology took up questions not dealt with in the new religion. Gnosticism did not begin with the appearance of the Christ figure; there were forms of this nearly forgotten faith in Egypt predating the Christian era and associated with Thoth, the ancient Egyptian god who presided over all priestly arts and sciences. Gnosticism, like alchemy, is rooted in hermetic philosophy and, like the latter, recognizes the mythical Hermes Trismegistus as its founder. This "thrice-greatest Hermes" comes down to us in the more or less Platonic language of the *Corpus Hermeticum*, in its Arabic and Latin translations. While the original documents have been lost, there seems to be no doubt that the texts we have are descended from a genuine tradition, and are in no way a pseudo-archaic fabrication of the Greeks.[3] The myths of the Near and Middle East contain elements that resemble those appearing in gnostic tradition. Furthermore, a branch of Jewish Gnosticism sets the stage for the development of the Kabbalistic systems of thought.

If early Christianity had its shadow, then Gnosticism was that shadow. Here I mean the *shadow* in the collective sense, as Jung used the term: "a moral problem that challenges the whole ego-personality"[4] — but when it appears as an archetype it forces man to come face to face with "the rare and shattering experience of gazing into the fact of absolute evil."[5] Christianity teaches goodness and light and the *separation* of the earthly and profane from the heavenly and sacred. Where Christianity tells of the One God who sends his only begotten Son to earth, the Gnostics confound every element of Creation, as well as the appearance of Adam, and of Christ as the Second Adam, with intimations of doubleness, androgyny, and the problematic presence of the feminine principle. The gnostic doctrine states that the Creator and his works were evil. Here meet and clash the views of the pagan, Jewish and Christian world. But the clash is not an open one because Gnosticism is a heretical doctrine, threatening to the powers of orthodoxy. For anyone who wishes to study Gnosticism today, the effort still will be set with trials and difficulties, since there are many confusing versions of tales, usually presented in cryptic language, and mostly in fragments that do not quite add up to a cohesive picture. Reading these texts is fascinating, however, for they show how deeply preoccupied with the problems of evil and dissension in the world were the philosophers, scholars and theologians in that day when, supposedly, "are the hopes of our forefathers fulfilled" with the birth of the Messiah.

Many gnostic myths deal with Creation and the world antecedent to man on earth, but they all follow a similar pattern. The first stage is the Beginning of beginnings, always in a Time beyond time. There was then an indescribable Totality which could only be spoken about in metaphors. Jung cites such an excerpt from a gnostic document attributed to Valentinus, which says: "In the beginning the Autopater contained in himself everything that is, in a state of unconsciousness." Another passage, this from Hippolytus, states that the "Father" is not only unconscious and without the quality of being—that is, neither psyche nor matter—but without opposites, neither male nor female, and therefore unknowable (*"le Père...qui est dépourvu de conscience et de substance, celui qui est ni masculin, ni féminin"*).[6] Though he has no form and is not man, he is called Man, and the Man is All, source of the Universe, unbegotten, incorruptible, everlasting.

In the second stage, the Totality conceives and begets a Unity, a single monad. Referred to as the Son of Man, this was "uncompounded and indivisible, yet compounded and divisible, loving and at peace with all things, yet warring with all things and at war with itself; as it were a musical harmony containing all things."[7] The Son of Man is also described by the gnostic sect, the Naassenes, as an "invisible point," an appellation fully in accord with the idea of the Monad. The emblem of the Monad is the *jot* or *tittle*, being simple and having been composed from nothing whatever, yet composed of many forms and many parts. "The Son of Man is one jot,* one *iota*, the one jot flowing from on high, full and filling all things."[8] The relationship of the *iota* to

---

*Here as I was writing these words, my mind wandered as I tried to conceptualize this mysterious "jot." My unconscious supplied a solution to the problem, for while typing the manuscript my finger slipped, and instead of "jot" I typed "joy," which surely could describe the Son of Man who "was composed of nothing whatever," is incorporeal yet "full and filling all things."

the Unknowable Absolute is the same as that of the Hebrew letter *yod* in the Kabbalah to the Mystery of Mysteries.

There is much symbolism about this *point*. It is seen as the center, from which proceeds the circle that is the soul. The point is the God-image; the soul creates the circle by circumambulating the God-image. The point is also a very small spark; the spark of the soul in semen and in milk which increases to power. In alchemy this point is the *punctum solis*, the mystical essence in an egg yolk that grows into a chick. For Gerhard Dorn, the philosophical alchemist, this point is the starting point of Creation. A point of light also the beginning of the possibility of Creation in the Kabbalah.[9]

Another Gnostic conceptualization of the Son of Man is that he is *Aipolos*, the pole (also a pun on the Greek word for goat herd, the one who must turn in all directions). Here again is the idea of a point (pole) that has no real existence, but about which the entire earth turns. This figure is symbolized by Mercurius, the ever-elusive trickster who is of essence but whom one cannot grasp; also Proteus, the shape shifter, in whom every quality exists *in potentia*.

The third stage occurs when the Son of Man, having within himself the potentiality of the Androgyne, becomes the One through which an opposite comes into being. Referring to the time before this God splits into his masculine and his feminine halves, there are the myths of self-copulation. In an Egyptian story of Creation we read: "I, even I, had union with my clenched hand, I joined myself in an embrace with my shadow, I poured seed into my mouth, my own, I sent forth issue in the form of Shu, I sent forth moisture in the form of Tefnut."* [10] All this takes place on the level of eternal life. The creative principle is still unconscious, self-occupied, the uroboric dragon who is locked with its tail in its mouth and cannot move anywhere. There is as yet no earthly creation, nor can there be because a creative principle without a compensatory destructive principle could do nothing but flood all existence. As long as eternal life is possible then nothing can come into being; creation demands the sacrificing of immortality. William Blake, deeply influenced by this gnostic idea, wrote:

> Thus one portion of being is the Prolific, the other the Devouring; to the Devourer it seems as if the producer was in his chains; but it is not so, he only takes portions of existence and fancies that the whole.
>
> But the Prolific would cease to the Prolific, unless the Devourer, as a sea, received the excess of his delights.
>
> Some will say: "Is not God Alone the Prolific?" I answer: "God only Acts & Is, in existing beings or Men."
>
> These two classes of men are always upon earth, & they should be enemies: whoever seeks to reconcile them seeks to destroy existence.
>
> Religion is an endeavor to reconcile the two.[11]

---

*When I discovered this material in my reading I was struck by its close resemblance to dreams and masturbatory fantasies brought to me by people with whom I was working analytically, people who had no awareness of the mythological parallels. (See Chapter 21.)

In the heresies of Gnosticism, we are permitted to reflect upon the lege. and images that the orthodox faith had rejected and excluded. We are told that the pole is the hub of the world wheel, and the wheel, or the circle it describes, is the *anima mundi*, the Soul of the World. Or, the division into opposites comes in another manner: the Godhead emanates from himself a heavenly light, female in nature, which is the divine Wisdom, called Sophia. Other pairs, or *syzygys*, are emanated by the Godhead, and these are able to reproduce through consorting with their opposites; the Godhead alone brings other celestial powers into being without any assistance, because he is complete within himself; that is, androgynous.

The Heavenly Sophia, upon seeing this, becomes envious, and she determines, as the Primordial Father did, to create a celestial sphere without a partner. She fails, and gives birth to a monster, called Ialdabaôth, and who also has the names Sacla and Samael. He is like a serpent and a lion in appearance, and one half of him is fire and the other half darkness. Sophia is deeply ashamed of the abortion she has produced. She conceals it in a cloud of light, so that none of the celestial powers may see it except the holy spirit, the Mother of the living, also called Zoë. Ialdabaôth, who has taken a portion of the celestial power from the Mother, makes himself the demiurge of the world below, creating the visible universe that we know. By uniting himself with the ignorance that is in him, he engenders also a long series of powers to govern the celestial firmament and the abyss.

This fierce fury of creation seems to be a ghastly parody on the Genesis creation myth, for when Ialdabaôth at last sees his creation completed, contemplating the angels all around him, he cries out in his pride: "I am a jealous god and there is no other god but me!" But, as the narrator of these myths points out, Ialdabaôth with these words admits the existence of a divinity superior to himself, for of whom would he be jealous if there were no other god?[12]

The whole tale is presented as a revelation by Jesus, who has not been crucified at all but has changed places and form with Simon of Cyrene, who

and is crucified in his place. Jesus returns to impart cer-
...achings to John and to others of his followers. The misera-
...ie earthy sphere is now in existence, according to this myth,
...as taken away all of the light powers of Sophia. Then Sophia
...s. After thirteen separate laments, her repentances at last reach
the ...., the Most High. He takes mercy on her suffering, and because
of his conc...rn for the world which has come into being through her pride,
he sends his Son, the Christ, to earth in order to redeem it.[13]

In another version of the gnostic tale of creation, Sophia, in the form of
a dove, descends into the waters below the firmament, and begets "Saturn,
who is identical with Yahweh."[14] Saturn is also called *"Sol niger"* (the black sun)
in alchemical literature, but here he is Primordial Man. Traces of Greek myth
are evident in the motif of creation by the dove resting upon the waters; and
we recall also the tale of the banishment of Saturn (Cronus) to the region
of darkness when the new king (Zeus) assumes power.

According to Saint Hippolytus, Simon Magus called the Primordial Man
*arsenothelys*, "male-female."[15] This word is compounded from the Greek *arsen*
(the male-masculine)[16] and *thele* (nipple-teat). *The* in Greek is the equivalent
of the Latin *fe* in "female."[17] As *Nous*, this gnostic representation of instinctual
wisdom beholds his reflection in the depths below, plunges down, and is caught
in the embrace of *Physis*, matter.[18] *Nous* becomes the demiurgic force responsible for the creation of the material world. There is here an alternative to the
Judeo-Christian view in Genesis of a God who creates the world and everything in it and looks around and pronounces it "good." The Gnostics saw the
Prince of Darkness as responsible for the evil in the world, either as an adversary of God or as that element needed to complete the traditional God-image.
God as Primordial Man, whether a God of Light or Prince of Darkness, is
in any case *arsenothelys*. Therefore man, earthly Adam, when he appears in
the image of the Creator, must be androgynous.

The Naassenes, a gnostic sect that takes its name from *Naas* (in Hebrew,
"serpent"), also hold that the universal Ground of Being, the Original Man,
is the Androgynous Adam. The serpent of Eden is viewed as a hero instead
of a villain because he revealed the secrets of the Tree of Knowledge that Ialdabaôth had jealously guarded from Adam and Eve. The couple becomes sexual, and therefore human, only when Eve is withdrawn from Adam's side and
Adam is able to come into a relationship with her. The cosmic drama of the
Naassenes contains three elements, as Eliade points out:

> (1) the pre-existent Logos as a divine and universal totality; (2) the Fall, which
> caused the breakup of Creation and the birth of Suffering; (3) the coming of the
> Saviour, who by his unity reintegrated the countless fragments which make up
> our present-day universe. According to the Naassenes, androgyny is one moment
> in a vast process of cosmic unification.[19]

A fragment of the gnostic document called *Little Interrogations of Mary*, and quoted by Epiphanius, shows how Christ as the "Second Adam" is brought into the orbit of sexual symbolism through a story parallel to that of the Edenic-Adam. Christ is supposed to have taken this Mary up to a mountaintop where, before her eyes, he produces a woman from his side and begins to have intercourse with her. If this crude symbolism offends our sensibilities today, it is not hard to imagine the effect it must have had upon the Christians of the third and fourth centuries. The author of the text must have been aware of this, for he writes that Mary was so shocked by what she had seen that she fell to the ground in a faint.[20]

Jung suggests that the symbolism in this legend may have been based on a visionary experience, and he cites *John 3:12* to make it clear that it is not to be taken concretely. When Mary questions Christ about the event, Christ responds to her: "If I have told you earthly things and you do not believe, how can you believe if I tell you heavenly things?" Christ is here informing Mary that he is speaking of a spiritual mystery, not because he is making a secret of it, but because its meaning is still hidden from consciousness. In bringing forth the woman from his side, Christ is not only playing the role of the Creator-God in Genesis, he is also demonstrating his androgyny in a powerfully dramatic way. The splitting of the Original Man into husband and wife means opening up the possibility of consciousness through a conjunction of the opposites in one's own being. This is what Mary sees in her vision: the counterbalancing femininity needs to be experienced emotionally in order to compensate what had been missing for her in the pure deified masculinity of Christ.[21]

Since the Christ figure is clearly androgynous here and has been shown to be so throughout medieval iconography, Jung raises the question of why is it necessary for the Lamb to come into a marriage with the Church! Why is this sacred marriage necessary when this state of his own being already includes the female![22] An answer to this is suggested by several verses from the Gnostic *Gospel According to Thomas*, of which two will be given here:

22

Jesus saw children who were being suckled. He said to his disciples: These children who are being suckled are like those who enter the Kingdom.

They said to Him: Shall we then, being children, enter the Kingdom? Jesus said to them: When you make the two one, and when you make the inner as the outer and the outer as the inner and the above as the below, and when you make the male and the female into a single one, so that the male will not be male and the female (not) be female...then shall you enter [the Kingdom].[23]

114

Simon Peter said to them: Let Mary go out from among us, because women are not worthy of the Life. Jesus said: See, I shall lead her, so that I will make her male, that she too may become a living spirit, resembling you males. For every woman who makes of herself male will enter the Kingdom of Heaven.[24]

The Christ as imaged in *The Gospel According to Thomas* is a living Christ. In him, the fourth stage of androgynous development is realized. He is always in the process of transformation, as well as being the agent of transformation for others. The key to an understanding of androgyny is in the recognition that androgyny is not a state to be attained, but rather an ideal to be sought and a way of life into which energy can be effectively directed. Androgyny is the act of becoming more conscious and therefore more whole — because only by discovering and rediscovering ourselves in *all* of our many aspects, do we increase the range and quality of our consciousness.

Gnosticism embraces convoluted and elaborate systems, and we have barely touched the surface of some of its motifs that relate directly to our theme. The reason I have mentioned this obscure material at all, knowing that it would have to be treated most summarily, is that it seems important to glimpse how Gnosticism gave itself to elaborate explanations and rationalizations and even dramatizations purporting to provide some rationale for the existence of principles in the world that either are not accounted for, or actually avoided by, the orthodox religious traditions. As far as I can determine, however, Gnosticism did not attempt to enter into the world and change the lives of people directly, as a way of expressing its doctrine.

Since we are concerned not only with the abstract problem of androgyny, but with the process of integrating its principles directly into pathways that will expand our energies and enrich our lives, it will be important to consider how the opposites were actually *united in a practical working system*. Such a system evolved from the insights of Gnosticism as well as from some of the ideas developed under the influence of the astrological mystique. The system was alchemy, a "science" that was either too wise or too naive to exclude the element of spirit from the hermetic vessels in which the work was carried on.

# Chapter 12

## The Philospher's Stone in Alchemy:
## The Androgyne Imprisoned in Matter

Gnosticism is *Mater Alchimica*, the Mother of Alchemy. Leading from gnosis to alchemy means that *Nous* comes down from the celestial space, in the form either of a dove or of a serpent, into the embrace of *Physis*. Dove or serpent, it does not matter, for both are preforms of Christ, and Christ is the symbol that stands as one of the stated goals of the alchemical process. The alchemists, who were also philosophers, never forgot the connection between the world of spirit and the world of matter. But it did not suffice for them to have gnosis alone. It was necessary to move beyond the knowledge of the doctrines concerning the mysterious metaphysical worlds. What was required was the alchemical work, the *opus*. Speculation had to find its analogue in matter. The whole secret of the process by which the opus is carried out is found in that same teaching of Hermes Trismegistus that inspired the adherents of Gnosticism. It is contained in the famous "Emerald Table of Hermes Trismegistus," the text of which was first found in the works of Jabir ibn Hayyan, one of the earliest writers in Western alchemy:

> I speak not of fictitious things, but that which is certain and true.
> What is below is like that which is above, and what is above is like that which is below, to accomplish the miracles of one thing.
> And as all things were produced by the one word of one Being, so all things were produced from this one thing by adaptation.
> Its father is the sun, its mother is the moon; the wind carries it in its belly, its nurse is the earth.
> It is the father of perfection throughout the world.
> The power is vigorous if it be changed into earth.
> Separate the earth from the fire, the subtle from the gross acting prudently and with judgment.
> Ascend with the greatest sagacity from the earth to heaven, the power of things superior and things inferior. Thus you will obtain the glory of the whole world, and obscurity will fly far away from you.
> This has more fortitude than fortitude itself; because it conquers every subtle

thing and can penetrate every solid.
Thus the world was formed.
Hence proceed wonders, which are here established.. [1]

So begins a work in which *that which is below is to be made like that which is above*, where human beings are to realize in themselves and in their work the refinement of nature and of matter by combining it with the essence of spirit. While the alchemists were working with material they were also "soul making". The work had always a seeming aspect of duality. It was expressed in a language in which everything had an apparently simple and practical description and in addition a fantastic symbolical description. If matter were base, as the gnostic doctrine had implied, and if spirit were imprisoned and held fast in matter, then it was the task of those who saw this to use all means possible to free the spirit from its bondage. Yet to be concerned only with spirit would be to miss the point altogether, for men and women are of this earth; there is no escape from corporeality. The alchemists committed themselves, therefore, to working with the materials of the earth, and to seeking their own soul development in the course of the process.

The duality of their vision was only a semblance, for in the long run what they were attempting to do was to synthesize a unitary world view in which physical facts and mystical experiences would have equal validity, playing an equally important part in shaping the affairs of the world. They did not succeed. Consequently, there developed two world views, one being rational, logical, and scientific, and the other mystical, intuitive, artistic and religious. The polarities that characterize the Age of Pisces are based to a large extent on the opposition of these two views.

Were we to accept the traditional stereotypes that have characterized the image of the masculine and the image of the feminine, it might be said that the rational-scientific world view was more "masculine" in nature and that the mystical-intuitive view was more "feminine." It could just as well be said, however, that the first view was more "creative" and the second more "receptive," or that the first view was more "active" and the second more "passive," or that the first was more "extraverted" and the second more "introverted." The important point to be made is that in order to have a complete view of anything, or a holistic approach to any problem, it is necessary to work with the opposites and find some way of bringing them into active confrontation. No more than a man or a woman can procreate without the help of the other, and no more than even a mythical god or goddess can create a material world without the help of something to relate to — if only its own emanation or the wind that blows about its formless being — can anything whatever be created or transformed without calling the principle of opposition into existence. When we use the terms "masculine" and "feminine" in our discussion of the alchemical work, it is important to realize that we are using them symbolically; that is, to represent opposing and often conflicting qualities in nature. We do not pretend merely to describe the sexual qualities of human beings. It was in the spirit of dealing with the opposites and their union that the alchemists approached the *opus*, saying: "Were it not for the earth in our work the air would fly away, neither would the fire have its nourishment, nor the water its vessel."[2]

The counterbalance to gnostic influence in the early history of alchemy was the body of pre-Socratic thought that culminated in Aristotle. Although this, too, contains a great deal of speculation, it was considerably more grounded in human experience and observation of natural phenomena. This line of thought has in its cosmogonic view features in common with those we have already discussed. There was thought to have existed before Creation a chaotic prime substance. This was referred to in alchemy as the *prima materia*. Only did this *prima materia* gain existence when it was given a form. As Aristotle defined it, form did not only mean shape, but it also had to be defined in terms of heat and cold, moisture and dryness. This follows the pattern of which we took note when we discussed the features of astrology. The four qualities were broken down into two pairs of opposites: heat-cold and dryness-moisture. Placed in form of a cross, they form a conjunction of opposites. Recombining these opposites then creates the four elements, another conjunction of opposites:

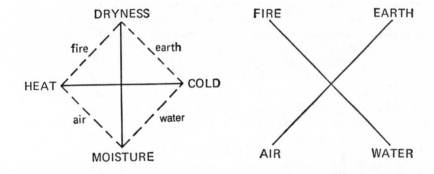

Aristotle had proposed that in each of these elements one of its two components predominated. For example, in fire, heat predominates over dryness; in water, moisture over cold. All living things are composed of quantities of all four elements in various combinations. It was thought that by substituting one of the qualities in the element for another that one element might be transmuted into another. The problem of the transmutation of substances seemed perfectly reasonable to these ancients, if only the technique could be discovered and the proper conditions for the work could be understood and carried out. The alchemists appeared to possess an insight which contemporary physics has only rediscovered in this century, that the person of the experimenter cannot help but have a profound influence upon the experiment. The alchemists also held that all metals in the earth have the potentiality to ripen into gold.

The presence of spirit in all matter was the transformative agent that would make this possible. The work of the alchemists was directed toward speeding up the process by which the spirit the matter could be released. What was required first of all was to obtain from the metals with which they worked the original substance, the *prima materia*.

Ostensibly they were working with the metals, the material substance of the work. Each metal had a correspondence to one of the planets and hence, as the alchemists understood it, had an affinity with the planetary powers: gold with the sun, silver with the moon, copper with Venus, mercury with Mercury, lead with Saturn, iron with Mars and tin with Jupiter. As can be imagined in those days when astrology was in full flower, each of these symbolic designations called forth a wealth of evocative images. The mythological terminology suggested processes in which the material itself represented for the alchemists the workings of the entire universe as well as providing a description of the inner experience of man the microcosm.

The idea of the transmutation of ordinary metals into gold would be more respectable in the eyes of the Church and the mainstream of society, it seemed to the alchemists, than would be the idea of transforming the human personality in a way that would gain higher spiritual powers for certain "realized persons." There was something surreptitious about this art, for was not the task of spiritual perfection the special providence of the priests and ministers designated by the Church? Was it not understandable, therefore, that the alchemists should have carried on their activities under the cover of a practical and potentially useful operation, so that the real work—which might have appeared threatening to the authorities—could be pursued undisturbed?

It was not, however, that they considered matter unimportant. Matter was the vehicle that carried the process, and most alchemists were involved in working with the material substances in the *laborium*, while at the same time being cognizant of the spiritual aspects of the work. Only a few concentrated on the spiritual aspect of the work entirely. The alchemist Gerhard Dorn, calling attention to the importance of the latter aspect of the work, warned that he who would acquire the chemical art must study the "true Philosophy" and not the "Aristotelian."[3] He insisted, "the arcane substance [soul] is one and the same, whether found within man or outside him."[4]

The history of alchemy is difficult to follow because the alchemists required secrecy in order to ensure their political survival. Their teachings, consonant with their own beliefs, involved liberating the individual from false concepts and preprogrammed ideas. If openly declared, the alchemists' libertarian views would have aroused the opposition of the established Church. It would not be so very different from what is engendered today from established institutions when a movement for liberation from some conventional stereotype begins to gain momentum. As a result of all this esotericism and obfuscation of the real goals, the efforts of alchemy were largely dismissed by the general public. This was not so much because people feared the consequence of a radical alteration in the physical and psychic structures of their world, but because they perceived the process as a *literal* one rather than as a *symbolic* one and saw it as much effort being expended after what was an impossibly vain and foolish hope.

Behind their smokescreen, the work of the alchemists flourished. While a misled public pointed to the fact that no gold was emerging from the *laborium* where the work was being performed, the alchemists shared with each other the precept, "our gold is not the common gold," meaning that their work was directed toward achieving the "philosopher's gold," which was not the perfection of matter but of the spirit. Matter provided both the metaphor and the vehicle for the transformative process.

If the metals could be broken down into their elements (earth, air, fire and water), the elements further broken down into their predominating qualities (heat, cold, moisture, dryness), and these qualities isolated and then recombined, it would be possible to return the substances to the original *prima materia*. Now comes the disturbing element of alchemical theory for anyone who believes in a Creator-God who has the power to rule the universe and to direct the course of human life. The intent of the alchemists, or so many believed, was to gain control of the prime matter and recombine it so that they could fashion substances of their own choosing and design. In other words, they would initiate their own process of creation. Now, of course, they were extremely careful to invoke God's help at every juncture, and to make it clear that they did not seek to do this alone but recognized the need to be in harmony with His nature and His plan, but all the same, they admitted that their work was an *opus contra naturam*. In this monumental task they were forever inveighing against *hubris*, the sin of pride against the gods, perhaps remembering the unhappy fate of Sophia. Still they were, in a sense, submitting themselves to the same risks as had that feminine emanation of the Godhead when she decided to risk an experiment in Creation on her own.

The alchemists often referred to their method as a "spagyric" art, a word compounded from two Greek words meaning "to take apart" and "to put together." Thus the process combined what are called today the analytic and the synthetic methods in chemistry. The terms "analytic" and "synthetic" are also applied by C. G. Jung to psychotherapy. Jung considered the aspect of the therapeutic endeavor that required the reduction of the complexes and symptom formations into their original components — for example, early childhood sexual traumas — an "analytic" endeavor. The recombining of the primal matter of the psyche in new ways, utilizing the archetypal or basic elements as structural components, he called the "synthetic" method. The first would be comparable to the task of extracting gold from the ore; the second to refining and synthesizing the finer substances by combining the elements.

It is again a process of working with the opposites. To accomplish the goal of integration, the manipulation of opposites is part of the technique. As Ralph Metzner has described it: "Analysis probes, goes into, takes apart: it is a masculine, dynamic function. Synthesis contains, combines, encloses: it is a feminine magnetic function. The first fusion of male and female energies, known as the *conjunction,* is the central process of alchemy."[5]

An important aspect of the alchemical work was that the combination of "female" and "male" principles referred not only to the ways in which the work was carried on, nor even to the materials that were used — each metal had a masculine or feminine association that corresponded with the planetary power: gold-sun-masculine, silver-moon-feminine, copper-Venus-feminine, iron-Mars-masculine, and so on. The work itself was carried out by a man and woman, the adept and the soror. Again, we are reminded of the Kabbalistic image of the king and his architect initiating and executing the Creation as a project that could not have been carried out without the participation of both. Pictures depicting the alchemical art often show the man on the right and the woman on the left performing the various operations in the vessel which is between them. The process is referred to as the "alchemical wedding" and it proceeds on many levels of understanding.

The crux of the process is the engagement with the *prima materia,* and this is symbolized in the problematic figure of "Mercurius" in whom all things were supposedly combined. The opposites are present in him at the start of the process, but not yet differentiated. Thus, the basis of the *opus* is an unknown substance, yet called by many names — half-chemical, half-mythological — such names as "animal of earth and sea," "chaos," "accursed of God," "Adamica," "Monad," "sea," "mother," "moon," "dragon," "microcosm." Also, it has the quality of ubiquity. Jung quotes Anaximander:

> I make known to you, ye sons of the doctrine, that the beginning of all creatures is a certain primary and everlasting and infinite nature which cooks and rules everything, and whose active and passive [aspects] are known and recognized only by those on whom the knowledge of the sacred art has been bestowed.[6]

Mercurius, also called Hermes, is not only the receptacle of the *prima materia* and the symbol for it, he also is the agent of transformation. Psychologically seen, he represents the agency of consciousness which, as it comes into being, increases our awareness of our own potentials for discriminating and evaluating. It also prepares the way for the reformation of the matter-substance-idea. Mercurius is frequently depicted as a hermaphrodite, an image designed to reflect the nature of Divinity, which is "All in One." The mythical teacher Hermes Trismegistus, in revealing his secrets to Asclepius, says: "God has no name, or rather he has all names, since he is at once One and All. Infinitely rich with the fertility of both sexes, he is continuously bringing to birth all those things which he planned to create." The young healer god then asks: "What, you say that God has both sexes, Trismegistus?" "Yes, Asclepius, and not God alone but all beings animate and vegetable."[7]

The elements with which the alchemists work are seen through the dark glass of symbol and metaphor as bipolar constructs: "sun-moon," "sulfur-salt," "king-queen," "heaven-earth," "fire-water," "living-dead," "open-occult" and, of course, "masculine-feminine." The process moves in stages that are often described as "death," "torture," "killing," "dissolving," all with the object of breaking the matter down into its original state. The work on the soul is an integral, though not always stated or understood, part of the process. This means being able to commit oneself to the work, to put into a secondary space the purely personal and ego concerns (the psychological concomitant of the earth-centered world view) and to see oneself as part and parcel of the entire universe. The image to be held before one is that every act by every person has an effect on all, changing the delicate balance that keeps the universe in motion. Therefore, it was considered necessary by the alchemists to conduct their work and their lives, which were really the same thing, as if the salvation of the world depended upon it.

The breaking down of substances into the *prima materia* would bring about the stage called the *nigredo*, which is characterized by the utter blackness of the original chaos. It is a period of destruction and despair, and it is absolutely essential to the process. It has its parallel in mystical literature as the "dark night of the soul" or in mythology as the descent into the underworld or the night-sea journey in the belly of the sea monster. The *nigredo* is akin also to what is experienced by an individual as deep depression, either suffering a physical illness or beset by a dis-ease, a weariness of soul. It is the bottom of the pit, where disorientation and weakness and hopelessness are the quality of life. Often this is the condition of people who seek the help of a psychotherapist. The kind of healing they seek is what the word "healing" essentially means; that is, "to be made whole."

The task requires the process of purification. The alchemists called this work the *albedo* or "whitening." It was not a single process but many, involving repeated separations, drying out, moistening, dissolving, coagulating, fermenting, combining and separating out, again and again. The object of this stage was to bring about a condition where a new union could take place between opposites which had been broken down through the agency of operations personified in Mercurius.

The psychological analogue for this *albedo* is the torture and agony that the individual soul experiences when the mode of life is no longer in keeping with the reality of the totality of the psyche. One is living a lie, or else life is felt to be without value or meaning; and it becomes necessary to examine every aspect of being, painful though that examination is. I have found no truer image of the agony this entails than that in Blake's *The Four Zoas*. Fallen Man has become separated from his feminine aspect, his "Emanation," and trembling and pale he cries:

> Why wilt thou Examine every little fibre of my soul,
> Spreading them out before the sun like stalks of flax to dry?
> The infant joy is beautiful, but its anatomy
> Horrible, Ghast & Deadly; nought shalt thou find in it
> But Death, Despair & Everlasting brooding Melancholy.
> Thou wilt go mad with horror if thou dost Examine thus

Every moment of my secret hours. Yes, I know
That I have sinn'd, & that my Emanations are become harlots
I am already distracted at their deeds, & if I look
Upon them more, Despair will bring self-murder on my soul.[8]

The vessel in which the alchemical process takes place is symbolized as the coffin of the impotent old king At the same time it is capable of becoming the womb in which the new seed would develop and where the resurrection can take place. Again, Blake speaks of Primal Man:

> Sing
> His fall into Division & his Resurrection to Unity
> His fall into the Generation of decay & death, & his
> Regeneration by the Resurrection from the dead.[9]

The synthetic phase of the psychological healing process is the analogue for the portion of the alchemical process that makes the "Resurrection" seem possible. The suffering that has come about as a result of either spiritual or physical disintegration provides the strength and substance for the distillation of the new orientation toward life. The individual who has experienced life from a single perspective, that of consciousness, has been felled by the violent attack of the unconscious or unknown opposite. The long process of coming to terms with the unconscious forces within the individual psyche, if carried out under the aspect of good fortune, grace or the proper conditions, brings the sufferer at last to a place where something new may be conceived.

In alchemical language this may be stated as the conjunction of sulphur and salt. Sulphur, characterized as masculine, is related to the sun. The alchemist Dorn said, "The male and universal seed, the first and most potent, is the solar sulphur, the first part and most potent cause of generation,"[10] and it is called the "homogeneous sperm," "the living fire," and there are numerous other designations. Salt is usually characterized as feminine, coming from the sea, whose tides are under the aspect of the moon. The importance of the feminine principle as partner in the process is made clear in the statement "he who works without salt draws a bow without a string."[11]

The conjunction of the opposites, under the agency of the figure of Mercurius, brings about a new union in alchemy. The opposites have been differentiated, and the newly formed substances purified. In terms of the development of the human soul, either through meditation or through psychological work, this corresponds to the differentiation of the various qualities that make up our own personalities. This means that we are able to break loose our idea of what we are from the self-images we have constructed in order to conform to what we imagine to be the expectations of our parents, our duties in life or our roles in society. It means that we end the confusion between our essential selves and the adaptive covering we pull over our faces to protect ourselves from the hazards of the normal events of everyday life. This covering, or *persona* as Jung called it, is absolutely as necessary as clothing in a winter storm; but equally necessary is it for us to know that the *persona* can be removed, and that the vulnerable being can stand exposure in situations where personal intimacy is possible.

A second aspect of the psychological analogue to the alchemical process is the facing of our personal *shadow*, which in its deepest darkness brings forth the image of the *nigredo*. We face our shames and guilts and the evil aspects of our own natures and we acknowledge ownership of them. But we do not need to wallow in the putrefaction of our own excesses and limitations. Instead, we are to work with them until we have accepted them as the realities of our nature instead of pathologies, and have done the best we could with them. The *nigredo* whitens; life lightens.

A third aspect of the psychological analogue to alchemy is the long and complicated process of discovering the contrasexual-other within ourselves. A man tends to find his femininity first in the woman he admires. He sees "the feminine" embodied in her. His initial tendency is to allow her, even expect her, to live that femininity for him. This does not only mean that the woman may be expected by him to perform the functions his societal group normally assigns to women. It does not even mean that he may expect her to function emotionally in the gentler and softer ways that seem less appropriate for men. At some point of the process of coming into the fullness of his own being, a man will have to withdraw these expectations from the woman or women in his life. This is not to say that a woman should not behave in the so-called "feminine" ways. What I am saying is that the man has to cease *expecting* that from her. The woman must be and has every right to be the person she is, and a man in working out the problem of the contrasexual opposites must learn to stop projecting his own confused and unrecognized contrasexual qualities upon women. If he feels a need for tenderness, then let him be tender himself, and see what that evokes from the world.

The woman who experiences the alchemical process in psychological terms, through working out the conjunction of opposites in her own nature, has a similar task. A woman who has been reared to believe that in order to be adequate as a feminine person her manner must be at all times gentle and sensitive, that she must be prepared to defer to others, especially to men, and that she must avoid competitiveness or strong expressions of opinion—this woman will have a difficult time of it if she attempts to enter the so-called "man's world" and deal with it on its own terms. She may be able to overcome her habitual reluctance to assert herself; nevertheless because of background and early training she may find that no matter how much she may achieve in the world, she continues to be devilled by a nagging feeling of inadequacy. If questioned, it develops that this sense of inadequacy means "inadequate as a woman," or "insufficiently feminine." The alchemical model allows, even encourages, her to accept the opposite element within herself, realizing the natural androgyny of the human psyche. As a woman striving to succeed in the world, yet torturing herself because she feels obliged to perform all the traditional feminine rituals whether she wants to or not, she fears that she must end up a psychological hermaphrodite — a hideous anomaly who hides first one aspect of her nature from view, and then the other. But if she can somehow come to the point of transformation, if she can accept that *both* parts of her nature are *legitimate*, then it become unnecessary to display either her "masculinity" or her "femininity." She can simply *be who she is*, a person in whom opposite tendencies can exist not as enemies but as lovers, with one aspect fertilizing the other, who can then carry the fruit of the union into a real existence.

In both cases, man and woman are moving from an ambivalent state, akin to the hermaphroditic image, toward the state of dynamic energy exchange that androgyny implies. Neither in the personal work of the individual on his or her own psychic development, nor in the alchemical *opus* performed under the guise of chemical operations with metals and other substances, was the conjunction of opposites the end of the process. The true goal, as stated at the beginning of the *opus*, was the making of "gold," but not the ordinary gold.

The end of the process would be the liberation of the new substance, for which there were many names. The "philosopher's gold" was also the "philosopher's stone," "the diamond body," "the golden elixir of life," "the panacea." Of all the names by which the longed-for culmination of efforts was designated, the one most expressive of the value placed upon it was this: the *filius philosophorum*, the son of the philosopher. Through this name we see that the human soul is the earthly counterpart of God's only begotten son, the Christ, who is given to men and women that they may know that they too are divine — as it is said, "it is no longer I who lives, but Christ who lives in me."

The mystery and the miracle is that through the *work* the *filius philosophorum* is produced. It does not simply happen, it is not a gift of grace (although grace may play a part), but it is the result of hard work and devotion and the application of man and woman to the process in the right spirit. That spirit is a free spirit, a spirit of experimentation, and of personal discovery through personal effort and personal commitment. It cannot be done by anyone for anyone else, for each person is the alchemist, working with his soror if he be a man, or her adept if she be a woman; and the soror or adept is within each of us. We share the work with this partner, who is the personification of a part of the psyche. This soul, in close participation with the unconscious, is freer than is the conscious personality from the uncompromising demands of the material world we live in. The soul is the part of us that bring us into balance with the rest of the cosmos.

We pause to reflect on the *opus* performed by the alchemists, and wonder if it has meaning for our times. It seems that the alchemists' purpose was to resolve the problem posed by Gnosticism, of how to contend with a world condemned to evil as a result of *Nous* having descended to earth and being captured in the embrace of *Physis*. If spirit, in all its complexity, is imprisoned in the abode of matter, then the alchemists sought to redeem that spirit through their work. Only if these efforts were successful could the *filius philosophorum* come into being—and analogously, only through devotion to the work could human beings become liberated from the state of unconsciousness imposed upon them by the continuing war of the inner opposites.

Alchemy reached its zenith in the eighteenth century, but by the time of the French Revolution interest in it was already waning. It foundered on its lack of any adequate knowledge of natural processes, and it quietly slipped into obscurity with the coming of the age of scientific materialism. The great rift between faith and knowledge grew ever more extensive. Jung described the polarity characteristic of the last years of the Age of Pisces:

> Faith lacked experience and science missed out on the soul. Instead, science believed fervently in absolute objectivity and assiduously overlooked the fundamental difficulty that the real vehicle and begetter of all knowledge is the *psyche*, the very thing that scientists knew the least about for the longest time. It was regarded as a symptom of chemical reactions[ironically!], an epiphenomenon of biological processes in the brain cells— indeed, for some time it did not exist at all. Yet all the while scientists remained totally unaware of the fact that they were using for their observations a photographic apparatus of whose nature and structure they knew practically nothing, and whose very existence many of them were unwilling to admit.[12]

Modern science, even with its electron microscopes, its computers and its space probes, could not find the "spirit," so science concerned itself primarily with "matter." Those scientists, like Jung and Einstein and others who were intensely occupied with human concerns, were thought to be somewhat unreliable when they strayed from what was supposed to be their area of expertise to champion a holistic world view.

Scientific materialism reached its peak in the twentieth century with a reversal of human values, epitomized at Auschwitz and Hiroshima. The opposites had been polarized as completely as one could imagine. In the midst of all this, a reaction has begun to set in. The new revolution in consciousness is slowly gaining in strength. In the creative process that will bring about a new age, we have the chance to evolve a higher form of existence through learning the lessons of the past. To paraphrase Pascal: the soul has its history, which history does not know.

# Chapter 13

## Adam Kadmon in Kabbalah:
## The Tree of Life as Androgyne

Since the planet was manufactured by larger forces, we can trace our lineage to the universe. This is not a matter of dreamy speculation but of fact. Hydrogen, oxygen, nitrogen, and carbon, the fundamental elements employed by life on Earth, are the most abundant chemically active elements in the universe. The calcium in our bones was cooked in ancient stars, then seeded into the dust and gas from which the sun and its planets formed. Earth's gold and uranium were spewed into deep space by exploding stars and swept up by the infant Earth, much later to cause us excitement and trouble. As the Nobel laureate biologist George Wald put it, "We living things are a late outgrowth of the metabolism of the galaxy."[1]

When today's "facts" are presented in literate prose, as Professor Timothy Ferris has done, the images seem in striking parallel to those described by the medieval mystic who gave form to the Kabbalistic *Book of Splendor*, the *Zohar*:

"In the beginning"—when the will of the King began to take effect, he engraved signs into the heavenly sphere [that surrounded him]. Within the most hidden recess a dark flame issued from the mystery of the *eyn sof*, the Infinite, like a fog forming in the unformed—enclosed in the ring of that sphere, neither white nor black, neither red nor green, of no color whatever. Only after this flame began to assume size and dimension, did it produce radiant colors. From the innermost center of the flame sprang forth a well out of which colors issued and spread upon everything beneath, hidden in the mysterious hiddenness of *eyn sof*.

The well broke through and yet did not break through the ether [of the sphere]. It could not be recognized at all . . .

When King Solomon "penetrated into the depths of the nut garden," as it is written, "I descended into the garden of nuts," he took up a nut shell and studying it, he saw an analogy in its layers with the spirits which motivate the central desires of humans, as it is written, "and the delights of the sons of men [are from] male and female demons."

The Holy One, be blessed, saw that it was necessary to put into the world all of these things so as to make sure of permanence, and of having, so to speak,

107

a brain surrounded by numerous membranes. The whole world, upper and lower, is organized on this principle, from the primary mystic center to the very out-
ermost of all the layers. All are coverings, the one to the other, brain within brain,
spirit inside spirit, shell within shell.[2]

The *Zohar* is the best-known book of the extensive Jewish Kabbalistic literature. The literature finds its sources in the traditions of the Jewish Gnostics,
mystics who speculated on, contemplated, and possibly even experienced in
an ecstatic way the ascent of the soul toward the Heavenly Halls. This belonged to a movement of profound spiritual intensity. It arose during the period
of the Second Temple (ca. 538 B.C.-A.D. 70), and has left us tractates of only
a fragmentary kind. In all probability these tractates were originally part of
a secret oral tradition, and were only later written down, and then only spo-
radically and partially. Much of what has been preserved in writing has not
yet been translated into English. When this is made available, a far deeper
insight into the origins of Kabbalism than we presently have will be possible.

The early writings centered mainly around *Merkabah* mysticism. The Vision of Ezekiel was the central fable of this tradition, and the description of
the *Merkabah* or Throne Chariot of God was the focal point of all meditation.
The movement of the soul toward the Throne of the unknown God was
described in terms of a journey through seven palaces lying beyond the seven
heavens, and there are involved elaborate fantasies of discussions such as might
be held between the keepers of the heavenly gates and the traveler. All of this,
as I write about it, gives me the strange feeling that it bears a more than ac-
cidental resemblance to questions raised in the article of Timothy Ferris quoted
at the beginning of this chapter. Here Ferris, in his "speculation on the possibility of interstellar communication," suggests that growing out of a 1971 U.S.-
U.S.S.R. conference on extra-terrestrial life derives "the notion that we humans may be destined to find ourselves micro-organisms in a mind wide as
a galaxy."[3]

In our day we are sufficiently enlightened to know that the hypotheses of
scientists deal with well-grounded data that brings us closer to Truth, while
the pre-Christian mystics were enmeshed in fantasies that grew out of their
own psychological needs and orientations, as well as their very limited knowledge of the facts of nature. So, of course, the old *Merkabah* mysticism with its
attempts to ascend to the throne of the Most High through all the heavenly
spheres sounds very primitive in comparison with today's astronomers' attempts
to initiate communication with intelligence in the galaxies. Yet one cannot
help but wonder, in those moments before sleep when anything seems possible, how our twentieth-century formulations will appear to the scientist of the
thirtieth century.

But to return to the Kabbalah. The tradition of *Merkabah* mysticism was
the foundation of the later work on the questions surrounding the creation
of the world, questions that are no less fascinating to the human mind now
than they were in ancient times. Sometime between the sixth and third cen-

tury B.C., there arose within the early rabbinic tradition *Maaseh Bereshith*, the esoteric discipline dealing with theories of cosmogony and cosmology. It was clearly stated that the speculative studies contained therein were not for everyone, but only for those who were specially called, and then the secret knowledge was passed from master to disciple in accordance with the latter's capacity to absorb and assimilate the highly charged material. The prohibition against wider dissemination of the information contained in the speculations was felt to be necessary because of the possibility of incorrect interpretation, which might then lay the scholars open to charges of heresy.[4] As we have seen before, the act of venturing into the mysteries beyond the conventionally recognized range of human knowledge inspires resistance from the orthodox establishment, whether that orthodoxy be religious or scientific. Today, there is very little government support available for interstellar communication.

The *Sefer Yetsirah* or "Book of Creation" has come down to us from the *Maaseh Bereshith*. Even the fullest version contains no more than sixteen hundred words. It outlines a doctrine that was understood to have been revealed by God to the patriarch Abraham at the time that he made his covenant with him, and the doctrine was then passed down orally by Abraham through his sons. The final chapter of the *Sefer Yetsirah* clearly seems to have been the result of a visionary experience. In it are disclosed the revelation of the ten *Sefiroth*, or numbers, which originally appear as forms of light; and then comes the description of the establishment of the Hebrew alphabet as a divine instrument of creation which in its totality is the foundation of all things.[5]

It is with the material on the *Sefiroth* that we will be primarily concerned here. This is a relatively small part of the extensive Kabbalistic literature that developed over the centuries, but it is an extremely crucial one, particularly in reference to the theme of androgyny. The doctrine of the *Sefiroth* is dealt with extensively in the *Zohar*. This *Book of Splendor*, formerly thought to have been a compilation of many authors and their works, is now considered by modern scholars to have been almost exclusively the work of one man, Moses de Leon, who wrote it in Spain, toward the end of the thirteenth century. In the *Zohar*, the two branches of Kabbalism come together, the *practical* and the *speculative*. The practical had mainly to do with magical, mantic, and numerical manipulations devised and practiced in order for the initiate to become skilled in using the power inherent in the Divine for purposes of living on this earth. The speculative branch, which concerned itself mainly with penetrating the veils of mystery surrounding the Light of Creation, is more relevant to our theme.

In the sense that the *Zohar* begins with the appearance of Light, it starts where alchemy culminates. The alchemical *opus* consisted in the long process consisted in the long process of dismantling the substances of the material world (and its psychological correlates) and returning them to the dark chaos where they had their origin. Long and patient efforts would be employed to bring this *prima materia* toward the goal, the philosopher's stone — not a stone in the common sense, but a "diamond body" or uncorruptible substance of "gold." The "philosopher's gold" pointed to the light of the sun — again a symbol for the universal power that rules over and infuses the "above" as well as the "below." If the goal of the alchemists was the liberation of the spirit (the redemption of the philosopher's stone from matter), then the goal of the Kabbalist was just the opposite; that is, to *incorporate* (in the literal sense of the word) the spirit into the body, into the human experience and into the material world. That spirit is expressed as Light, and Light is the beginning of the Kabbalah. Everything we see, everything we have, everything we do, is to be infused with the divine spirit as manifested in Light. It is not something we have to do or have to make, in the way that the alchemists had to perform their work. Rather, it is a state in which Nature and the world exist, a harmonious state in which we find ourselves. Our task, and the Kabbalah points the way to it, is to become conscious of the manner in which we exist within the cosmic scheme. The Kabbalah describes how the divine universe emerged from a state of chaos into a designed order. It suggests how human beings can become aware of this celestial model and, guided by it, transform their own sense of inner chaos into the inner order inherent within it. Self-awareness and awareness of the divine element in ourselves awaken us toward an end, a goal in which the order within ourselves reflects the universal order. This universal "harmony of the spheres" has been a human dream ever since the Chaldean astrologers looked up and marveled, and imagined a Zodiacal Man as the prototype of every human man and woman.

Plato began with the "idea" and saw objects in the sensible world as images of "ideas" or "archetypes." The *Zohar* carries the investigation further. It asks, what precedes the idea? How does the first nebulous, dimly recognizable flash first emerge into consciousness? How does it shape itself in the mind even before it is possible to give verbal form to it?[6] Gnosticism's concern was with *Nous*, the fallen spirit embodied as intellect or creative power or energy, alienated from its supernal origins and held in the grip of *Physis*, matter. The task of alchemy, building on Gnosticism, was the redemption of the spirit, and its purification and separation out from matter so that what was below could be reconstructed upon the model of what was above.

Now, as we look at Kabbalism, we will see that once more we face an engagement of "above" and "below." But in this view, the perfect order of the heavenly spheres has been disturbed through no fault of human beings. According to the tradition, all this happened in that mythical time before creation had been completed and when no human being existed. As reflections of a universe that has already been damaged through the exercise of its own overwhelming and uncontrollable power, we humans experience the shattering fragmentation of our own natures. Through devoting ourselves to the comprehension and interpretation of the divine plan or intentional order of the universe, we may discover the pathways we need to traverse in order to heal ourselves. In doing so, we may utilize the opportunity to participate in the reunification of the entire cosmos. In the Kabbalistic tradition, the human being does not work *for* God in order that human kind may be redeemed;

nor does he make of himself a sacrifice in order to redeem the stone or the living Christ. In Kabbalah the work is *with* God; that is, we are to put ourselves into that relationship with God in which through a constantly operating system of energy exchanges and a mutual relationship of intense loving, God and his manifestation in the human being interact to redeem each other.

I have difficulty, naturally, in communicating what I mean by "God" and what I mean by "Love" in this context. By neither word do I mean a lofty abstraction, or a shorthand expression for a philosophical concept. Nor do I mean, by either word, something that is entirely anthropomorphic. The term "symbolic" comes closer if we mean by symbolic the use of a word that evokes a strong emotional reaction — pointing to a whole complex of ideas that have unusual significance and that also carry the sense of the weight of more than what is known — a quantum of mystery, if you will. So the term "symbolic" only hints at the meanings of "God" and "Love," and it is not sufficient. There is another element that is far more palpable than the "symbolic," an element that enlivens the individual when he even touches the word, that fills him with a longing for contact, for interaction, for giving and for receiving, and sooner or later for bringing something new into being. So then this creative force, which is embodied in the terms "God" and "Love," is nothing more or less than the profound *energy* that moves the stars and also the human being, whether the person turns toward the heavens in awe and wonder, or sees the enrapturing beauty in the eyes of one who is dearly loved. Therefore, we will understand the erotic elements in the Kabbalah, on the several levels in which they appear, not merely symbolically but as referring to real relationship, to passionate love relationship between human beings and the universe, and between men and women, and among men, and among women, and in the most intimate and real sense, between the masculine and feminine elements in each individual.

Before discussing the cosmogony as put forth in the *Zohar*, I want to draw attention to the concepts of "masculine" and "feminine," as I will use them in writing about the Kabbalah. I have a dual purpose here. The first is to make more comprehensible the way in which these terms are used throughout Kabbalistic material. The second has to do with an application for our own day, and perhaps to relieve some of the pressure on those who object to the designation of certain characteristics of the personality as "masculine" and "feminine." The so-called sex gender "stereotypes" from which so many men and women today are seeking to be liberated, may be often inapplicable to present-day society because of the rapid sociological change that we are currently experiencing. Gender roles no longer depend so completely upon an individual's biological sex as they did in ancient and medieval times.

In the days of the *Zohar*, for example, there was for all intents and purposes *no practical difference* between sex and gender. Man's function was to penetrate the world, through labor and through intellect, and to initiate action through what might be expressed as "the sowing of the seed," an expression that could be equally well applied to his function as father of the family and to his function in the world. Woman's function was to receive the seed; that is, to be receptive, to provide the atmosphere in which growth could take place. She was to support and sustain the man, and give him the rest and peace he required in order to take on his responsibility in the world. She was occupied in the main with childbearing and rearing and maintaining the religious spirit in the home and, since women did not regularly survive their husbands, the problems of the woman alone in her middle or later years did not exist. Women had little concern for "the second half of life," in our terms. They sought no "second career" after their children were grown. Anatomy and gender roles for both man and woman were consistent in those days to a far greater degree than they are today. So it is perfectly natural that in speaking of "qualities," as I will do when I discuss the "masculine" and the "feminine" manifestations of God in the *Sefiroth*, imagery will be used that was as close to the individuals who conceived it as their own bodies and sexual experience. Since in that time eroticism was not separated into profane and sacred types, it is not surprising that the erotic language expresses the living presence of spirit in human life in a way that cannot be characterized as only symbolic. The passion is real. If I wanted to put it in terms more acceptable to scientific and psychological investigators, I could call it "energy." Energy is generated through the interaction of opposites.

Before there was matter or any created thing, or any Creator to conceive of a creation; before all that, there was Mystery. According to Kabbalah, It cannot be described, as It had no qualities whatever. The name that was given to It was *En Sof*, which translates into "limitless" or "boundless."[7] The *En Sof* precedes the God of the Bible, or any of the gods of creation. The *En Sof* is everywhere, and yet there is no place where It can be found. Since It cannot be defined, scholars have attempted to say something about It by saying what It is not, but even this defies comprehension. Being composed of no-thing, It is "nothing," and this is difficult to conceive of inasmuch as the *En Sof* was imagined to have filled the great All, outside of which nothing existed. Being limitless and filling All, before creation could begin it would be necessary for there to be primordial space in which a finite world (or worlds) could be placed. They say that the *En Sof's* first act was a contraction into Itself. This withdrawal left the primordial space, which nevertheless contained something of the divine presence. Thus, the *En Sof*, which was limitless, began the creative process by a first act, in which it placed a limitation upon itself.

The second act of the *En Sof* was that of emanation. A small dim spark, a point of light, issued forth from the Infinite, and gradually took form and glowed as a flame. The form taken was a configuration that existed, yet did not exist materially in the sense in which we think of a material existence. It existed as fire exists without having substance. Then, out of the glow it could be seen that the light coalesced into the form of Adam Kadmon, the Primordial Man. This was not Adam of the Garden but, as we will see, was the celestial archetype after which Edenic-Adam was fashioned.

Another reading of this act is that the original point of Light extended and there shone forth in it seven letters which did not solidify but remained fluid. Afterward Darkness issued forth, and it also did not solidify but remained fluid and in it seven other letters appeared. Then there issued the Firmament, in which eight letters took shape, and this also remained fluid for a time and placed itself between the seven letters on the right and the seven letters on the left. When the Firmament took shape and solidified as the vault of the heavens, the twenty-two letters of the Hebrew alphabet also solidified, and in that moment the Holy Torah was engraved. This Torah, the mystical symbolic Torah that was conceived before the world, was to become the source of all the knowledge that would come into being. This corresponds to the Word that, in the Christian Bible, existed "In the beginning."

What was engraved first were the words: "Let there be light," which was understood as the calling forth or sowing of seed. Whereupon *El Gadol* (great God) emerged from the primal ether on the Right, and *El Gadol* was masculine in nature. "And there was" signified Darkness, which is called *Elohim*, and which appeared on the Left, and is feminine in nature. Then comes "Light," signifying "that the Left was included in the Right and the Right was included in the Left."[8] Primordial Man, Torah, or the God of Genesis—whatever tradition we read discloses that the Androgyne was the beginning of Creation. As above, so below.

The Kabbalah reformulates the entire Genesis story of Creation in terms of the *Sefiroth*, the ten mystical numbers or emanations of light that streamed forth from the original point of light which the *En Sof's* first acts had brought into being. It is said that the lights of the *Sefiroth* burst forth from the eyes, mouth, nose and ears of Adam Kadmon. At first these ten *Sefiroth* were only concentrations of light, totally undifferentiated, and without the qualities that were later assigned to them. The *En Sof's* original plan of creation was that these *Sefiroth* would become more heavily concentrated and so be able to receive the beams of light from the eyes of Adam Kadmon. The first three *Sefiroth* called *Kether, Binah* and *Hokmah* received the light without difficulty, but when it came time to fill the vessels of the seven lower *Sefiroth* the intensity of the streams of light was so great that it burst the vessels, so that the light from the eyes of Adam Kadmon, as well as the lights that had composed the vessels, shattered into myriads of sparks and fell into the realm of the shells. These were the wastes of the "primordial Kings" who represented the several creations that God had made and did not like, before he finally made that creation of which it is said, "And God saw that it was good."[9]

The idea of several successive creations of the world, of which our own is the latest and the least perfect of all, is not unique to the literature of Kabbalah. It also existed in Greek mythology; it is found in the four *yugas* of the Hindu world cycle, and in other places.

The "necessary interplay between the yes and no of the creative process" is offered in the following Talmudic analogy,

First, the Holy One, Blessed be He, tried to create the world according to the

measure of mercy [grace] but it fell apart. Then he tried to create it according
to the measure of justice [*din*, judgment] but that too fell apart. What did he do?
He took an equal measure of mercy and mixed it with an equal measure of justice, and the result was our world.[10]

*Justice* and *Mercy* in the sefirothic schema, represent feminine and masculine
elements, respectively, and so it is clear that without a harmonious balance
between these two, the world could not have been created. The entire schema
of the *Sefiroth* are traditionally represented as a diagrammatic "Tree of Life"
consisting of a central column containing four *Sefiroth*, a right column containing three and a left column containing three. The mixture of the masculine and feminine *Sefiroth* provide a most interesting interplay of elements which
combine into a perfect model of the Androgyne.

The three *Sefiroth* of the column on the left are designated as "feminine,"
the three on the right as "masculine." The central column of four *Sefiroth* shows
*Kether*, the *Sefira* at the top, as "masculine," *Malkuth*, the lowest *Sefira*, as "feminine," and the two between as androgynous (or, in some versions, *Tifereth* is
"feminine" and *Yesod* "masculine").

In another image traditional within Kabbalism the *Sefiroth* are depicted as
the parts of the "body" of Adam Kadmon. Some Kabbalists say that the body
of Adam Kadmon was the first manifestation of the ray of light that emanated from the *En Sof*, and that the *Sefiroth* were in turn emanations from the
body of Adam Kadmon. With this latter idea in mind, let us consider the
doctrine of the *Sefiroth* as related to the body of the Primordial Man.[11]

*Kether* means "crown," and is the topmost of the *Sefiroth*, associated with the
head. It is also called the source and is masculine.

*Hokmah* means "wisdom," and is shown on the right side of the head or at
the right shoulder. It is also the brain and it is masculine.

*Binah* is "intelligence," and is shown at the left shoulder or the heart. As heart,
it means the kind of intelligence that consists of understanding. *Binah* is
feminine.

These three, *Kether*, *Hokmah* and *Binah*, comprise the first triad, which is concerned with the head and its thinking function. Thought was not only to be
a rational process, it was to be related intimately with the feeling function.
This triad is called *Neshamah*, the first and most sublime state of the soul.

*Hesed* means "mercy" or "love" and is visualized as the right arm of Adam
Kadmon. It is masculine.

*Gevurah*, "judgment" or "power" belongs to the left arm, and is feminine.
While this does not necessarily conform to the modern stereotype of the feminine, it nevertheless corresponds to a containing power that is needed to keep
in balance what the writers saw as the overflowing tendencies of the masculine, especially as regards mercy or love.

*Tifereth*, "beauty" is the chest of Adam Kadmon. *Tifereth* is the offspring of
*Hesed* and *Gevurah*, is androgynous and mediates between the two parents. The
three together constitute the second triad of the *Sefiroth*, and corresponds to

*Ruach*, the state of the soul concerned with the moral and intellectual world.

*Netsah*, as "victory" or "endurance" is the right leg and is masculine; while *Hod*, as "majesty" or "glory" is the left leg and is feminine.

*Yesod*, which is called "foundation" is represented by the genitals, in which the male and female organs are combined. *Yesod* in union with *Netsah* and *Hod* comprises the third triad, the state of the soul called *Nefesh*, which has to do with the material world. The other two triads in the schema relate to higher levels of existence.

And finally, there is *Malkuth*, the "feet," which is also called "Kingdom," and symbolizes Adam Kadmon's harmony or wholeness. *Malkuth* is feminine, and is related to earth.

As a rule Adam Kadmon is imagined as being seen from the back, with his right and left sides corresponding to our own. It is of this image that the following passage in Exodus (33:19-23) is said to refer. After Moses has asked to look upon the glory of the Lord, the Lord responds:

> And he said, "I will make all my goodness pass before you, and will proclaim before you my name 'The Lord'; and I will be gracious to whom I will be gracious, and I will show mercy on whom I will show mercy. But," he said, "you cannot see my face; for man shall not see me and live." And the Lord said, "Behold, there is a place by me where you shall stand upon the rock; and while my glory passes I will put you in a cleft of the rock, and I will cover you with my hand until I have passed by; then I will take away my hand, and you shall see my back; but my face shall not be seen."

Once more we discover in the hidden or esoteric doctrine the image of the cosmic God who presents himself as the androgynous model for the human psyche, which is composed of consciousness and soul. The necessarily androgynous *Self*, as Jung understood the term, is that center of psychic totality which is the product of the conjunction of the opposites. The conscious aspect corresponds to the ego-image which in men is masculine, and in women, feminine, for who would wish to be perceived as other than what he or she really is? And yet we are more than our conscious selves; that inward extension of our being which we call "soul" (and which Jung called "anima" in men and "animus" in women) carries those qualities that are not naturally a part of consciousness. Therefore, they are experienced as "other" or "contrasexual." That inward part, the soul, becomes conscious only through the spiritual task, the *opus contra naturam*.

Another configuration of the *Sefiroth* conceives of the ten together as the Tree of Life, with its crown, *Kether*, in the heavens and its roots in earth, *Malkuth*. There, below *Kether*, the crown, which is the God of Creation, are the two attributes: *Hokmah* (wisdom), the masculine principle, situated on the right, and *Binah* (understanding or intelligence), the feminine principle, situated on the left. *Hokmah* and *Binah* are called "two friends who never part." Their union produces the life energy that sustains the universe. *Hokmah* is the primal flash of mind, the impregnating seed, while *Binah* is the vessel in which this seed receives its form. In *Hokmah*, perception is attained through a quick flash, it is the spark of generation; *Binah* is expressed as labor and meditation. The intuitive thought of *Hokmah* is assimilated into *Binah*, where it has the opportunity to develop and grow, and where it may be sheltered until the time is right for it to be brought forth. It is said that every idea that springs from

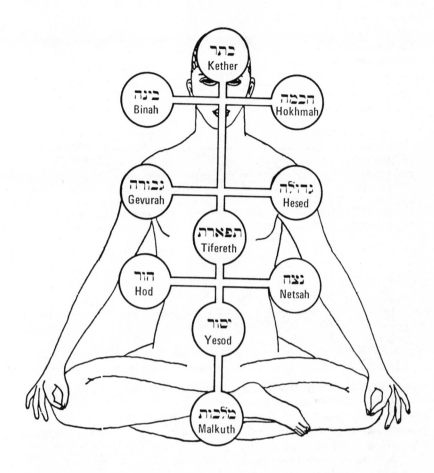

wisdom requires a period of gestation before it is ready for exposure in the world.[12]

From this interrelationship the rabbis extracted formulae for the behavior of women. But clearly, another interpretation is possible. The "two friends who never part" cannot refer to man and woman, for inevitably these part in one way or another, and eventually in death. The two friends, in my view, must be consciousness and the soul, the two friends within each individual. The first is the awareness which is a product of Logos (thought and words), while the second is a product of Eros (feeling and action). What may well be meant by the expression "two friends who never part" is the recognition of that individual and personal androgynous core which reflects in human beings the Logos and Eros of the Divine Androgyne.

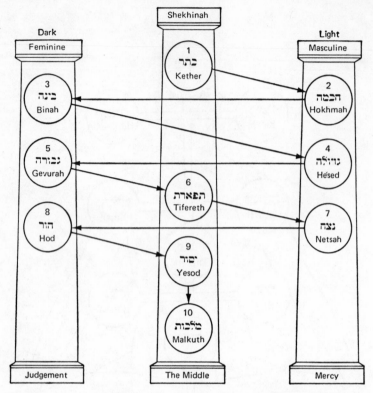

"On earth as it is in Heaven," the masculine and feminine opposites are not always united; therefore human beings often feel at odds with themselves and experience nameless longings that seem to be impossible to succor. There is a celestial archetype that speaks to this, and one expression of it may be traced back to the concepts of Isaac Luria, the sixteenth-century Kabbalist, and his followers. It explains that the original unity and wholeness of the androgynous Primal Man has been torn apart, and consequently the harmony of the *Sefirotic* world has been disturbed. The feminine part of Primal Man, Adam Kadmon, was represented by the *Shekhinah;* together they formed the totality of the *Sefiroth*. The *Shekhinah* had been split off and in this way Primal Man had become divided into male and female opposites. One of the grandest and deepest conceptions taken from this is the doctrine that states:

> Just because of this split, God needs man, whose task it is to reunite the riven opposites within the divine personality itself. From this point of view the exile of the Jewish people receives a deep and special meaning. For this exile of the people corresponds in the "upper world," so to speak, to an exile of the Shekhinah; who went into exile with them. The return of the Jewish people from exile, therefore means, in Jewish mysticism, the redemption of the Jewish people; it is above

all an earthly image, and likeness of an inner-divine drama of redemption, of the homecoming of the Shekhinah to God... So, while man needing redemption strives to restore the disturbed world order, he is at the same time working toward the redemption of God and his union with the Shekhinah, and thus toward the restoration and realization of the wholeness of God.[13]

The *Zohar*, in referring to the *hieros gamos*, the sacred marriage between God and the *Shekhinah*, points clearly to the corresponding condition of the human personality which cannot be fully realized in its wholeness unless the contrasexual element is raised to the level of conscious acceptance. We read in the *Zohar*:

> ...when they [the masculine and the feminine] unite, they look as if they were one body. From this we learn: the masculine by itself is like only one part of a body, and the feminine also. But when they join together as a whole, then they appear as one real body.

And again:

> The *matronita* united herself with the King. From this, *one* body resulted. Thence comes the blessing of this day. Therefore we know: what is only masculine or only feminine is called only part of the body. But no blessing rules over a faulty or incomplete thing, but only over a complete place, not one that divided, for divided things cannot long endure or be blessed.[14]

There is and still remains in Jewish tradition a completely worldly way of experiencing the divine mysteries of the sacred marriage. Some of the old secrets have been lost, and there are new generations who have not learned the meanings of the prayers and the practices, but there still remains the ritual. A ritual, even when its myth has disappeared and its *raison d'être* has been forgotten, still has its effect upon the human spirit, if only to remind us that we are connected to a sphere beyond the boundaries of consciousness, and even beyond the boundaries of sex and gender. This knowledge exists in the world, not only in the abstractions of philosophers and scholars. The Sabbath ritual in Judaism provides an example.

Only vaguely, if at all, is it remembered that the family gathers to mark the holy union of God, the Most High, with his Heavenly Wisdom, the *Shekhinah*. But all know that a sacred marriage is taking place in the microcosm, for the Sabbath is referred to as a "bride, radiant and lovely," in the prayer that bids people to "Come, welcome the Sabbath." The home is prepared for her appearance, everything is clean and shining, a festive meal is prepared, and all members of the family are wearing their best attire. The Sabbath Bride is celebrated in her union with Jacob, the Patriarch of Israel. But on a more personal level, the wife has prepared a delightful feast for her husband and children, and there is wine to add to the holy joy of the occasion. The husband, in loving appreciation, recites the passage from Proverbs (31:10-12) which begins:

> A good wife who can find?
> She is far more precious than jewels.
> The heart of her husband trusts in her,
> and he will have no lack of gain.

The husband and wife, through the Sabbath celebration, experience the inner union, the husband with the *Shekhinah* in her earthly manifestation as the Sabbath Bride, and the wife in her loving worship of God as manifested through the Patriarch. After the spiritual union has been consummated by each one, husband and wife, in themselves, the two are ready to enter into sexual union with one another. The spiritual union has been blessed in all its erotic significance, and now the erotic union between husband and wife may be likewise consecrated in the shadow of the spiritual expression that has been allowed to take place. It is incumbent on the husband and wife to have intercourse on the Sabbath.

Through their sexual union, the earthly couple not only fulfill themselves and each other, they also bring the creative process from heaven to earth, and in so doing they participate in a creative process which re-creates God. In man and in woman there is, as in God, "a union of the active and the passive, procreation and conception, from which all mundane life and bliss are derived."[15]

The harmony of this conception has been realized over and over by those who were attuned to it and once more, in our generation, it has been given musical and verbal form in the magnificent *Kaddish Symphony* of Leonard Bernstein. The feminine voice heard throughout the symphony represents the *Shekhinah* in her earthly form. She calls for a new covenant that will once more affirm the promise of a holy union that is experienced as transcendent, but is also immanent, personal and available as human experience. Her last prayer at the conclusion of the symphonic service:

> Look tenderly again at me, at us
> At all these growing children of God
> Here in this sacred house,
> And we shall look tenderly back to you.
> Oh my Father, Lord, and Lover,
> Beloved Majesty, my Image, my Self,
> We are one, after all, you and I,
> Together we suffer,
> Together exist
> And together we re-create each other.[16]

# Chapter 14

## Purusha-Prakriti, Siva-Sakti,
## Yab-Yum and Other
## Manifestations in the East

The spiral of thought swirls gently around and I see that I am nearly back to the point from which I began my lengthy excursus. What gave me the impetus to follow the hidden river of androgyny that flows under the surface of our Western world was, first of all, my *opinion* that modern psychosexual theory does not take into account the fact that on some level *we are all androgynes*; and secondly, the challenge put by C.G. Jung that woman should hold her opinions at a distance, look at them critically, and investigate their backgrounds in order to uncover the primordial images.

The sense of being back where I started from has to do with the weather as I wrote this. The afternoon at my summer cottage in Wisconsin was extremely hot. I found myself adjusting bamboo shades and curtains to keep out the sun's rays and let in the breeze, and while doing this I had a sense of *déjà vu*. Not until a little later in the evening when I went out on the balcony and saw the full moon shining over the treetops and felt the cooler but still heavy air, did I realize what that sense was about. I remembered how it had been when I had visited a friend on a desert plain in northern India half a dozen years ago; how after the torturously hot afternoons, when the relief of evening came, my bed would be placed out on the balcony where the air was moving and I would enjoy resting under the brilliance of the moon, looking up at the frozen stars.

A flood of memories returned. It had been my first trip to the Orient, and there I had found myself in touch with a society so different from my own that it amazed me at every turn. For one thing I saw that India was able to tolerate ambiguity in a way that I had never known in the West. This came to mind as I recalled a visit I made with my Indian friend to a Hindu temple in a small city, where my curiosity about this tolerance was stirred in a surprising way. We removed our shoes and left them on the steps of the temple, then my host guided me into a small anteroom to the right of the main sanctuary. Five or six men were seated there on the floor in meditation posture and no one stirred as we entered. We silently took places and found our own meditative space. It required a little while, for I felt a bit awkward being the only woman there, apparently the only stranger and a foreigner at that. Besides, I was wearing a short skirt, hardly the ideal garment for the half-lotus position in an Indian temple. Nevertheless, I did manage to get comfortable and to drift into a somewhat dreamy state, when all at once I became aware of a large black ant crawling up my bare leg. My immediate instinct was to crush it beneath my thumb, but as I reached out to do so I had a sudden intuition that led me instead to brush the creature off gently without doing it any harm. I felt as if the eyes of all India were upon me at that moment, and I had not failed the test.

I was ready to go with the group of men when they finally arose and walked into the sanctuary. We sat toward the rear of a large room in a circle by ourselves. One of the men would read something in Sanskrit from a large book (which I later learned was a section of the *Upanishads*); then another would comment at length on the passage. Then another reading, and one or more interpretations, and so on for a long, long time. As this was proceeding in one corner at the rear of the temple something entirely different was happening in front. Upon a large dais behind an iron grillwork railing were three richly caved statues of gods, all seated and draped in fuchsia-colored silks, and laden with necklaces of gold and jewels and ropes of pearls wound round and round in splendid array. Men and women in a perpetual stream walked up to the rail, bowing and even prostrating themselves low before these sacred images, sprinkling themselves with holy water, waving wands of incense. What was so striking to me was that the people who venerated the images seemed to pay no attention to those who were reading the sacred scriptures, nor did the latter look up to notice those who made obeisance before the images. It was clearly acceptable for each person to worship according to his own desire or custom, and there was no question as to who was "right" and who was "wrong." There was room in the temple for anyone who might choose to worship there.

Coming as I had from a Jewish background in which the graven image is anathema, what seemed strange to me was not so much seeing the expression of a colorful polytheism — I had known that Hinduism had its pantheon of gods and goddesses — but that there seemed to be this easy tolerance between those who enjoyed the more concretistic representations of the holy and those who did not. I asked a few questions and learned that the Hindu religion was monistic, although to the casual observer like myself it appeared to be completely polytheistic. Monism is, however quite different from the monotheism of the Hebrew or Christian faiths. As I came to understand it, in India, monism is the belief that there is only one reality in the universe, Brahman,* an unknowable eternal principle, beyond life and death, beyond

---

"Brahman (neuter) and Brahma (masculine) are not to be confused with each other. The former refers to the transcendent and immanent Absolute, the latter is an anthropomorphic personification of the Creator-Demiurge. Brahman is properly a metaphysical term, Brahma mythological." (H. Zimmer, *Myths and Symbols in Indian Art and Civilization*, p.123).

beginning and ending. Brahman is "one without a second," of which the entire phenomenal world, with all its color and diversity, is an expression. Brahman belongs to the same order, the Absolute, as does the *En Sof* in Kabbalah, or the *chaos confusum* in alchemy, in that It is beyond the differentiating qualifications of sex, beyond all limiting individualizing characteristics whatever. Heinrich Zimmer, writing on *Myths and Symbols in Indian Art and Civilization,* describes Brahman as

> ...the all-containing transcendent source of every possible virtue and form. Out of Brahman, the Absolute, proceed the energies of Nature, to produce our world of individuated forms, the swarming world of our empirical experience, which is characterized by limitations, polarities, antagonisms and co-operation.[1]

Zimmer states that the noun *Brahman* is neuter. Here his editor has introduced the following footnote by Dr. Ananda K. Coomaraswamy, who supplied a number of supplementary notes to complete the work after Zimmer's death:

> It must be understood that in Sanskrit grammatical gender is not always a sign of physical sex. Gender infers function, sex infers form; so that an individual may be masculine from one point of view and feminine from another. For example, Prajapati (the Progenitor, m.) can be referred to as "pregnant," Mitra "inseminates Varuna," Brahman (n.) can be regarded as the "womb" of life; and as in Christianity, "this man" and "this woman" are equally "feminine to God." Absolutely, Brahman although grammatically n., is the principle of such differentiation; just as in Genesis the "image of the God" is reflected in a creation "male *and* female." In general, masculine gender implies activity and procession, female gender passivity and recession, the neuter a static or absolute condition. Essence and nature are respectively m. and f., logically distinct, but "one in God," who is "neither" this nor that, and therefore "It" rather than "He" or "She" specifically.[2]

Brahman stood behind the Creator and the Creation, obliterating any difference between them, in the sense that we with our limited and finite perceptions perceive that difference. As in the mystical tradition of Judaism the *En Sof* preceded any God of Genesis, so Brahman preceded all appearances of Creation for the Hindus. Therefore, they could not describe Brahman, but could only move around their own concepts and say what cannot be said of It:

> The disciple asked: Om. By whose will directed does the mind proceed to its object? At whose command does the prana, the foremost, do its duty? At whose will do men utter speech? Who is the god that directs the eyes and ears?
> The teacher replied: It is the Ear of the ear, the Mind of the mind, the Speech of speech, the Life of life, and the Eye of the eye...
> The eye does not go thither, nor speech nor the mind. We do not know It; we do not understand how anyone can teach It. It is different from the known; It is above the unknown.
> That which cannot be expressed by speech, but by which speech is expressed— That alone known as Brahman, and not that which people here worship.

> That which cannot be apprehended by the mind, but by which they say, the mind is apprehended—That alone known as Brahman, and not that which people here worship...
>
> The teacher said: If you think: "I know Brahman well," then surely you know but little of Its form; you know only Its form as conditioned by man or by the gods. Therefore Brahman, even now, is worthy of your inquiry.
>
> The disciple said: I think I know Brahman.
>
> The disciple said: I do not think I know It well, nor do I think I do not know It. He among us who knows the meaning of "Neither do I not know, nor do I know"—knows Brahman.[3]

Knowledge of Brahman, that is, Nirguna Brahman (the unmanifest), the foundation of all knowledge, remained through Hinduism the guiding principle, in the light of which creation, man, and all the gods and goddesses were seen as multiplications of manifestations of the first principle. Since this principle could be manifested in every way imaginable, there was no conflict in the mind of the Hindu over the multiplicity of its emanations.

As with the *En Sof* in the Kabbalah, the image of light, or sparks, is preeminent:

> As from a blazing fire, sparks essentially akin to it fly forth by the thousand, so also, do various beings come forth from the imperishable Brahman and unto Him again return.[4]

Brahman, that is to say, Saguna Brahman (Brahman manifest), now manifests as Purusha, who is at once the Universe *in potentia* and the androgynous Creator-Creatrix from whom is born the animating spirit in all the living. He compares to other imaginings of Primal Man:

> He is the self-luminous and formless Purusha, uncreated and existing both within and without. He is devoid of prana, devoid of mind, pure, and higher than the supreme Imperishable.
>
> Of Him are born prana, mind, all the sense organs, ākāsa, air, fire, water, and earth which supports all.
>
> The heavens are His head; the sun and moon, His eyes; the quarters, His ears; the revealed Vedas, His speech; the wind is His breath; the universe, His heart. From His feet is produced the earth. He is, indeed, the inner Self of all human beings.[5]

From this we are able to see that in the first place the Totality contains the Two in the One, *prana*, the inner energy of the mind or "subtle body," and the elements of the material world. The opposites manifest themselves in innumerable forms and ways, and exist always in their relationship to one another. In contrast to the illusion of stability of the material world which one feels in the West, with our trust in matter and quantification and the appearances of things, we sense that in the world of the Upanishads the eternal flux is the only reality.

I came to India with my Western orientation, and I saw before my eyes conditions of living that would be intolerable even in the worst slums of our American cities. I found arising within me an urgency to call attention to this disgraceful situation, to the need to change things, to "improve them." When I injudiciously gave voice to this, my criticism was gently turned away with what seemed to me to be indifference. I realized that what had appeared to me as a status quo that needed to be radically altered, appeared to the Indian as a moment in an eternally cycling process which was moving according to ageless principles hardly susceptible to alteration by man, but which were, nevertheless, always in motion and always undergoing transformation. The Indians saw the world as a construct of the Great Goddess whom they call Maya, who measures out time and space, both in an important sense delusory.[6] Unlike me, they saw the "status quo" within this vast tradition.

While in India I happened across Gopi Krishna's autobiography of his inner life, *Kundalini, the Evolutionary Energy in Man*. I had picked up the book from my host's bookshelf. The electric blue color of the binding attracted me, but as is the case of some books printed in India, there was no title on the cover, so I had no way of knowing what the contents might be. The very first page of the text gripped me and held me bound, as I read the account of Gopi Krishna's sudden and unexpected inbreak of psychic energy (*prana*) that struck with such force that the man's entire personality structure was shaken to the very core of its foundation.

Gopi Krishna was a well-educated public servant, living with his wife and family in Srinigar, in Kashmir. He was a respected member of the Hindu minority in this largely Muslim area. He had been practicing daily meditation since the age of seventeen, hoping gradually to attain a higher level of consciousness beyond the conflict of opposites, but it was not until he was thirty-four when the dramatic breakthrough into a new form of consciousness took place. Then it occurred with devastating suddenness, in no way resembling anything he might have anticipated. As he described it, he had been sitting for hours in meditation, his attention draw toward the crown on his head, contemplating an imaginary lotus in full bloom, radiating light. Intensely concentrating, he suddenly felt a strange sensation below the base of the spine, at the root of the sexual organs. The sensation was "so extraordinary and so pleasing" that his attention was forcibly drawn toward it. The moment his attention was withdrawn from the lotus, the sensation ceased. Thinking it to be a trick played by the imagination to relieve the tension, he again fixed on the lotus and, as the image grew again clear and concentrated, the sensation reappeared, this time so intensely that again his attention was drawn toward it. At that very moment it again disappeared. Now he withdrew attention and again turned his concentration upward, and though by now his heart was beating wildly, he attempted to regain his composure and fix his attention on the lotus. When completely immersed he again experienced the sensation, but this time maintained a rigidity of attention and did not allow it to leave the point where he had fixed it. Now the sensation again began, and this time it grew in intensity until he could keep from wavering only with a great effort. He wrote, "Suddenly, with a roar like that of a waterfall, I felt stream of liquid light entering my brain through the spinal cord."

Gopi Krishna related how the illumination grew brighter and brighter, the roaring louder. He experienced a rocking sensation and then felt himself slipping out of his body, entirely enveloped in a halo of light. In his own words:

> It is impossible to describe the experience accurately. I felt the point of consciousness that was myself growing wider, surrounded by waves of light. It grew wider and wider, spreading outward while the body, normally the immediate object of its perception, appeared to have receded into the distance until I became entirely unconscious of it. I was now all consciousness, without any outline, without any idea of a corporeal appendage, without any feeling or sensation coming from the senses, immersed in a sea of light simultaneously conscious and aware of every point, spread out, as it were, in all directions without any barrier or material destruction. I was no longer myself, or to be more accurate, no longer as I knew myself to be, a small point of awareness confined in a body, but instead a vast circle of consciousness in which the body was but a point, bathed in light and in a state of exaltation and happiness.[7]

The experience left Gopi Krishna numb and weak, his limbs stiff and all but useless, and for days restless and exhausted. He was bereft of his powers of concentration and his previous capacity for leading a well-ordered life in the practical world. While he was losing all warmth and feeling for his wife and children there burned within him a vast internal glow. Sometimes it seemed as if a jet of molten copper mounted up through his spine, dashing against his brain and showering into a cascade of sparks or swirling into a glowing pool of light. He was aware of having touched some lever in an unknown mechanism which so overpowered him that he feared for his sanity. Terrified and shaken, he still managed to continue going through the motions of his worldly life as well as he could, using all his will to keep from succumbing to the raging power within. Trained in objectivity, he kept careful observations of his own condition. He recognized that he was undergoing a crisis with a real physiological basis involving the entire nervous system from the brain to the smallest organ, and he made every possible effort to understand what was happening to him.

Gopi Krishna had read in the popular books on yoga some descriptions of the Kundalini Yoga, all borrowed from ancient writings on the subject, and never written by individuals who had claimed to have the experience themselves. In them it was stated that Kundalini represents the cosmic vital energy lying dormant in the human body. She is coiled like a sleeping serpent around the base of the spine a little below the sexual organ, closing with her mouth the aperture of the *susumna*, a slender duct rising through the spinal cord to the conscious center at the top of the head. When roused, the Kundalini flashes upward through the *susumna* like lightning, carrying with her the vital energy of the body, which for the time being becomes passive, cold

and lifeless. As she joins her divine spouse, *Siva*, in the last or seventh center, in the brain, the embodied Self is freed from the enchainment of the flesh and passes into the state of rapture known as *samadhi*. The state was described as deathless, full of bliss, and enjoying supreme consciousness. Only vaguely did the books contain any mention of the dangers involved in this yoga, and then they were not explained.

All the knowledge Gopi Krishna had gathered on the subject did not approach in meaning the experience itself—the experience that became a part of his consciousness and attention over a period of several years. He became utterly sensitive to the periodic movements of the Kundalini, how she carried with her "extremely subtle, brilliant particles of some immaterial substance, shooting up and down, this way and that, combining to present an appearance of a circling, shimmering pool of light." The inner fire was understood to be the essence of life energy, the "subtle body" that structures the whole of Yoga. This essence is *prana*, which was born of Purusha in the beginning, along with all material things of the world. According to yogic doctrine, *prana* is neither mind nor intelligence nor consciousness, but rather the driving force behind all of them, an inseparable part of the cosmic energy or Sakti. The designation Sakti is, strictly speaking, defined as the Creatrix of the universe, and Prana-Sakti, to which we refer when we speak of the Kundalini, represents the carrier of the Sakti-energy. Gopi Krishna calls attention to the correspondence of the Sakti-as-energy with that energy which present day science is coming to consider to be the basic substance of the physical world. It may not be too far off to suggest that the concept of Sakti-Prana bears a resemblance to the Freudian idea of *libido*, which is sexual in its nature and provides the driving and motivating force underlying most human activity. Sakti-Prana differs, however, in carrying a spiritual implication, the aspect Freud scrupulously avoided in speaking of *libido*.

We need only to note these correspondences and differences, not to prove or disprove them on scientific grounds. We are concerned with the *idea* in human awareness, and particularly in the Hindu culture, that allows the life force which dances through the otherwise inert physical body of a person to be given a feminine designation. Sakti-Prana is described in yoga parlance as the life principle of Creation, a mysterious stuff that animates the cells and organs of living bodies. Sakti-Prana regulates the mechanism of the body and builds it in the womb; it draws the breath. It maintain the surface consciousness that thinks of itself as master while utterly unconscious of the invisible activity of the real mistress of the abode. The meaning and importance of Sakti is expressed in the saying, "Siva without Sakti is a corpse."[8]

Gopi Krishna has devoted much of his life since that initial catalytic experience to trying to understand the process that fosters the awakening of the Kundalini. He is actively engaged in both philosophical and scientific research at his own Research Foundation for *Kundalini* which he founded, seeking to demonstrate that a specific psychophysiological mechanism in the body of man is responsible for the evolutionary process in man. He has shared his work with Professor Carl Friedrich von Weizsäcker, Director of the Max Planck Institute for the Life Sciences in Munich. In his Introduction to Gopi Krishna's book, *The Biological Basis of Religion and Genius*,[9] Professor von Weizsäcker has made a profound analysis of Gopi Krishna's Kundalini experience and of the psychobiological effect of Kundalini. Noting the measurable physiological changes that occur in individuals who — through discipline and the gaining of control over the mechanisms of breathing, of seminal emission, and of concentrating attention — von Weizsäcker realized that the rising of the Kundalini brings about an innervation of the entire body as well as an achievement of an altogether superior level of consciousness. He stresses the evolutionary aspect of Kundalini Yoga as evidencing the important consideration that the evolution of the human species does not occur merely in biological terms; it must also include an evolution in consciousness, which will improve the quality of human *experience* as well as that of the physiological mechanism. As in Darwinian theory, a selection process takes place in the *evolution of consciousness*, a process that is equal in its import to the *evolution of the structure of the human body*. Those individuals tend to survive who are best fitting for survival both physiologically and in terms of the development of their consciousness. Longevity, it seems, depends more upon the level of awareness and understanding of the world than it does upon sheer physical adaptability. Hence, it would seem that it is necessary to concentrate even more upon the improvement of the quality of consciousness than upon the strictly material aspects of life.

In practice, Kundalini Yoga offers a method for raising the level of consciousness in the person who is able to experience it and who has been adequately prepared for it. This yoga is a method for internalizing sexual potency and the energy derived from it. Semen is not meant literally here, but rather that aspect of sexual potency which is inherent in the *prana* that is activated in the genitals and is experienced as sexual potency when discharged in orgasmic sexual relations. But when this *prana* (energy) is drawn inward and upward, instead of being discharged outward, it becomes available to infuse one's own cosmic consciousness. The idea sometimes expressed, that the "seed" is somehow channeled to the brain in Kundalini Yoga, is erroneous; the language may be vague and metaphoric but it attempts to convey the sense that prana, the feminine evolutionary energy, is not "matter" as such, but rather something like the "life" in matter. *Prana*, and the channels through which it may pass, are thought of as a "subtle body"—really more in the psychological sense than in the biological sense—in contrast to the "gross" or material body. This is not to say that *prana* does not have its profound effect on the material body; it clearly does. We may go so far as to say that all experience, as we come to it subjectively, lives in us through being activated by this energic principle.

I have seen little said in the writings about Kundalini Yoga concerning a woman's experience of it. It is made clear that a man may experience this "self-fertilization" through the inner relationship with the feminine energy principle, but what of woman? We must remember that the term "feminine" does not only apply to woman, but in some instances to a certain kind of experience which has the quality of "otherness" as viewed by a man. For a woman, the stirring of the Kundalini could be experienced as a phallic penetration, because for her it is the phallic activity that arouses her female sexuality, energizes her, and endows her with the precious gift of *prana*. The woman who can achieve the yogic control through the discipline of meditation and other practices involving her breathing, her thoughts, and her sexual response must have developed her contrasexual aspect in a similar way to that of the man who undergoes the discipline. It would appear, then, that she would experience the awakening and movement of the Kundalini, but in terms of her own female experience. If a man experiences something like the filling of the womb, then the sense of bearing bodily witness to the male orgasm must come alive in woman.

What is so strongly potent about Kundalini is the realization which it brings of the possibility for some individuals to come to a unity within themselves, a unity consisting of the interplay of energy and matter, the feminine and the masculine, the bodily experience and the spiritual experience. This path is difficult, arduous and demanding, but Kundalini Yoga offers one possibility for achieving one's androgynous potential. It requires a rigidly ascetic discipline; it leads its adherents to the experience of our temporal world as illusory and of little value in comparison with the attainment of non-dual awareness of the "Undivided Whole," the non-separability of the created and the Increate.

Gopi Krishna's experience of Kundalini lies firmly within the tradition of the Hindu Tantra which, along with the Buddhist Tantra, provides the major Eastern path to the sublime union of the Masculine and the Feminine. Tantra is difficult to define, and still more difficult to understand, for as in the example of Kundalini Yoga, it is not presented in direct language. Much of it has been concealed or deliberately obscured so that those who were not sufficiently mature or developed in consciousness could be protected from the dangers inherent in the powers and insights that it might activate. Tantra belongs to the esoteric disciplines. We can only speak of it in a general way, and can only hope to hint at the experience it holds for those whose lives have prepared them for it. There are many varieties of Tantric practice and, again, different levels of consciousness are achieved depending on the goals and capacities of those involved in it.

The Tantric tradition, in both Buddhist and Hindu forms, holds that there are two primary opposites, the static principle and the dynamic principle. The static principle is essentially cognitive; encompassing wisdom, realization, beatitude and spiritual illumination. The dynamic principle is described as conative; that is, placing emphasis on movement, energy and activity. In Buddhist tradition it is also compassionate and is identified with method and skillful means. In the Hindu Tantric tradition, *citta* or mind, the static principle, is embodied in Siva; that is, in the Masculine. The dynamic, that is, power and primordial energy, is attributed to Sakti, the Feminine force. The association of activity with the Feminine is a departure from the stereotype we expect out of our own Western culture, where for so long the Feminine principle has been identified with passivity. The Hindu's association of the Feminine with activity may be traced to the very strong religious element of Magna Mater worship that prevailed in India in the pre-Aryan era, and especially in the south. With the coming of the Aryans and their Vedic mythology and philosophy, the worship of male gods began to come into prominence, a development not unlike those that occurred in Greece and among the Hebrews. The invaders and settlers in much of India, coming down from the north, had assigned a trifling position to the goddesses. Nevertheless, they did not extinguish the goddess worship, but rather assimilated it into a religious synthesis in which "Prakriti," that is, the active principle, was merged with the active principle of the pre-Aryan society, namely the Great Goddess. Similarly, the Vedic "Purusha"—inactive, conscious, witnessing—was merged with Siva, the god who was often represented by the image of the lingam (phallus). Thus, the saying in Hindu Tantra, "If Siva is united with Sakti, he is able to assert his powers as Lord; if not, the god is not able to stir."[10]

The Indian and Tibetan Buddhist Tantrics, unlike the Hindu Tantrics, ascribed the dynamic principle to the male and the static to female. The Tibetan Mother (*yum*) is the carrier of "wisdom" (Tibetan *ses rab*, Sanskrit *prajna*), and the Tibetan Cosmic Father (*yab*) of the "means" (*upaya*). The latter is invariably a form of the Buddha. The Buddhist Tantras of India and Tibet stress the union of *prajna* the *upaya,* and there is saying, "Upaya without prajna is blind; Prajna without upaya is ineffective. Both of them fulfill themselves in union with each other."

There are exceptions to the Buddhist Tantric patterns of gender assignment to specific qualities. Perhaps the most notable is the persistent idea that the woman is to initiate courtship. Even up to the present, in Sanskrit poetry we read that the woman comes up to the tryst and prepares the rendezvous. Courtship initiated by the male is considered crude. This probably is a remnant of the pre-Aryan tradition that has continued into a religion in which otherwise the male has the more decisive role.

Again we come to the realization that it is not so important which sex carries certain specific responsibilities or attributes. *The vital point is that there must be opposition between two differentiated entities in order for the dynamic process to set in and to express itself by creating something new.* Each element — whether Masculine or Feminine — must be understood as comprising a set of qualities, a certain way of being or doing which resists confusion with its opposite. The clear difference is what attracts, for the mystery of the "other" promises to fill a longing for completion, in the world as in the self.

Tantra includes many variations in practice and belief, which may encompass the entire life style of those who become involved with it. It is set about with ritual and magic, with myth and philosophy, and there is a whole complicated order of signs and emotive symbols. Nor are there any art forms that do not find expression in Tantra; neither painting nor music, nor sculpture, nor the dance. All of these serve to heighten the sensitivity to what Tantra is in its essence — a spiritual vision of the inevitable and fateful bipolarity of all of life, natural and untransformed as well as Enlightened. Perhaps the Hindu Tantra emphasized the invariably sexual nature of the natural cosmos while the Buddhist Tantra stressed the androgynous being of the transformed, enlightened individual. But Tantra is unlike other religious systems, especially the orthodox Brahmin tradition which asserts that our world is a meaningless illusion that we must learn to reject along with all its pleasures. Neither does Tantra dwell on the urgent misery of the human condition, nor does it attempt through oppressing the body and the mind to escape from consciousness of or interest in worldly matters.[11] Tantra does not completely deny the validity of the ascetic approach, but it declares that there is no need to immolate the body and to suppress human feelings in order to gain release from any attachment to the world. In fact, some nineteenth-century Tantrics have stated that many of the miseries of the poor and the unenlightened in India have been caused by the hatred or indifference to the world that had been instilled into the majority of the people by the orthodox ascetic philosophies.

Tantra asserts that instead of suppressing the sense pleasures, the joy and the suffering of the phenomenal world, these should be approached more and more directly and openly, without fear or hesitation. Abandoning the security of conceptual reference points, even those of a "spiritual" nature, the yogi is required to bare his heart, his naked being, to the awesome reality of the natural world. According to the Tantra, the idea that the world is an illusion from which one must escape is itself a delusive mental construct that must be given up. Freed from that most subtle of all bondage, the yogi opens and communicates directly with the energies of the manifest universe. Here arises a reverence for the cosmos. Sense pleasure and joy are therefore cultivated in Tantra, without reference to any possible gratification or ownership on the part of the ego, but purely and simple for their own innate, sacred quality. On one level, worldly experience is the Tantric path, since its power, when confronted nakedly, provides the energy of the spiritual quest. On another level it is the "goal" of practice, because the abandoning of "higher," disembodied goals of the non-Tantric traditions leads to the epiphany of the phenomenal world as radiant with the "Absolute."

The final aim of the Hindu Tantra is the realization of that Cosmic union which exists only in the Supreme Being called "Ishvara." Ishvara is the One spoken of as Absolute Being, without qualities; It is unknowable and indescribable, without beginning and without end. It contains all the dualities and polarities gathered into the state of total unity. The name is different; the image, by now, familiar.

Creation, in Hindu Tantra, bursts forth from the explosion of the Primal Unity. In that act of violence the two principles of opposition separate, and incarnate in Siva and Sakti. With Absolute Unity shattered, existence is now relative; and there comes into being a state of duality that brings with it suffering, illusion and bondage. The Hindu Tantric seeks the reunification of the two opposite principles — Siva and Sakti — in his own body or hers. Although techniques differ, and sometimes a partner participates, the goal is not dissimilar to that of Kundalini Yoga. There we saw that Sakti, in the form of the serpent, may be awakened by certain yogic practices; and that when this occurs, she moves through the channel (susumna) by way of seven energy centers called cakras up to the top of the skull, where Siva dwells. In that last center, "the lotus," she unites with him. Through the cultivation of this yoga, the yogin would move in the direction of transformation into a living embodiment of the play of Siva and Sakti.[12]

In his discussion of Hindu Tantric literature, Eliade stresses that "'androgynisation' is only one part of a total process, that of the reunion of opposites." He speaks of "opposing pairs" that have to be reunited: the Sun and the Moon have to be made one; also the two mystic veins that circulate on either side of the central susumna — the ida and the pingali — and they bear the two breaths, prana and apana.[13]

The reunion of opposites here means that we are to consider on many levels of life and consciousness the meaning of the coincidentia oppositorum. It is the age-old ceremonial that is ever new and alive: the hieros gamos or sacred marriage of ancient Greece which was a sacrificial offering of childhood's innocence to the god; it is the mystical marriage of Gnosticism; the chemical wedding of alchemy where the alchemist worked hand in hand with his *soror mystica*; it is the union of God and Shekhinah; Israel and the Sabbath; Christ and Jerusalem. All of these are implicit in the Hindu Tantric rite that culminates in *Maithuna*, the mystic marriage, and yet there is an important difference. In Tantrism the union of opposites takes place in human experience, furthermore in the flesh, but the ceremony transcends the ordinary limitations of human expression of the body.

When we speak of the rite of *Maithuna* we speak of a mystical eroticism that was known from Vedic times; but it remained for Tantrism to transform it into an instrument of salvation.[14] Immortality, liberation from death, is the ultimate goal of cosmic love. For mortal beings to experience love on a cosmic scale requires a transformation of the very nature of being. To participate in *Maithuna*, even if only once, raises the yogin and his *nayika* (the devout woman) to a divine condition where they experience a state of bliss in which they are able to contemplate the Ultimate Reality directly.

The preparation for the technique of *Maithuna* begins long before with the diligent practice of Hatha Yoga. The beauty of the body must be carefully cultivated, for here is the temple where the divine ceremony will take place. Purification is required, through various kinds of internal cleansing and through the *asanas* (postures) which enhance the beauty, strength and control of the body. Hatha Yoga conditions the will to master the physical body in order to transmute it into a divine body. Other preparations consist of meditation and ceremonies that will make the ritual possible and fruitful. The yogini is a woman who has been instructed in the nature and meaning of the ceremony by a guru, and whose body has been consecrated by a rite of touching certain parts to identify them with similar parts of the Deity and thereby potentiate them.

It is said that every naked woman incarnates Prakriti, the female clement in the original and divine creative process. In approaching the naked woman, the yogin is to look upon her with the detachment and awe one feels in contemplating the mysterious secrets of nature, the wondrous ability to bring forth creation. Unless this gaze is accompanied by the terrifying emotion one feels in the presence of the divine that is about to reveal itself, there will not be a rite, but only a secular act. The woman-Prakriti is to be transformed into an incarnation of Sakti. As the woman becomes the goddess, the yogin must become the god. The two will join as father-mother of the world. The yogin, utilizing the divine model of Siva, will seek to realize in being the ideal of pure Spirit, motionless and serene.

In preparation, the two people retreat to some secluded place, such as a forest. Here the couple will spend many months in each other's company. The yogin will become accustomed to the body of his mistress, and will follow the rules of adoration and self-control until he is able to master his bodily response and he reaches a state of detachment where he neither desires her nor does he not desire her. He will have passed beyond the level of consciousness in which he demands personal or sensual gratification for its own sake. When at last they join in sexual union, the yogin is joined with the goddess, the yogini with the god. Because they have transcended their mundane mode of existence, there is, accordingly, a near immobilization of breathing and of thought. Throughout the sexual union there is never to be an emission of semen. The texts are clear about this, for otherwise the yogin would fall from his divine incarnate being to that of a common libertine. His sensual pleasure, like his body, is the vessel in which the opposites can come together in union. The fire, as the two lips of the vulva are called, stimulates the flow of the semen, which nevertheless is supposed to be held immobilized, or reabsorbed by the yogin in a process of self-fertilization. The yogini, also, allows her sexual energies to circulate within herself. Likewise the regression is enhanced by the arrest of the breathing, and by the stilling of all thought. It is said in the Hindu Tantric texts that through this rite some achieve the union within themselves of "sun" and "moon," of Siva and Sakti; that they are able to transcend time as we know it and to emerge into a Cosmic Time in which are relived the periodic creations and destructions of the universes (the cosmic "days" and "nights"). Through the transcendence of the opposites, the Divine Androgyne once again comes into being. In Eliade's words:

> By arresting his breathing, by "unifying" it in the *susumna*, [the yogin] transcends the phenomenal world, he passes into that unconditioned and timeless state in which "there is neither day nor night," "neither sickness nor death"— naive and inadequate formulas to signify "emergence from time." To transcend "day and night" means to transcend the opposites...it is the reabsorption of the cosmos through inversion of all the processes of manifestation. It is the coincidence of time and eternity on the purely "human" plane, it is the reintegration of the primordial androgyne, the conjunction, in one's own being, of male and female — in a word the reconquest of the completeness that precedes all creation.[15]

How shall we, so far from those strange Tantric rites, feel our way into some glimpse of understanding of this experience? Veiled as the writings are in mystery, consisting as they do of endless variations, and bound about with intricacies of rule and custom so that they are truly unapproachable to any except the practitioner himself; how can we hope to get an inkling of their meaning? It may help us to realize that although some people did actually perform the rite of *Maithuna* in its specific and concrete form, there were others for whom (as in alchemy) the rite was an internal image to be meditated upon, visualized, and taken as a guiding model for the inner life.

We, too, can meditate upon the mythic image. We can imagine what it must be like to sit immobilized, in sexual union with the god. How still one must be, to feel within oneself the shape and form of Divinity, to know with that deep inner knowledge that encompasses the totality of oneself, body as well as psyche — undivided, that there is an immortal Presence within, around, and flowing through oneself. Experience it as Sakti-Prana if you will; the air you breathe is charged with it. Being in touch with that immortal body means being able to be alone yet not to be alone. It means reunion with that Primordial Androgyne that is the womb of God, the ancestor of the psyche. But it does not mean sinking back into that undifferentiated state where we were androgynes but we did not know what we were.

Over the centuries we have become conscious of our own evolution, and human consciousness has evolved. A new kind of consciousness is emerging in our times. Gopi Krishna says that Kundalini is the evolutionary force that exerts the power that is capable of transforming the human spirit, and that we can learn her ways and discover how to apply her energies. This powerful element in life, that fills it with dynamism and makes growth possible, that is the embodiment of flux and change and transformation, is called by other names as well: Sakti, Eve, Sophia, Aphrodite, the Shekhina, Anima, Muse — there is no end to the list. She is the Eternal Feminine, or she is so viewed by the men who were the mythmakers. They realized that only through the mystery of the Other could their own creative thrust find response, and that only through union with her could they participate in making life fruitful in spiritual sense. The great cosmic myths, as Tantra teaches, can be directly experienced by certain individuals who are enabled by their fate to consecrate themselves to the task. The vision occurs in a magical moment when, after very long preparation, the human beings slip off their gross bodies and lose themselves in the cosmic space where they have always been, but have not seen it. During the mystical union that at last becomes conscious, the Masculine principle and the Feminine principle are intimately engaged with one another. It is a moment of conception, and what is conceived is the child of the human spirit.

# Chapter 15

## Dynamic Union in Tao

Great Tao is beyond description. Great argument uses no words. Great goodness is not kind. Great integrity is not incorruptible. Great courage is not aggressive. Tao that is manifest is not Tao. Words that argue miss the point. Perpetual kindness does not work. Obvious integrity is not believed. Aggressive courage will not win. These five are round and mellow, yet they may become square and inflexible.

Knowing enough to stop when one does not know is perfection.

Who can understand an argument that has no words and Tao that cannot be expressed? If a man can understand this, then he may be called the treasure house of heaven. Pour into it and it will never be filled; pour out of it, and it will never be emptied. Yet no one knows why this is so. This is called the hidden light.[1]

I return to the state of the Uncarved Block. The circle moves round and comes back to the point from which it started. I have made a long journey in search of the androgyne, and have only touched down at various points, as if taking an excursion around the world in eighty days. My glances have been cursory, I have not been able to pause as long as I would have liked, to drink in the atmosphere of each setting of the myth. Nor will I apologize for the insufficiency of my efforts, though I am aware of it. If it requires effort to study, to learn, to explore, to immerse oneself in an idea, then all efforts are inevitably insufficient. I have tried to respond to the challenge I saw in the writings of Jung concerning the functions of *anima* and *animus*. Specifically, what started me on the way was the statement that woman should explore the grounds of her opinions. I have addressed myself to the opinion I hold along with many other contemporary women and men, that it is time for people to free themselves from the sex and gender roles that have so long remained as stereotypes in our Western world. I found it necessary to look into the question: why has woman accepted a role in which she is locked into a certain image of femininity? Why has she let this happen to her? Meanwhile, over the years since Jung characterized woman's consciousness as being "still wrapped in the shadows of non-differentiation," woman's intellect, her capacity for clarity, her productive activity, and her generally competent functioning in a world until only recently designated as "man's," have been widely recognized. Yet, as we complete our circumambulation of time and space, we come back to where we began: however a society defines the Masculine principle and the Feminine principle, always there *is* a difference.

It seems to me that where our Judeo-Christian view went wrong was not in its differentiation between the masculine and the feminine natures; this differentiation has been made in every society. Our error was in becoming *fixated* in the male-dominance fantasy, the ruling idea of a patriarchy based on belief that an omnipotent male deity was prototype for created man. If woman came along as an afterthought to help man, or rather if she could be convinced that was how it was, then the power principle could be safely maintained in the hands of the male establishment, and women would be obliged to function harmoniously with the men, supporting and complying with their use of power.

If we can put our grimness behind us and see the humor in the situation, we realize that it never worked that way. Power does not function in a vacuum. It needs resistance, contradiction, opposition — all of these, if we look at them critically, are forms of receptivity. Leonardo da Vinci understood this when he said:

> Force is a spiritual power, an invisible energy arising from motion which by impact of violence from without causes bodies to be distorted or displaced, imparting to them a marvelous animation; it compels all created things to assume new shapes and places. It runs with fury to its own desired undoing, expending itself the opportunity offers. Slowness strengthens it and speed weakens it. It is born of violence and dies through liberty.[2]

The male-dominance fantasy, which has such a questionable basis in history and myth, is a fantasy, just that; only not everyone in our society has realized it yet. The interdependence that exists between the Masculine principle and the Feminine principle is what undergirds the interdependence that exists between men and women. When this interdependence is violated, and when the innate equality in value of the Masculine and Feminine principles is violated, there is much suffering for both men and women.

The essential relationship of these principles to each other, and their collective relationship to the overriding oneness of all things, finds some of its most exemplary expression in the imagery of the Tao. This is why I said that it is necessary to return to the "state of the Uncarved Block" for a few observations before ending this journey backwards in time, and preparing to change direction.

"The Tao which cannot be named" is the emergence in Chinese philosophy of the awareness of the Ultimate Principle in which the uncreated coheres, until creation gives it form and shape and endows it with energy. Out of the nameless, faceless, Imponderable comes an undifferentiated Unity, to which a quality can be ascribed and a name given. The description is visual rather than a matter of words, reflecting the fact that Taoism is so deeply identified with Nature, and so little concerned with the intellectualizations that ensnare those who attempt to explain her.

The image is the familiar T'ai chi, the circle out of which develop the principles of reality, the one pole being the light (Yang) and the other the dark or shadowy (Yin). Richard Wilhelm, who brought the archaic *Secret of the Golden Flower* from China to the West in translation, noted that some European scholars have turned first to sexual references for and explanation of the Yin and Yang, but that the characters refer primary to phenomena of nature. He explains that in their original meaning, Yin is shade and therefore the north side of a mountain and the south side of the river, which ordinarily lie in shadow; while Yang is the south side of a mountain and the north side of a river, which receive the direct rays of the sun. However, both Yin and Yang belong to the undivided One, as the river is one river and the mountain one mountain. So the T'ai chi corresponds to that androgynous principle wherein the two lie in the matrix of the One, but are not yet separated. The T'ai chi is not visualized in human shape, as were its counterparts Celestial Man, Adam Kadmon, or the figure of Siva-Sakti in eternal union. Nor was it translated into matter, as in the alchemy of the West. Nevertheless, the abstract symbol carries a meaning similar to all of these: it refers to the central monad from which creation ensues, creation being termed "the ten thousand things."[3]

Yang and Yin only have their effect in the world of phenomena. There Yang appears as the active principle, initiating and conditioning, while yin appears as the passive principle, derivative and conditioned. Yin and Yang begin with the principles of darkness and light, but these opposites are expanded into all the polar opposites, including the sexual designations of Yang for the Masculine and Yin for the Feminine. As we know from our own experience, light is only light relative to darkness, and the darkness finds its meaning in terms of the light. The two are qualities of the One. This applies, of course, to the Masculine and the Feminine: in Tao they are aspects of the One, and Taoism teaches that the inner nature of humanity corresponds to the heavens; that is, that the individual person is a phenomenal form of the Tao. Yet immediately before birth, or even at conception, the opposites in the human organism begin the process of splitting apart, and it is out of this continuing division that the sense of the duality of life arises. It brings with it the experience of pain and disintegration, which one tends to try to heal by seeking satisfaction in the temporal world.

Yin and Yang belong to a Chinese cosmology that includes the archaic sciences of astrology and alchemy. In it we recognize archetypal principles associated with the same and similar disciplines in the West, which is hardly strange, since all societies tend to base their philosophies on their observations of nature and the interpretations drawn from these observations. The familiar elemental quaternity is here in Taoism also, with Yang being thought of as cold and dry, Yin as warm and moist. The two are present in any given situation, it is only the particular distribution of the qualities that give each situation its unique character.

The *Tao Tê Ching* is the sacred teaching of Taoism, and is popularly ascribed to the legendary master Lao-tzû who was supposed to have lived around the sixth century B.C. The sage was said to have looked old at birth, having spent seventy years in his mother's womb, and because of his immense wisdom he was put in charge as historian and keeper of the archives in the state of Ch'u. Confucius came frequently to consult with him concerning the ancient rites, but inevitably received a rebuff. Nevertheless, Confucius always spoke of him with profound respect. Unfortunately, his high opinion of Lao-tzû was not shared by the princes whom Lao-tzû served, since they did not understand his teachings, so that he had to flee the country, as he said, "disguised in coarse garments and hiding in his breast the jade of wisdom." As he came to a mountain pass, the keeper of the pass begged him to write down the essence of his teaching before he disappeared behind the mountain, and so he hurriedly wrote down the two volumes of the *Tao Tê Ching*, before departing for his unknown destination, or so the legend goes.[4]

If we were to characterize the *Tao Tê Ching* we might say that it is primarily a "Yin" book, for it counsels the wisdom of uncertainty and the power of yielding. The following passage will illustrate this quality:

> The best charioteers do not rush ahead;
> The best fighters do not make displays of wrath.
> The greatest conquerer wins without joining issue;
> The best user of men acts as though he were their inferior.
> This is called the power that comes of not contending,
> Is called the capacity to use men,
> The secret of being mated to heaven, to what was of old.[5]

The *I Ching*, one of the five Confucian classics, is a philosophical work and a guide to life based on the principles of Yin-Yang. This Taoist work, unlike the *Tao Tê Ching*, is more in the nature of Yang, in that it not only serves as a guide, but even may be consulted as an oracle or a fortune-telling device. Indeed, this probably was its original function, and since its recent wave of popularity in the West it begins again to serve many people in those capacities. But the major thrust of the *I Ching* is to name the "Tao that cannot be named," to assign various qualities to aspects of life, to provide patterns for discovering the meaning in a given situation, and for inferring modes of response to the situation.

The *I Ching* was set into its final form about the second century A.D. It was structured on a binary system, with a straight line ($-$) signifying the Yang principle and a broken line ($-\,-$) representing the Yin. In diagrammatic form the Yin and Yang symbols are frequently shown surrounding the circle of T'ai chi, which equals the One, the void, the matrix. Yin and Yang, the negative and the positive, combine into eight possible trigrams, which can then be paired, with sixty-four hexagrams resulting. The sixty-four hexagrams constitute the readings of the *I Ching*, suggesting the infinite variety of combinations of Yin and Yang that might he possible if the doubling and redoubling were continued.

Of all the possible hexagrams or combinations of Yin and Yang, the first two provide the key. These are the first hexagram, ☰ which is composed entirely of straight lines and is pure Yang; and the second hexagram ☷ which is composed entirely of broken lines and is pure Yin. All the other hexagrams have their complementary elements within their own structures, and hence are independent; but the first and the second, being of single nature, need each other for completion. The first hexagram is composed of six Yang lines, and is designated *The Creative*. Its image is "heaven."

> These unbroken lines stand for the primal power, which is light-giving, active, strong, of the spirit. The hexagram is consistently strong in character, and since it is without weakness, its essence is power or energy... Its energy is represented as unrestricted by any fixed conditions in space and is therefore conceived of as motion. Time is regarded as the basis of this motion. Thus the hexagram includes also the power of time and the power of persisting in time, that is, duration.
>
> The power represented by the hexagram is to be interpreted in a dual sense — in terms of its action on the universe and of its action on the world of men. In relation to the universe, the hexagram expresses the strong, creative action of the Deity. In relation to the human world, it denotes the creative action of the holy man or sage, of the ruler or leader of men, who through his power awakens and develops their higher nature...
>
> The beginning of all things lies still in the beyond in the form of ideas that have yet to become real. But the Creative furthermore has the power to lend form to these archetypes of ideas...[6]

*The Creative*, powerful as it is, can do nothing by itself, anymore than could Ophion, the serpent, bring the created world into being unless there were a Eurynome to dance upon the waves and to receive his embrace. Therefore *The Creative*, the carrier of power, is totally impotent unless coupled with *The Receptive*, the image of which is "earth":

> This hexagram is made up of broken lines only. The broken line represents the dark, yielding, receptive primal power of yin. The attribute of the hexagram is devotion...its image is the earth: It is the perfect complement of *The Creative* — the complement, not the opposite,* for *The Receptive* does not combat *The Creative* but completes it. It represents nature in contrast to spirit, earth in contrast to heaven, space as against time, the female-maternal as against the male-paternal. However, as applied to human affairs, the principle of this complementary relationship is found not only in the relation between man and woman, but also in

---

*Hexagrams that are opposites in structure are not necessarily opposites in meaning

that between prince and minister and between father and son. *Indeed, even in the individual this duality appears in the coexistence of the spiritual world and the world of the senses.* [Emphasis mine.][7]

It is evident that what is qualitatively different about *The Creative* and *The Receptive* is the Masculinity of the first and the Femininity of the second, and what is equally important is that both of these qualities are present in the intrinsic nature of each human being regardless of sex. These qualities are not necessarily culture-bound or culturally conditioned, as some contemporary sociologists assert, except insofar as the trends of society follow the necessities of Nature. The Creative, the lingam, the spark, the thunderbolt, Hokmah, Nous, Naas, Ophion, Logos, all belong to the archetypal nature of the Masculine. When this Masculine archetype becomes manifest in a woman, as it surely does, it needs to be recognized as the fertilizing "other." This Jung saw, when he called this archetype *animus*, meaning the Masculine element in the psyche of the female. Conversely, The Receptive, the yoni, the vessel, the sea, Binah, Sophia, Zoë, Eurynome, Physis, all belong to the archetypal nature of the Feminine. When the Feminine archetype becomes manifest in a man, she must be recognized as the conceiving other. In making this clear differentiation of psychic contents, Jung called this archetype the *anima* when experienced by a man.

Others[8] have suggested that both men and women possess "anima" and "animus." I think this a misinterpretation of Jung's intent, which, I believe, was to recognize the intrinsic psychobiological difference, with all its implications, between men and women as being *primary*, and the equally important presence of the "other" which is *not* biologically but psychically based, as being *derivative*, rather than *intrinsic*, and therefore *secondary*. To put it another way, men are born with a penis which simply and naturally is used for penetration, while women need to develop their phallic potential in order to penetrate the world. Therefore, I feel that the use of the terms *anima* and *animus*, when intended in the "Jungian" sense, should be clearly understood as referring to the *contrasexual* archetype, because it is the very *otherness* that lends these archetypal factors their force and dynamism. By attempting to merge these elements in the human psyche, we have concocted the very monstrosity we have been seeking to avoid: the homomorphic creature which found its way into the decadent writings of the Romantics and the paintings of the Symbolists as the pale aesthetic hermaphrodite, and which today reappears in our own culture with much glitter and twang as the sexually ambivalent rock star.

The psychic qualities that we have come to conceive of as "masculine" and "feminine" are grounded in mythologems that follow the pattern laid down by nature. These mythologems form the bedrock of the collective unconscious. The qualities they embody tend to work their way through the layers of the individual psyche upward into the attitudes of society, which is to say, the "collective consciousness." Our culture has reinforced these masculine-feminine themes for various reasons. In my view, cultural patterns tend to derive from the intrinsic nature of the total human organism rather than the other way round. I do not deny that society—or rather, people in societies—have often exploited these innate tendencies to the advantage of certain individuals or interest groups or political entities. But in general, the characterization of psychological qualities as "masculine" or as "feminine" originated on the far side of recorded history, and they have proceeded to develop in remarkably consistent patterns throughout the world.

The *I Ching* points to an *apparent* dualism through the coexistence of these opposites within an individual, but it states:

> ...strictly speaking there is no *real* dualism here, because there is a clearly defined hierarchical relationship between the two principles. In itself of course the Receptive is just as important as the Creative, but the attribute of devotion defines the place occupied by this primal power in relation to the Creative. For the Receptive must be activated and led by the Creative; then it is productive of good. Only when it abandons this position and tries to stand side by side with the Creative, does it become evil. The result is opposition to and struggle against the Creative, which is productive of evil to both.[9]

Two examples from my analytic practice come to mind which show the interrelatedness of the two principles as they appear in contemporary society. Both concern women who have very strong creative impulses. The first is competent in confronting the extraverted world, has many talents and is much sought after, but she rejects most of the opportunities for self-expression that come to her, and she frequently refers to herself in depreciating terms. She says, "I fear that if I express my real *animus* strength, I'll overtake my husband, but even worse, I'll overcome my feminine side. The active and the passive are still split apart in me; I feel I have to function in one mode or the other, instead of potentially being both." I speak with her about the relationship of yin and yang in woman, how yin takes the lead and allows the woman to be what she is, authentic as woman, but she can also be strongly supported by her yang, which through its relationship *as other* stirs her creativity but does not distort it into a hermaphroditic confusion. We speak of the fact that the bodies of men and women all produce both male and female hormones, so in that sense we are all androgynes. But we are born as male or female, and society reinforces the dichotomy, the *other* tendency gets repressed. The recognition of androgyny represents "the return of the repressed," and offers the potentiality for wholeness.

The other example is of a poet who has written in excruciatingly personal terms about her own sexual experiences, so that one feels nearly crushed by the writhings of her vagina or drowned in her sea of menstrual fluid. As an analyst, I have long ago gotten over being squeamish about things I hear in my consulting room, but her reading her own work to me, deeply moving as it was, made me want to leave the room and head for the nearest shower. I tried to explain to her why I felt her poetry would not be accepted for publication. I talked about how extremely personal it was, how it related to her inwardness to an extent that one felt that reading it was raping her privacy, how she left nothing whatever to the imagination. I fumbled around with my clumsy critique for several minutes, knowing that although I was feeling an intense response to her material I was unable to express it clearly or succinctly. The woman immediately understood. She gathered up her papers; and as she was leaving the room she said it all, absolutely correctly, in just three words uttered on my threshold: "Too much Yin."

The legendary Taoists, besides being philosophers, poets, painters, nature worshippers, magicians and sorcerers, were also alchemists. Among the many esoteric practices in which they engaged, there was a certain advanced yoga which was so abhorrent to the Confucian authorities as to bring great disrepute upon its Taoist adepts. The vehemence of the criticism was hardly deserved, since the yogic practices that were involved demanded strict seminal continence, for which the absence of lust was essential. The Taoist art of sexual yoga is beautifully described by John Blofeld in *The Secret and Sublime*, and it is from his report that this summary is taken.

In preparation for the practice of dual cultivation, the yogin is taught the means of achieving stillness through thought control assisted by yogic breathing. Profound and regulated breathing accumulates the precious *ch'i* (cosmic energy identical with the Sanskrit *prana*) which is said to lengthen the human life span and refine the body's substance. This goes together with thought control, through which deepened consciousness leading to the inner mystery is won. Nothing can be accomplished until one can withdraw the play of thought and maintain dispassion regardless of the peculiar nature of the phenomena that may occur. Those who have been able consciously to behold the Tao in a formless state undergo a change in personality which may appear incomprehensible to others—circumstances which seem dangerous to others, *they* recognize as laughably absurd, and thus true sages may be taken for halfwitted fellows grinning at daydreams. For the sage, "hand in hand with anxiety and fear, ugliness is put to flight. Gems sparkle on dusty roads; puddles appear as pools of lapis lazuli; tough weeds acquire fragile beauty; dung takes on the charm of delicately mottled amber."[10]

The purpose of the Yoga of Dual Cultivation was to distill within the adept's body a golden liquid from which the elixir leading to longevity, immortality and mystical union with the Tao could be formed. A Taoist alchemical manual states:

> At each copulation of heaven and earth draw to yourself the secret sources of *yin* and *yang*, in other words when you and your partner come together, combine the two vital fluids and draw them into your body.

This yoga, which was the cause of much defamation of the Taoist adepts, may be interpreted on three levels:

First, the transmutation of cinnabar and lead into the miraculous elixir of immortality; second, the creation within the crucible in one's own body of a golden pill or foetus, as means of cheating old age or death; third, a similar form of internal alchemy depending on an ingredient derived from sexual intercourse.[11]

The first and even the second seem to parallel the opus of Western alchemy. Furthermore, these two interpretations were applied in China to matters of politics and military strategy as well as to the individual's attainment of personal tranquility, since all things are said to function in accordance with the same patterns and rhythms.

The practice of creating an "immortal foetus" or internally compounded elixir would not be possible for anyone who had not banished sensuality and desire from his or her mind. The instructions are couched in veiled language in the texts, so as not to tempt those who are not prepared to engage in this yoga. If the adept is male he is told to select a female partner in the best of health, whose charms, however, are such as not to inspire inordinate affection. There is a saying: "Silver weighing fourteen ounces is desirable; it should never have been subject to smelting." This is to be read as a girl of fourteen who has hitherto been a virgin. Ideally, the practice of sexual yoga should be embarked upon in one's sixteenth year for then, provided one has never had an emission, one's vitality is said to be unimpaired. The most essential requirement for the male is the conservation of the semen, which must on no account be ejaculated. Second in importance to this, the ability to make the partner repeatedly expend her Yin-fluid, draw it into his own body and concentrate it in the lower Cinnabar Field (abdomen) where the mingled fluid unites with spirit and ch'i, and becomes a compact mass. This can be made to rise through two channels parallel to the spine through the several *cavities* which are not exactly equivalent with the Hindu *cakras*. The inexactness of the correspondence does not invalidate the system, because what is being dealt with is not simply anatomy as we know it, but the *subtle* anatomy which is psychically and even metaphorically perceived and experienced.

In this form of Taoist yoga, it is understood that the adept may as well be a woman as a man. If the adept is a woman, all that has been said concerning the man applies in reverse, with the difference that she will require many partners, for the male essence is easily exhausted.

There is also a Taoist form of internal alchemy that is practiced without a partner and bears some resemblance to *Kundalini* Yoga. Here, too, the yoga is based on the principle of preventing the generative force that is produced in conjunction with the semen from being dissipated. As soon as it moves toward its usual outlet, it is driven backwards by means of the inner fire which has been kindled by regulated breathing, and it is forced upward through the *channel of control*, passing through three *gateways* until it reaches the head. By means of a ritual of exercises including a special form of breathing, the generative force is cleansed and recirculated into the *lower cavity* which acts as a lighted stove supporting a cauldron of generative force ready for transmuta-

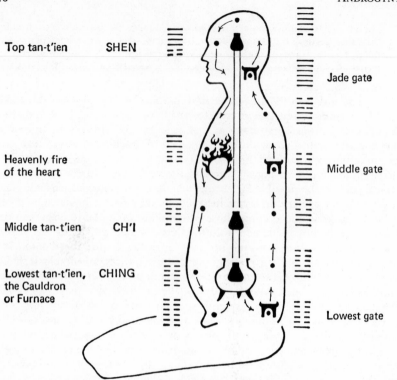

Top tan-t'ien          SHEN

                                                    Jade gate

Heavenly fire
of the heart                                        Middle gate

Middle tan-t'ien       CH'I

Lowest tan-t'ien,      CHING
the Cauldron
or Furnace                                          Lowest gate

tion into vitality. The vitality, driven by the breathing and inner fire, soars up and flows down again repeatedly and with ever-increasing speed. The cosmic spirit in the brain causes spirit to develop and its bright light to become manifest. What takes place is "an internal copulation of the positive and negative principles," through which the "golden elixir" is distilled. The entire process is described in precise details in the old alchemical manuals, but the language is indirect and accessible only to the initiate. Yet enough of this material has come to light so that we can read in it parallels to all the processes and practices of Western alchemy. There is the important distinction, however, that in Taoist Yoga the laboratory wherein the process takes place is the body of the adept, and the "matter" that is to be transformed is not base metal but the physiological substances and their subtle essences. The immediate goals are long life, rejuvenation and immortality; the ultimate goal is oneness with all that is.

Sexual yoga was practiced by the Taoists in the Yoga of Dual Cultivation or in an individual meditation, in the Buddhist Tantra of Tibet or India, in the Hindu Tantra or the Kundalini experience, altogether only by a very small proportion of the populace. The methods were secret and were for the most part imparted orally to those who were spiritually or psychologically ready to receive them. As previously indicated, part of the preparation consisted of a regime of arduous discipline designed to harden the human body which served as vessel. In recent years these disciplines have been cast out of their homes. The Tibetan lamas were forced to flee their lofty heights before occupation by the Chinese Communist armies; the Taoist meditations have been all but drowned out by the wave of new thought in China today. In a society that seeks to raise the general level of great masses of people, there is little time for the patient process of maturing and refining in the highest possible degree the essence of the single human soul. India, too, has her eye on the mechanized societies of the West, and in learning so much from us, much of her attention and respect has been drawn away from her own secret treasures.

The irony is that while the East expends its efforts to assimilate so many of the materialistic values acclaimed in the West, it is in the United States that efforts have been made to rescue some of the people who carry with them the greatest esoteric traditions of the East. A few far-seeing persons have responded to the need to record and preserve the old literature and culture of Asia. Consequently, the disciplines may come to a rebirth in our own country and in our own time, if only those who possess them are careful in the way they disseminate what they have. Our Judeo-Christian ethic has not prepared us to experience in a bodily way the tremendous power of the spirit; we will need to change much in our attitudes and ways of living before we will be able to attune ourselves to the possibility of learning what these wise men have to teach us. Yet the importance of their existence and the importance of their presence among us is hard to overestimate. Not only have they understood the necessity for consciously integrating the opposites, and especially the Masculine principle with the Feminine principle, but they have worked out explicit rituals for living out the integrative process within the body of the person. In doing so, *they have dissolved the dualistic concept of psyche and soma.*

If we take seriously this dissolution of the dualistic concept of psyche and soma, we are led to the inescapable conclusion that many other seeming dualities that we were taught to believe are realities in the objective world, may not be so at all. The polarities that characterized the Age of Pisces may give way to the conjunction of the opposites in the Age of Aquarius. What if we were to heal the splits between mind/body, spirit/nature, intellect/emotion, religion/sexuality, masculinity/femininity? What if we saw, as it is presented in the *I Ching*, that the seeming dualities are all functions of our limited human vision, that in reality there is unity; in unity, reality? How would these ideas, once assimilated, transform our way of relating to other human beings, transform our own sexuality, and transform our deeply personal relationship of ego to Self?

We in the West cannot be successful if we try to imitate the practices of the East, or act out our fantasies of what those practices may have been like. They arose out of their own matrix as a natural development, just as our practices emerge from our own background. We have at hand, however, all the ingredients we will need to perform our own new alchemical opus. We have the capacity to find ways to transcend the dualities into which we have fallen and to recover our own wholeness. We need to become aware of the Undivided, the great One, which preceded all the gods and all the theologies. We need to find ways to live our lives as persons who are undivided in ourselves—we need to find ways to fuse the opposites within us.

# PART 2
Today and Tomorrow

# Chapter 16

## Androgyny in Motion:
## T'ai Chi and the Hollow Brush

Again I fly through space, this time through the night.

I have been on a long journey and now I am returning home. The route is from west to east.

In the beginning I was outward bound, to lecture and to lead a seminar in California. I was outward bound in more than the literal sense. My task had been to lay open to view some matters which I had been working on, studying and thinking through. The flight itself, the moving outward and away from my geographical center and starting point, had taken place in the brightness of the morning.

Now I return homeward. I had journeyed toward the west like Blake's sunflower, "who countest the steps of the Sun." And it had been there that the unexpected had occurred. Without bidding I had discovered the physical and psychological edge of the land, the hint of the androgynous presence.

There had been no time for my own reading or studying on the trip. While I carried the "image" of the androgyne within me, I saw it outside of me reflected wherever the opposites came together. This occurred in discussion after discussion, where new ideas clashed with older ones, and where a few could perceive that the new had retained within it the seed of the old, and the old carried within it the seed of the new. The symbolical representation of the T'ai chi is not only a model for the way things are, but it is also a model for the way things grow. Perhaps even this is not a contradiction in terms, for in a certain way of seeing, "growing" is the way things are.

Finally, toward the end of my trip, I saw it. No longer as a symbol on a page of paper, no longer as a concept or idea: I saw the androgyne as living motion. It was not an invisible dance of the atoms in space, although I am certain that what I saw was an embodiment of that, whatever else it may have been. And it was not Siva dancing; but it did not exclude the dance of Siva either. The androgyne sprang to life as both the dancer and the dance, in a way more beautiful than I could have anticipated or imagined.

The place was the ferryboat S.S. *Vallejo*, moored in the harbor of Sausalito just beyond the Golden Gate Bridge. I had driven down the dusty roads along the edge of town to the waterfront. I had found the rickety old pier and crossed the gangplank that connected the large wooden vessel of uncertain vintage to the land. Walking along the narrow deck, I entered at last a large central area midship to find a class in progress. About twenty men and women were gliding through the movements of a dance. In the center I saw Al Chung-liang Huang, T'ai chi Master.

The teaching was in the man, in his dance, in his every movement, in his calligraphy, in his face, and in his life. The life as graceful, undulating rhythmic motion, appeared to be a dance that had neither beginning nor end. Chung-liang is neither old nor young. His very being expresses the meaning of movement and change without pause or cessation. He gives expression to the principle of life itself, that is, to the breath of life, the *ch'i* that flows through life and enables life to flow. When Chung-liang dances, the circular process of life is made manifest. Each movement in T'ai chi flows into the next, which is its opposite. One never has the sense of "first you do this and then you do that." Change is the only constant, from one movement to another, from initiation to completion, to rest, to initiation again. The energy never stops, never pauses, never appears to be blocked. The *circulation of the light*, a goal sought in Chinese philosophy, takes place before my eyes. It takes place in the body of this man, the body that seems to float in air one moment and to be fully grounded the next. He presents a curious combination of lightness and weight, of the strength of a great tree and the yielding fluidity of a forest stream. Although in continuous movement, the body is always in balance; the balance is always asymmetrical, so that at any moment the design formed by the body is in the process of turning into its opposite.

If there were a ritual dance of the androgyne, T'ai chi as performed by this master could be that dance. It is neither a masculine dance nor a feminine dance. It has the strength and grace of both. The energy flows forth from its spring, its center within the body. The center, called the *tant'ien*, is in the lower abdomen, just below the navel. It is considered to be both a reservoir for the *ch'i* and also the center from which our body movement originates. *Tan* means distilled vital essence, and also the rich red color of blood. *T'ien* means field or place. Therefore the *tant'ien* is the field of energy, the center of the vitality. The energy moves out from this place, is disseminated into the world, is drawn back out of the world and pulled together, and is returned to this place.

The moving outward portion of the cycle belongs to the phase of the Masculine, Yang, the moving inward to the Feminine, Yin. Each cycle of movement reaches or thrusts or stretches or glides upward or outward as Yang; then it falls as gravity takes over; it falls, and is scooped up and returned to the center as Yin. It is put forward and it is drawn back in again and it is not depleted. All of movement, life energy itself, can be seen as Yin and Yang flowing into each other. When Yin and Yang flow in and out of each other in continuing rhythm, the thrusting of the one is met with the yielding of the other. In the natural shift of balance that is constantly occurring, the one is always becoming the other. The changing is a continuing process: there is no moment when it ceases to occur. T'ai chi is not only an image handed down to us from the sages of ancient China, nor is it simply the essence of the Taoistic approach to life as brought to the West. It is an active principle that is expressed as sheer beauty in the life and art of the T'ai chi master himself, and it is an active principle that can be discovered in the life of anyone who can become conscious of its presence so that he or she may cultivate it. It is the way of the androgyne. It is a way of moving through life as life moves through you — there is a real sense of the *circulation of the light*. The movement is not restricted to the dance, although the devotion to the dance as an active form of meditation is a very good way of becoming conscious of the process. *Ch'i* is present here and can be recognized as being present in all of life.

The afternoon after I watched the dance, *ch'i* found expression in another art form in the calligraphy lesson. I observed Chung-liang at the low table he had made especially for this work. Seated on a small round cushion, the T'ai chi master began the careful process of making his own ink. Through the meditative action of grinding the ink on a stone in a circular motion, his own energy was transferred to the black substance with which he was working. He described what he was doing as he went along. "The preparation of the ink...serves as a centering process...I make an environment for myself where I can take my time to do this...it's like being a potter, kicking the wheel and centering the clay...There's no need to rush." As he sat erect, his spine was a hollow tube through which his energy was flowing. Though his posture was formal, there was nothing rigid about it, and there was grace in his stillness. He took the brush in hand and held it upright in front of his body, exactly parallel to his spine, the tip pointing downward at the paper. He curved his fingers about the bamboo handle, holding it with the *t'ai chi fist*—"the empty open fist that is neither tense nor limp." He dipped the brush into the ink, smoothing the hairs to form a point. "This is as if a million different thoughts collect to one thin center point. The smoothing of the brush on the stone is another centering process."[1]

First he made several circles in the air, feeling his way through in relation to the dimensions of the paper. When he was ready, the movement in the air descended to the paper without changing its rhythm as he traced a perfect circle on the page. The brush was a metaphor for Chung-liang's body, the paper for the earth, and the dance became the circle inscribed. With four swift, sure strokes he divided the circle into eight pieces, like slices of a pie. Here was the frame within which he would draw the Chinese characters that represented the hexagrams of the *I Ching*. He began with *Ch'ien*, which is translated in the *I Ching* as *The Creative*. He filled circle after circle with the ideogram, *Ch'ien*, while he spoke of the many varieties of meaning that were inherent in it. His brush moved deftly from left to right and from above to below. The character was drawn at first in discrete strokes, over and over. Then he showed us how the strokes could be allowed to flow together into a cursive script which abstracted its essentials and glided through them without lifting the brush, so that their form was changed but their essence remained clearly recognizable to anyone who knew even a little of the language. T'ai chi is flowing with the stream of energy.

Chung-liang proceeded to the second hexagram of the *I Ching*, which is *K'un, The Receptive*. Again, his hand, his body and his words were a living expression of the meaning of *K'un* in its many aspects. And so, he demonstrated another and another of the hexagrams, while speaking of their origin and their symbolism. It looked so easy, this dipping into the ink—and this sweeping of the brush across the paper. As a visitor to the class I was permitted to try it for myself, and it was anything but easy. I made repeated attempts, but my figures were clumsy and gross in comparison with his finely articulated ones. I saw that his "easy" grace was the product of a lifetime of practice. I learned that both his parents had been calligraphers in China and that he had begun learning the art from them when his Western contemporaries were learning to print their ABC's. But while the Western child was taught to be satisfied with legibility and adequacy, this youngster in China was given a model of excellence and grace to emulate.

T'ai chi, the dance of life, can be done with the whole body, it can be turned into a work of calligraphy on a sheet of white paper, it can find its way into the act of painting, into music, into the cultivation of a garden, and into the act of love. Always it is the art of asymmetrical balancing, in which the flow between the opposites is so exquisitely smooth as to be almost undiscernible. The energy is never spent; it is always put forth and then draw back. When the dancer stops he has more vitality than when he began.

I think of T'ai chi in terms of my own journeying. The night's return journey to the east takes on the meaning of T'ai chi. I can no longer see my two voyages as two: flying out West to deliver some lectures and visit some friends, then turning around and coming home again to study, to work with people, to write. I can no longer see my life as an alternation between periods of extraversion and introversion. The polarity which was so clear in the concept dissolves in the experience.

I fly eastward through the night in a direction that seems to counter the sun's, yet when I regard my movement as circular instead of linear I see that I am not going counter to the sun's way at all. I am embarked on the classical night-sea journey. I have been in that place where the sun dropped into the waves of the western sea to cross the underside of the earth in the pit of darkness. The hour is late, and my fantasy turns to the *nigredo*, the timeless space, the chaotic void. *Nigredo* is the place of *Sol niger*, the "black sun," which is not a sun at all but a negative sun, an absence of light, a black hole in a void wherein exist the potentialities for the emergence of that energy which can coalesce into bodies like suns.

The blackness of the night sky urges me to reflect on the meaning of *nigredo*. It is not the beginning of Creation but rather the Beginning of beginnings. The beginning of Creation forms the bedrock of a myriad of mythologies. People of every culture have asked three questions: Where did this earth and all the celestial bodies come from? Wherefore Life? What is Man? Collectively, each culture has found answers and has expressed them in its own language. Each creation myth is different, yet there are striking resemblances among them. From the few examples of such myths that I have sketched, it was possible to discern certain patterns that repeat the primary motifs: first the primordial undifferentiated wholeness of the One; next the differentiation of the two within the One and their polarization; then the splitting apart through some primal catastrophe or creative act, the separation of heaven and earth, or of above and below; and then the banishment to earth of the "other" aspect of the primordial Oneness. After the Fall, Primordial Man will serve as an androgynous prototype for a human race which it will create or which will be created through it. He is the Primordial Androgyne, the one who says, "Let us make man in our image." These words are pronounced in a thousand tongues and a thousand ways. Genesis is only one of them.

The creations of the Primordial Androgyne are not only separated out and polarized as male and female, they are also polarized as day and night. Yet the reality is that there is no day without a night or a night without a day. For every sun there is a black hole in the universe, for everything that "is" there is an "is not," for every "I" there is a "you." And, if I see "you" in your transpersonal aspect you become for me a "Thou." Jung once said that for everything we assert is true, it is possible to say that the opposite is equally true. If I have traversed the concave arc from the East to the West, I can now traverse the convex arc from the West to the East, and it is all the same journey, the circular journey toward wholeness.

As we perceive what I would like to call the "day world" we register it in three dimensions. We are taking in the world of Creation, that is to say, the world as far as we can define it through the data of our senses and through all the elaborate technological prostheses that we apply to the human body in order to increase the range of its data-gathering potential (for example, microscopes, telescopes, electroencephalographs, computers). We understand the day world essentially through the process of manipulating the data we have gathered together. For this we require certain kinds of processes, in the

main logical, linear, sequential and focused. We are concerned with analyz-
ing, that is, taking apart; and with synthesizing, that is, putting together—
often in new ways.

The "night world," on the other hand, appears to transcend the three-
dimensional as it dreams its dreams and experiences in other ways the lower-
ing of consciousness and the free flow of unconscious contents. The night world
is the one in which materials come together and make their own patterns,
incorporating things that were not thought to have belonged together, challenging the rational, producing the unexpected. It is a world in which fantasy
and imagination are given unlimited space.

The role of brain structure and function in determining two different modes
of consciousness has recently been the subject of significant research. "Day"
and "Night" have been used as metaphors in talking about the aspects of bimodal consciousness. Arthur J. Deikman, in considering the infinite variety
and rapid shifts of psychological and physiological states in an individual, concluded that there are two primary modes of organization: an "action" mode
and a "receptive" mode. The action mode is the one that is organized to
"manipulate the environment, while the receptive mode is organized around
intake of the environment rather than manipulation." He points out the need
for recognizing the relativity of the different modes, rather than assigning absolute primacy and validity to the one with which we are most familiar; namely,
the "action" mode.[2]

It has long been known that the brain of higher animals, including man,
is a double organ, consisting of right and left hemispheres connected by an
isthmus of nerve tissue called the *corpus callosum*. Ronald E. Myers and Roger
W. Sperry discovered that when this connection between the two halves of
the cerebrum was cut surgically, each hemisphere was able to function independently, almost as if it were a complete brain. The separation of the
hemispheres provided an opportunity to explore whatever differences in function there might be between them. The experiments that followed pointed
to a specialization that developed in human beings by the age of four or five
whereby the left hemisphere became more proficient in the speech and language functions (in right-handed persons), thus winning for itself the label
of being the dominant hemisphere. Further tests and experiments showed that
the right hemisphere, which controlled the left side of the body, functioned
better in tests requiring motor co-ordination such as arranging blocks to match
a pictured design. The separation experiments showed that it is possible to
create two independent spheres of consciousness. In normal human beings,
however, the *corpus callosum* acts as a bridge whereby the different perceptions
are swiftly transferred back and forth from one hemisphere to the other, making
it possible to integrate separate kinds of learning within the brain.[3]

In the early part of the present century, most brain research emphasized
the superiority of the left hemisphere functions of the brain, primarily the
intellectual, verbal, analytic capacities that tradition has associated with the
masculine mind. This side has been called the "propositional mind" by

researcher Joseph E. Bogen. But more recently findings in research have increasingly demonstrated the importance of the functions of the other side of the brain, what Bogen has called the "appositional mind." He points out the tendency in the right cerebral hemisphere toward mediation of superior kinesthetic functions, as well as spatial perception, interpretive ability, and especially musical ability.[4] Many of these attributes have traditionally been associated with the feminine. But this side and its functions have by no means been as thoroughly investigated as the other, and its capacities have yet to be determined with any certainty.

Interestingly enough, the scientific findings parallel very closely the conceptions of the duality of human consciousness as expressed in the literature and traditions of other cultures. In a study of the myth and symbolism of *left* and *right*, G. William Domhoff finds that the left is often the area of the taboo, the sacred, the unconscious, the feminine, the intuitive and the dreamer.[5] And Bogen cites some more illustrations of this point:

> Great literature has characteristically concerned itself with this issue. For example, it has been said of Dostoievski that "The anguish arising from the dual nature of man rings forth in great chords throughout his work."
>
> Not all mental duality is anguished: Dr. Samuel Johnson is said to have been much annoyed by dreams in which he found himself in repartee with an antagonist of superior wit. "Had I been awake," said he, "I should have known that I furnished the wit on both sides."
>
> Andre Gide averred: "There is always a struggle between what is reasonable and what is not." It is perhaps because we live in a society in which rational thought is held in particularly high esteem that the "other" is often considered to be base or undesirable even when it is un-named. More likely this evaluation is not cultural in origin, but arises from the fact that the hemisphere which does the propositioning is also the one having a near monopoly on the capacity for naming.[6]

The complementarity of the two modes of consciousness is the central thesis of Robert Ornstein's summary[7] and anthology[8] of work done in this field of research. Ornstein expressed the view that it is the polarity and the integration of these two, the intellectual and the intuitive, that underlie some of the highest achievements of mankind. He brings together in a chart the ways in which various people have described the two modes of consciousness, not as a final characterization, but as a way of making a bit clearer the Day-Night metaphor.

We recognize in Ornstein's chart the residue of many of the older myths as well as the basic material contributing to recent and possibly still-current beliefs relating to human nature and especially to the purported nature of "the masculine" and "the feminine." Ornstein calls attention to the fact that most of the older myths, and especially those coming out of the esoteric traditions, have specialized in the tacit, holistic and receptive mode, the mode that is identified with Night and is largely inaccessible to language and reason. He contrasts this mode with that of modern science, which is primarily

## THE TWO MODES OF CONSCIOUSNESS

### A Tentative Dichotomy[9]

| WHO PROPOSED IT? | | |
|---|---|---|
| Many sources | Day | Night |
| Blackburn | Intellectual | Sensuous |
| Oppenheimer | Time, History | Eternity, Timelessness |
| Deikman | Active | Receptive |
| Polanyi | Explicit | Tacit |
| Levi, Sperry | Analytic | Gestalt |
| Domhoff | Right (side of body) | Left (side of body) |
| Many sources | Left hemisphere | Right hemisphere |
| Bogen | Propositional | Appositional |
| Lee | Lineal | Nonlineal |
| Luria | Sequential | Simultaneous |
| Semmes | Focal | Diffuse |
| *I Ching* | The Creative: heaven masculine, Yang | The Receptive: earth feminine, Yin |
| *I Ching* | Light | Dark |
| *I Ching* | Time | Space |
| Many sources | Verbal | Spatial |
| Many sources | Intellectual | Intuitive |
| Vedanta | Buddhi | Manas |
| Jung | Causal | Acausal |
| Bacon | Argument | Experience |

verbal, logical and identified with Day. What is essential to Ornstein is the importance of understanding how these two modes interact in daily life. On the basis of his own research and his work with his colleague, David Galin, he states:

> ...in most ordinary activities we simply alternate between the two modes, select-ing the appropriate one and inhibiting the other. It is not clear how this process occurs. Do the two systems work continuously in parallel, and merely alternate control of the body, or do they truly time-share the control? Clearly each of us can work in both modes — we all speak, we all can move in space, we all can do both at once; yet in skiing, for instance, an attempt to verbally encode each bodi-ly movement would lead to disaster.[10]

Throughout his book, *The Psychology of Consciousness*, Ornstein has interspersed his report of scientific investigation of the two sides of the brain with a series of charming Sufi parables. These point to the polarities of human nature in which knowledge acquired through study and disputation is pitted against the earthy wisdom that comes from shrewd observation of nature and the reflec-tion of the mind upon experience deeply lived. His most important contributions in this book, it seems to me, are his clarifications of the polarization that characterizes the passing age, and his recognition of the need for integrating the two modes of consciousness. The epilogue of his book contains a plea for creating a dialogue within the individual with the hope of reuniting the divergent functions. As a way of approaching this task, he suggests that we return to some of the old myths and esoteric practices of the past. He seeks the redemption of that diffuse kind of thinking, that sensitive employment of the feeling, sensation and intuitive functions, which has fallen by the wayside in the rush for information about the way things work. We have been so busy taking things apart and putting them back together again in order to learn how to manipulate them, that we have lost sight of wholeness in and of itself, and of the place of wholes in their natural setting.

Ornstein would seek to bring together the two sides of human consciousness that he calls "Day" and "Night." It is a man's way of looking at the process, a "masculine" way, if you will. It makes the assumption that our *primary* mode of functioning is our "daytime" consciousness, and that this is what has become overextended and one-sided. This modality needs to be balanced by bringing to bear upon it the "night-time" consciousness, which is called "feminine," so that we may find a better balance within ourselves. He sees phenomena as predominately Day or Night, as Light or Dark, as Yang or Yin.

It is all different with Tai ch'i master Al Chung-liang Huang. Never for a moment did I sense that it was either a Day consciousness functioning or else a Night consciousness. I could not identify his way as either masculine or as feminine, which was why I suggested that he embodied the androgyne in a very real corporeal sense, and spiritually as well. As Chung-liang dances, it seems that his body flows in a different aura; that if anything, he moves between a "dawn consciousness" and a "dusk consciousness," always in the process of change, either moving into the light from out of the darkness, or else withdrawing into a growing inwardness that comes as the daylight falters. Chung-liang is already in the Aquarian Age. He is not, however, split off from the past. All the training and the discipline that came out of his background and his ancestry provides a base beneath him; it is his earth from which he can spring upward in bounding freedom, his earth to which he can return and find it resilient and yielding. He carries within his being the spirit of the Tao, which is ageless and also as relevant to the time to come as it is to the moment in which it is experienced. The new androgyny incorporates the modes of the past, and evolves beyond them.

The life and work of Chung-liang is only one of many examples I could have chosen of people and of movements that are in the vanguard of the new consciousness. Individuals arise in every field — in the various religious traditions, in psychology, in physics, in molecular biology and genetics, in the arts — who share the task of bringing the new consciousness to an ever-widening circle of people. The most astounding and encouraging fact about all of this is that where once the people who sought to reunite the spiritual aspects of human beings with their practical, mechanistic and "scientific" aspects came

almost exclusively from the fields of religion and philosophy and the arts, today a growing number of scientists have joined these others in their efforts.
It seems that scientists have discovered, in the process of expanding their knowledge to an unbelievable degree of vastness and complexity, that no matter
how many times their information is multiplied, there will never be an end
to all the mysteries. They have come face to face with the need for another
kind of knowing, which comes from within as much as from without the human psyche. At long last, the "two cultures" are on speaking terms with one
another.

# Chapter 17

## Dynamics of Androgyny:
## The Systems View

As we move into the Age of Aquarius (which may come to be designated as the Age of Androgyny), no one should be surprised to discover that a new myth is emerging. Naturally it manifests as have all the other myths, in the guise of a "sacred truth"; only this time the truth is designated in terms of a science: the systems view of the universe. Systems theory does not announce itself as a mythology; no mythology ever does. Nor does it attempt to integrate the mythologies of the past with a neorational approach to the present and the future. The systems theorist does not to bring together the fragments of truth that supposedly have been dispersed about the planet over the generations. He does not propose to heal the breaches or to bridge the polarities. None of this is necessary, according to systems theory, because, after all, the universe is not lying in fragments at the feet of the philosopher. Nor are the polarities "worlds apart" in reality. The world is characterized by a remarkable degree of consistency and coherence. If we do not see it that way, it is because of the limitations of our own capacities — the elephant is not divided into pieces because the blind men are only able to sense its parts.

Systems theory tells us that since the universe is already organized, we do not have to "make sense of it." We only have to perceive what is before our eyes and make some fairly obvious inferences on the basis of our observations, our past experience and our increasing technological capability. We need to recognize that we are members of an interrelated series of systems which all obey the same principles and have a common theme. We are not only involved in a process called *cosmic evolution*, we are part and parcel of it and we could not withdraw from it if we tried. According to Buckminster Fuller, a leading systems theorist:

> *What seems to be important at the moment is never what is really going on.* For the bee, it is the honey that is important; for Nature, what matters is the cross-pollination the bee effects in going after the nectar. So also, 99 per cent chromosomically programmed humans have been doing the right things for the wrong reasons.

What we think of as side events are really Evolution's main events.

None of this was planned. It was like the gradual assembly of the chicken inside the egg, to the casual eye chaotic and uncontrolled. Humans do not see the logical interrelatedness of big evolutionary development. Planning is still not incumbent on us, not the way "Planners" think of planning. How events and discoveries will cohere is utterly unforeseeable. The one sure thing is that cohere they will. The "Planner" incarnates the human mistake of supposing that Universe is waiting for human beings to make the major evolutionary decisions.[1]

Fuller is the generalist par excellence. For most of his eighty years he extracted principles from the universe, and then presented these principles in au understandable way to an audience that ranged from technical experts in their fields to children from four years up. One of his favorite principles is *synergy*, a word that means the unexpected interaction of parts in combination. As he explains it, *wholes* always contain behaviors you couldn't have expected when the parts were strewn in front of you. The way to begin understanding a watch is not to dump its loose parts out of a bag. You have to start from the whole watch, and even if you end up disassembling it, you'll not forget that when it was together, it ticked. The tick is a synergetic dividend.[2] When we begin to think in terms of "systems" or "wholes," instead of discrete entities or parts, the concept of energy takes on new meaning.

The specialist handles problems through piecemeal analysis by simplifying the information he has available. It is assumed that the forces of "bodies" calculated are acting in sequences of interacting pairs, for example, the right and left hemispheres of the brain. For some purposes this is a workable assumption. It can give us data on specific interactions and can aid us in developing techniques for manipulating and predicting them. However, since real things tend to be far more complex than this kind of analysis can handle, the specialist's approach does not give us a true picture of many things. Ervin Laszlo, a pioneer of systems thinking in philosophy, explains why science has had to shift its sights to the systems view of the world:

> Man himself is composed of some five octillion atoms, and his brain, of ten thousand million neurons. A hydrogen atom is composed of a proton and neutron in its nucleus and one electron in its shell, but the number of forces acting within it are so complex that mathematicians need multidimensional spaces to represent them. And atoms more complex than helium (which has two orbital electrons) contain three or more "bodies" in their shells and our mathematics are incapable of solving the three-body problem—that is, handling equations of motion for more than two objects moving under mutual influence. In other words, we are quite incapable of proceeding with the rigorous techniques of specialization for any phenomenon more complex than a helium atom.[3]

The beginning of the twentieth century marked the breakdown of mechanistic theories, even in physics, the science where they had been most successful. With Einstein and Max Planck, sets of interacting relationships began to replace concepts of energy and matter as the center of attention. Relativity took over in field physics and quantum theory in microphysics. Useful as the newer laws of physics were, they remained insufficient to explain the complex interactions that take place in living organisms. Thus, new laws had to be postulated, especially for biology, to replace the old dualism of a "life principle" or a "life energy" which "powered" the organism. The concept of dualism began to give way to laws of integrated wholes. The new laws did not contradict the basic laws of Newtonian physics, but complemented them; that is, they provided a wider paradigm into which the previous theories, as well as new data that could not be accounted for by the old theories, could be incorporated. Warren Weaver, in viewing the parallel developments in physics, chemistry, biology, sociology and economics, described contemporary science as the "science of organized complexity." The study of the nature of these complex organizations is the field of systems theory.

The systems view offers another solution to the problem of grasping the complex nature of things: it takes them in integrated chunks. Instead of looking at one thing at a time and noting its behavior when exposed to one other thing, it looks at a number of things as wholes and observes their behavior under diverse circumstances. This is what we tend to do naturally in any case, as when we deal with business enterprises as companies rather than as individual workers and employers, or when at night we recognize constellations without knowing the names of the individual stars.

In a certain sense, the holistic view of the new systems theory parallels the holisms of the earlier protosciences. In astrology, alchemy, and even in Gnosticism and the Kabbalah, the world was seen in terms of a unified and consistent process, which proceeded according to some evolutionary pathway that was gradually and imperfectly revealed to human beings. According to the old mythological view, all creation stemmed from Primordial Chaos. Somehow, in that mass of confusion, a spark of light coalesced and emerged out of the darkness gathering energy about itself and emanating energy from itself. In the old myths the Beginning was *in* the Totality, and from the Totality sprang forth that energy which became the Monad, the original elemental creative force. The manifestation of the Monad took different forms at different times. We have seen how the celestial God and the patriarchal ideology took the place of an Earth Goddess and the matriarchal ideology; both of which were preceded by a religious situation that was neither matriarchal nor patriarchal. M. Granet calls this primordial condition "the neuter aspect of the holy Place."[4] The "holy place" was perceived as "an undifferentiated religious power, the primordial *Grund* which preceded and supported all subsequent manifestations."[5]

The old mythologies were expressions of human involvement with the natural forces in the universe, and especially with the creative process by which new entities were continually being brought into existence, and existing entities were continually being transformed. One primary function of religious speculation has been to induce the recognition of our need, as human beings, to put ourselves into a relationship with those evolutionary forces which we observe with the subjective eye. We have long been told that if we go against "God's will" we are bound to stumble on the path. The interpretations of "God's will," or the "law of Nature," which the religions offer us were based on intuition and tradition. The religions sought to penetrate the complexities of phenomena by insight or revelation. Imaginative and inspired as the holistic theologies became, they could not stand the confrontation with actual experience which modern science demanded.

Gradually the rational-scientific view began to supplant the earlier protoscientific mythologies, however without disposing of them completely. As modern science began to develop its picture of the universe on the basis of testable patterns of research, the mythological-religious or intuitive views were put aside. Along with them, concepts of ethics and social justice were eliminated from science as tending too much toward the subjective. In a world in which only simple interactions could be definitely tested, modern science developed its picture of the universe as a magnificently designed giant mechanism, obeying elegant deterministic laws of motion. This was the nature of Newtonian physics, a science that proceeded to attempt to understand events by breaking them down into their elementary interactions.

If the mythological view was "subjective" with the "subject" attempting to learn the ways of Nature and to come into a harmonious relationship with her, then the view enforced by Newtonian science was an "objective" one, with the human being standing, so to speak, outside of Nature and observing her. Thus, scientific experiments were designed to provide the greatest measure of objectivity; and since the subjective element tended to creep in as an unknown whenever an experiment became too complex to account for all its variables, experiments had to be designed around the analysis of more and more simple components of events. The paths of science and religion diverged ever more widely.

The earlier mythological theories were holistic but highly speculative; modern scientific thinking reacted by being empirical but atomistic. Neither was free from error, the former because it used faith and insight in place of empirical inquiry, and the latter because it sacrificed coherence in favor of detailed facts. According to systems theorists, the present and newer choice over atomism, mechanism, and uncoordinated speculation is the shift toward rigorous but holistic theories. This means thinking in terms of facts and events in the contexts of wholes and forming integrated sets with their own properties and relationships.[6]

If one can follow this trend and begin to think in terms of whole systems, it may be possible to find a way out of the maze created by the old categories of "masculine" and "feminine." This would require a shift in thinking about the "masculine" and the "feminine" in two very basic ways. The first way would be to shift the common assumption that a specific quality of the personality may be described as either masculine or feminine. It would be necessary to cease thinking of the mysterious entity called "masculinity" as a heap of individual traits and characteristics such as aggressivity, directness, clarity and all the rest, and of "femininity" as a heap of the opposite traits. People would realize that the development of the many psychological tests that purport to determine the valence of "masculinity" or "femininity" in an individual are but vestiges of an atomistic science that pretends to understand a whole by an examination of the heap of its disembodied parts. The second way to move beyond the old categories would be to alter our assumption that since there are certain "feminine norms" and "masculine norms" which have been generated by a particular society, all males and all females in that society may be expected to develop in accordance with those norms. The societal images of masculinity and femininity—as something we can observe and define, and in accordance with which we can shape our behavior—derive from the very tendency to differentiate and categorize, a tendency that negates the concept of wholeness in human personality. Wherever a human being is described today, whether in a novel, on a driver's license, or in a personality measurement test, the first and most prominent means of identification is invariably sexual. I do not undervalue the importance of sexuality as a characteristic of being. Nor do I undervalue sexuality as a major channel for energy in its physical and psychological manifestations. However, I believe it is time to re-examine the customary superimposition of the sexual designation upon every aspect of human life, and the accompanying assumption that what we are used to calling "masculine" and "feminine" are basically related to sexuality *per se*.

There is another way of thinking about the Masculine and the Feminine and that is in terms of systems theory. I have been capitalizing Masculine and Feminine in order to differentiate this usage from the ordinary one which refers to qualities of the two sexes and to the metaphors derived from those qualities. As applied to natural systems, the Masculine and the Feminine refer to the dynamics that underlie the interaction between systems and their subsystems, and between systems and their supersystems. As we noted in connection with Yang and Yin, the term Masculine can be applied to one direction of energy flow and the term Feminine to another. It will become apparent that no system can work without a dynamic concept of energy infusing every part. But first, a brief description of the systems view of nature, the way in which modern science organizes its observations and its knowledge.

The systems view deals with what are called "natural systems." A natural system is a system the nature of which is defined not so much by what is in it, as by the way in which its parts or elements are *organized*. A natural system further has the quality of being like all other similar natural systems in terms of its functional organization, and it is this organization that differentiates it from other natural systems. For example, if the parts that go to make up an automobile were in various warehouses connecting to an assembly plant, these would not constitute a natural system. But, when the automobile is put together, fueled up and running, it is a natural system. It is an automobile, and in terms of its functional organization it is like other automobiles. This is why we are able to recognize it as an automobile. It is something more than an aggregate of parts. It consumes gasoline and it works; it runs. Or, to take a human example, eleven unrelated people in an area would not necessarily be thought of as a natural system; but a football *team* would be a natural system since it consists of an organized body of individuals, each performing in a certain defined relationship with all the others. In this sense, one football team is a natural system comparable to other football teams. A subsystem within the team might be an individual player, who would be seen as a system in and of himself and comparable to other players. The team itself might be seen as a subsystem which, with similar such subsystems, would comprise the supersystem of the football league. *Energy can be visualized as flowing within each system, man, team and league, as well as flowing between systems, their subsystems and the supersystems into which they are organized.*

Laszlo[7] proposes four non-varying principals of organization ("organizational invariances") which are said to characterize natural systems. Each has its relevance to the principle of androgyny.

1. *"Natural systems are wholes with irreducible properties."* He differentiates between "wholes" and "heaps." In the suborganic world, the atom may be said to be a whole, a discrete structure. We know that the atom as a whole has certain properties, and that the properties of the atom are not reducible to the properties of all its parts added together. If we took the neutron, proton and electron of a hydrogen atom and combined them in any arbitrary way, we would be unlikely to reconstitute the hydrogen atom. The properties of the hydrogen atom equal the properties of the parts *plus* the exact relations of the parts within the structure.

On the organic level, suppose we consider a human personality as a system. The particular characteristics or traits of the individual are not in themselves unique, but the way they interact is, and this is what makes each personality a distinctive whole. Masculinity and Femininity in the human being are two irreducible properties, distinct and different, which produce a dynamism through their interaction with each other. On the superorganic level, systems also interact as wholes communicating with other such wholes. What we said of automobiles and football teams as functional entities could be said also of national governments or ecological systems.

2. *"Natural systems maintain themselves in a changing environment."* Although the constituent parts of a system may change to adapt to changes in its environment, the system itself has an astonishing capacity for survival under difficult circumstances. In the suborganic world, under electron bombardment the atom becomes "excited" when it absorbs the extra energy from outside, and it radiates off the "excitation potential" when it returns to its normal (ground energy) state. Living organisms interact with the environment through input and output channels that exchange air, water, food and wastes and carry sensory information and communication. These organisms maintain themselves. They often perform repairs in case of damage, and these repairs are called "heal-

ing" and "regeneration." Of course they eventually run down through age and die, but usually not before they have managed to perpetuate themselves by a form of super-repair called "reproduction." So it may be said that the human organism is able to heal itself when its energy flow has diminished. Through various means, ranging from medicine to human relationship (psychotherapy might be one example of this), Yang and Yin energies may be brought into a more productive relationship. Individuals, by working on themselves, or through interaction with helping individuals, may become "well" after having gotten "sick," that is to say, people may bring order out of the disorder within themselves. Male and female, man and woman, also receive energy from each other and discharge energy into each other. This may take place on different levels: on the intellectual level, new ideas are synthesized; on the creative level, new artifacts; and on the procreative level, new human beings. All of this occurs as a response to a feeling of disease, of stress or tension. Many of the adaptive features of the organic world are paralleled in the superorganic area, where governments persist even though the entities of the governors and the governed may change, and forests continue to maintain themselves although individual trees may grow old, become diseased and die.

3. *"Natural systems create themselves in response to the challenge of the environment."* This third constant is the most vital one for our argument. As Laszlo describes this process of "self-creativity," he is not referring to some mysterious quality, innate in entities with "spirit" or "soul." He is talking about self-creativity in a more modest sense, as the principle behind evolutionary development. If natural systems were merely to maintain the status quo throughout the range of circumstances they encounter, there would be no evolutionary development, nothing like progress and change. But this is not the case—natural systems evolve new structures and functions to offset threats from their environment or to improve their way of interacting with it.

Essentially, there are two kinds of change, which must be differentiated. There is the preprogrammed change, such as takes place in the evolution and growth of an embryo within its mother's womb. All the information the infant needs to proceed in its developmental pattern is already coded into its genes by way of the DNA molecule at the moment of conception. Its progression along the established pathways is the process of ontogenesis. The other kind of change is phylogenesis, meaning the evolution of the species from one generation to the next. Through phylogenesis nature advances in a creative way, with systems transforming themselves as they constantly respond to challenges from other systems. We are in a process of continuously combining and separating and recombining Feminine and Masculine energies, distilling and excluding more and more dissonance (chaos), producing more and more harmony (order). In the biological sector, the transformations are known as "mutations," and some are more successful than others. Laszlo compares them to Broadway plays: the more successful ones have longer runs, the less successful close soon after opening night.

The all-important question is raised: does evolution have a purpose, fulfill a plan, or strive toward some end-product or final stage? Is there some general blueprint that all things by nature strive to achieve, or is it all a matter of chance, of trial and error?

The consistency of patterns and laws as they have been discovered through observation and reflection seems to point to the conclusion that there is some vast over-all plan for the universe which sets a general direction of development. To comprehend its total nature seems ever beyond us since our capacities for understanding are limited by the senses and intellects with which we are endowed, or, to put it another way, by nature of the information coded into the double helix of our genetic structure. So, in a sense, we unfold blindly according to a plan that we did not conceive — and we may observe the entire universe, from atomic particles to galaxies, doing the same.

But on another level, we as individuals are in the process of changing in every moment of our lives and to some degree, at least, we experience ourselves as planning those changes. We are always, it seems, at the fork of a road, and we are in every waking moment — and even in our dreams — deciding whether we had better go this way or that in order to meet the exigencies of survival or to achieve our longer-range goals. In one sense, we are determined by our constitution and must function within the limitations of that constitution. In another sense, we are free to design our lives and to create the means of going beyond many of our limitations. We can plan, and it appears that our planning makes a difference. The evolution of technology has been one means of providing for a changing existence in a changing world, but it is not the only means. The evolution of consciousness is another means of bringing about change in our existence and way of life. The latter means has been disconnected from the areas of concern to natural scientists in the Western world for several centuries, but it is beginning to be reconnected now.

4. *"Natural systems are co-ordinating interfaces in Nature's hierarchy."* To find our own place in Nature's hierarchy, we conceive of ourselves as individual human beings. Within each human body operate several organic subsystems: the respiratory system, the digestive system, the neurological system, and so on. Each such subsystem has its own subsystems operating within it according to established patterns, all the way down to the cells. The cells can also be seen as being composed of subsystems in the suborganic world; their subsystems are molecules and atoms. The hierarchy reaches above and beyond our individuality, too. We are subsystems in social systems such as the family, and families are subsystems within communities and so on until the whole human race is seen as the supersystem under which all subsystems of human groupings are ordered. The human race is, however, only a subsystem, in terms of animal life, animal life is a subsystem in the system of living organisms. And so on and on with each system in the hierarchy incorporating the systems below it. Each system is constantly under pressure from within and without. Those systems that adapt themselves to the changes, themselves change in the direction of evolution, while those that are unable to adapt diminish in strength and eventually disappear.

The changes that occur as systems go through their evolutionary development appear to be the result of planning; that is, of attempting to conform
to the pattern of the whole. The failed adaptations fall away, like the dinosaurs
of history or the antediluvian giants that peopled the earth "once upon a time."
Naive rats learn to use the mazes built by experimental psychologists to get
food for themselves. They are participants in an evolutionary movement forward, powered by an evolutionary energy which gives impetus to all movement and change. The effect of this is that formerly autonomous systems
become subordinated to control from above, without fully surrendering their
autonomy. Systems incorporate into supersystems: clans into tribes, tribes into
communities, communities into city-states, city-states into federations, federations into nations, nations into families of nations. A similar process takes
place on the suborganic level and on the supraorganic level as well. The energy that powers the evolutionary process tends toward organizing systems in
the direction of greater complexity and of increasing cooperation among like
systems. Systems combine with others in higher-level systems, but the small
units are still there, continuing to exercise their essential functions. The
strength and power that a well-functioning organization of systems supplies
creates that extra dividend of synergy which enable it to survive where less well-
organized systems or separate entities could not exist separately. This is the
implicit meaning in "United we stand, divided we fall." The universe is the
One, the whole, the supersystem within which all other systems are coordinated. The universe is the ultimate system: we cannot fall out of it. A human
being is, in the last analysis, a coordinating interface system in the multilevel
hierarchy of nature.

Laszlo summarizes the systems view of nature:

> ...The systems view of nature is one of harmony and dynamic balance. Progress
> is triggered from below without determination from above, and is thus both definite
> and open-ended. To be "with it" one must adapt and that means moving along.
> There is freedom in choosing one's path of progress, yet this freedom is bounded
> by the limits of compatibility with the dynamic structure of the whole.[8]

From a human standpoint, the key to adaptation is a recognition that although each individual is a self-contained system, no one could long survive
without being open to an ongoing infusion of energy from outside the system. As much as we are dependent upon air, food, water, material goods and
communication, so are we psychologically dependent upon other people for
the infusion of new ideas, new relationships, new loves. Formerly autonomous
systems within human beings, the Feminine in man (*anima*) and the Masculine in woman (*animus*), become subordinated to the control of the totality of
the psyche, which has been called the *Self*, without losing their authority. But
the *Self* is not a closed system. As William Blake reminds us, "All deities re-
side in the human breast."[9]

Now let us change pace and retreat from this sketch of a contemporary scientific approach to a passage from the *Inner Chapters* of Chuang Tsu, the Taoist sage of the sixth century B.C., who also reflected on these matters:

> A boat concealed in a ravine and a fishnet in a swamp appear to be safely hidden. But at midnight a strong man may put them on his back and walk off with them. But if you hide the universe in the universe, there is no way to lose it. This is the ultimate reality.[10]

Modern science agrees with the ancient sages of the East although it expresses, in terms far more sophisticated and complex, that what holds the universe together is the mysterious non-individualized something we call "energy." This sounds as if it were caught in the dualism of matter and energy, the belief that matter has to do with "things," and "energy" is what pushes these things around. From the point of view of a human being, one can only observe *directly* the operations that *seem* to be of this sort. Indeed, Newtonian mechanics were based on the assumption that physics consists of a mere description of experimental facts or something deducible from such a description. Modern science has gone far beyond this conception, however. We realize today, as Einstein has emphasized, that the physical scientist arrives at his theory only by speculative means. Our nature as human beings determines what we are able to perceive.

If we could arrive at an Archimedean point outside the universe and view it, we could see the universe in its totality—where it begins and where it ends. But since this is an impossibility in view of our being part and parcel of that "total" system, we can only extend our perceptions by every device we are clever enough to invent, from the most powerful microscope to the telescope with the greatest reach. From our point of view within the galaxy, the distant galaxies recede from our vision. The universe expands faster than we can develop machinery to explore it; and the more we strike out from the small field of knowledge which we as individuals can encompass toward the *Mysterium Tremendum* which seems to most of us eternally incomprehensible, the more we can understand the feeling expressed by T. S. Eliot:

> O dark dark dark. They all go into the dark,
> The vacant interstellar spaces, the vacant into the vacant...
> I said to my soul, be still, and let the dark come upon you
> Which shall be the darkness of God. As, in a theatre,
> The lights are extinguished, for the scene to be changed
> With a hollow rumble of wings, with a movement of darkness on darkness.[11]

We perceive matter and energy as separate, but through the speculations of contemporary scientists we have come to realize that matter and energy are inseparable. They are not different entities, but two aspects of the same. We are told that the views of modern physics are totally new. Yet the sound of the theories, when we listen to them with our inner ear, echo faintly remembered themes heard long ago.

The notion that there is nothing static, nothing abiding, but only the flow of relentless process, with everything originating growing, decaying, vanishing and being reborn in another form—this wholly dynamic view of life of the individual and of the universe is a fundamental conception of later Hinduism. The illusory quality of matter, as viewed by someone who has managed to overcome his subjectivity, is the essence of the concept of Maya. In the cosmic dance of Siva, all the features and creatures of the living world are interpreted as momentary flashes from the limbs of the Lord of the Dance.[12]

Where does it all come from, this ever-present, ever-flowing energy that permeates the universe? George Gamow supports the "Big Bang" theory of the creation of the universe, the idea that a great primeval explosion many billions of years ago started the whole process. In the speculations in his book, *The Creation of the Universe*, Gamow speaks of a time when all the matter in the universe was concentrated in one incredibly dense mass of matter for which he used the term *Ylem*, the Greek word for primordial matter. The temperature and the pressure of the *Ylem* became incredibly high until it contracted and then expanded into an unimaginably monstrous explosion. Eventually the stars congealed from the expanding dust and gases, and the universe continued to expand as a continuation of the motion imparted to matter by the initial explosion. Gamow believes that the motion will never stop.[13]

Reason suggests that there is something awry with a concept in which everything goes outward, but which does not account for its inward return, and this sets us off on a whole range of speculation. Fuel for speculation is provided by the physicists themselves, who with all their knowledge admit that they do not have any final answers. They speculate; they come to their hypotheses often through intuitive insights or through leaps of consciousness, and even at times through the solutions delivered to them by the unconscious process that manifests itself through the dream. I am emboldened to allow my own speculations to run, and to create my own metaphors for the energic fires that keep the universe cooking and so transforming itself. It is not necessary to assume automatically that just because a theory is newest, it is necessarily best. I remember Laszlo's remark to the effect that in evolution's experiments the most successful ones, like Broadway plays, are the ones likely to have the longest runs. One might add that some ancient theories, like dramatic classics, are revived and again attract large audiences.

The *second law of thermodynamics* states that entropy, the measure of a system's disorder, tends to remain constant or to increase as changes occur within the system. But as the experimental physicist Franz Exner pointed out as early as 1922, this principle was deduced by experience and experiments with *macroscopic* phenomena, and the application of the principle to the microscopic world is no longer justified on the basis of experience. When once one is able to break free from the limitations imposed by the facts and conditions that can be observed directly, hints and hunches for our speculations may be seen to emerge out of some of the older mythologems that have curiously persisted over millennia. Meanwhile, the "truths" of earlier sciences have been superseded by the fruits of more recent investigations. It appears that although the universe ought to run down, according to the principle of entropy, and people ought to wear out much more quickly than they do, and order ought constantly to be undermined by chaos—quite the opposite seems to be taking place. Even the principle of the conservation of energy is of little help here. The universe, if anything, is winding up: learning continues to increase somewhat faster than forgetting; structures in society become more complex and more delicately coordinated; we learn to replace depleted sources of energy by recycling or discovering new sources; we plan in advance how to reconstruct communities felled by natural catastrophe, and we are often able to repair even the damage done to the earth by man, its most intelligent and most selfish creature. *It appears that the universe is winding up instead of winding down.*

Physicists today find it impossible to talk about modern concepts of energy solely in terms of thermodynamics. They no longer believe with Helmholz that the sum total of the energy in the universe is constant or that what runs down through entropy cannot be regenerated. No more is there the old reverence for "equilibrium" when speaking about energy. Life does not exist in a state of equilibrium. Equilibrium is now defined as a thermodynamic state in which there are no macroscopic changes. We did not know this before physicists began studying microcosmic phenomena, because from all we can observe directly in the world around us there are no macroscopic changes in terms of energy. Until physicists began investigating microcosmic phenomena, it appeared that one could exist in a universe of closed systems that were relatively static. But the discovery was made that there are subatomic changes. If a system can be observed with an electron microscope, it will be seen that there is constant movement of elementary particles. However, the movement in one direction is exactly the same as the movement in the opposite direction, which produces the impression that there is no movement at all. But this movement, this very fine oscillation, is the very essence of energy. Since it balances itself out, this movement is not visible when viewed macroscopically. This is why energy produces an eternal flux, which is called *life*. Without the flux there is equilibrium, and equilibrium is tantamount to death.

The spark that appeared in the void beyond time has not dimmed, it has only become brighter. The universe drew its energy from that spark, or so believed the philosophers of ancient times and others who held this imperishable belief through all the ages. Perhaps the "Big Bang" theory is only a recent version of an old myth. Gamow's great explosion may have issued from the spark of light that appeared in the Beginning of beginnings in the chaos that was unformed and void, before the universe came into existence. If there is matter and anti-matter, if there is light and darkness, would it not be conceivable to speak of universe and "anti-universe"? Is this not another way of saying that if what characterizes the universe is the tendency toward order, then what characterizes the "anti-universe" would be the tendency toward disorder? Then "anti-universe" would be chaos, for chaos is characterized by formlessness and disorder. In the moment that the chaos concentrated itself sufficiently to extrude a form, even an invisible point of light with energy enough to pierce the abysmal darkness, the Beginning of the universe was taking place — and the duration of that moment may have to be measured in billions of years. Art often precedes science in its intuition.

> For in this Period the Poet's Work is Done, and all the Great Events of Time start
> forth & are conciev'd in such a Period, Within a Moment, a Pulsation of the Artery.
>                                                                            Blake[14]

The old "etheric" theory of the classicists does not sound so improbable now as a way of conceptualizing the process of creation. I speak of creation as a process and not as an event, for reasons that will shortly be seen. Imagine that the anti-universe, the chaos, is not an entity separate from the universe, but rather the complementary aspect of the universe as it is ordinarily conceived in the human mind. So, if a conception of the universe involves the interaction of negative and positive energies, then the anti-universe, or chaos, might be seen to correspond to "the neuter aspect of the holy place." If energy in the universe as we know it emerged from the chaos we cannot know, is it not possible that it returns to that chaos?

In terms of human experience, observed from our vantage point on earth, the sun is seen as the direct source of earth's energy. This observation is affirmed over and over in the mythologies of many peoples, who equate the sun with the sun god as the source of energy and therefore the source and creator of life and of the world. Contemporary science affirms that in the suborganic field of microphysics, solar energy is manifested in the nucleus of the atom. In terms of energy, one could see this emerging energy as a positive charge.

Another way of describing the outward flow of energy from the source in which it is generated would be to call it Masculine. Here we are not thinking of the designation in sexual terms at all, but clearly as a description of a certain quality of energy flow. It is Masculine in the sense that a fountain is Masculine. It has qualities of pushing out, thrusting, disseminating and dissipating itself. This Masculine flow of energy would completely exhaust itself if this process were to continue indefinitely. But as it proceeds it becomes part of a process that does not run down but finds a way to replenish itself. It is a process comparable to the Taoists' "circulation of the light." The Masculine energy, Yang, as it begins to diminish, gradually flows over into its opposite. It is taken over by the Feminine energy, Yin, into which it flows. Where the Masculine energy spills over in its profligacy, the Feminine energy gathers up. The Feminine energy principle could be seen as the negative charge inasmuch as it exists in a complementary relationship to the positive charge of the Masculine energy principle. Another way of conceptualizing it would be to say that the Feminine energy flows along the concave arc of the circle as the Masculine energy flows along the convex. The Feminine is the internal flow of energy, complementing the external flow of the energy of the Masculine. In microphysical terms, the Feminine energy would be represented by the electron and the Masculine energy by the nucleus of the atom.

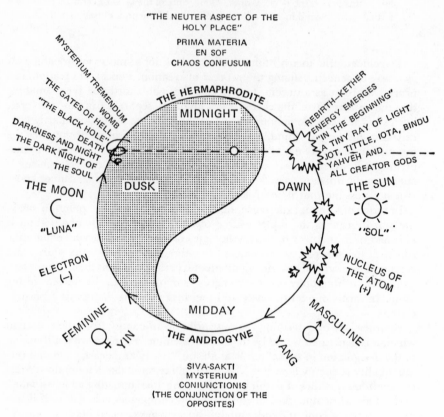

THE "ANTI-UNIVERSE"
(4TH DIMENSION)

"THE NEUTER ASPECT OF THE
HOLY PLACE"

PRIMA MATERIA
EN SOF
CHAOS CONFUSUM

THE HERMAPHRODITE
MIDNIGHT

MYSTERIUM TREMENDUM
THE GATES OF HELL
WOMB
"THE BLACK HOLE"
DARKNESS AND NIGHT
DEATH
THE DARK NIGHT OF
THE SOUL

REBIRTH—KETHER
ENERGY EMERGES
"IN THE BEGINNING"
A TINY RAY OF LIGHT
JOT, TITTLE, IOTA, BINDU
YAHVEH AND.
ALL CREATOR GODS

THE MOON
☾
"LUNA"

ELECTRON
(–)

DUSK

DAWN

THE SUN
"SOL"

NUCLEUS OF
THE ATOM
(+)

MIDDAY

FEMININE ♀ YIN

THE ANDROGYNE

MASCULINE ♂ YANG

SIVA-SAKTI
MYSTERIUM
CONIUNCTIONIS
(THE CONJUNCTION OF THE
OPPOSITES)

WHEN YANG HAS REACHED ITS GREATEST STRENGTH, THE DARK
POWER OF YIN IS BORN WITHIN ITS DEPTHS, FOR NIGHT BEGINS
AT MIDDAY WHEN YANG BREAKS UP AND CHANGES INTO YIN.

I CHING

THE UNIVERSE AS WE KNOW IT
(3RD DIMENSION)

It is as though the whole universe were engaged in the Yoga of Dual Cultivation. As in Taoism, we are not speaking of a real duality here, but of a Oneness that exists because of the complementarity of the two principles which are mutually defining:

Under heaven all can see beauty as beauty only because there is ugliness.
All can know good as good only because there is evil.
Therefore having and not having arise together.
Difficult and easy complement each other.
Long and short contrast each other.
High and low rest upon each other.
Voice and sound harmonize each other.
Front and back follow one another.[15]

Masculine and Feminine kinds of energy also follow one another and are essential to one another, yet there is no sharp line between them. From any point as we observe the circular path in our imagination, it appears that energy is in the process of moving from the Masculine to the Feminine, from the Sun toward the Moon, from light into darkness. Duration is not the consideration here, but rather the idea that the flow is continuously taking place. The process is nearly instantaneous when we speak in terms of the speed of light, and nearly endless when we speak of the lifetime of a star. But even the stars have a beginning and an ending to their individual lifetimes, and in between these they undergo an evolutionary process.

The *black hole* is now believed by astrophysicists to be one of the possible final outcomes of stellar evolution. Stars, like other systems, tend to become increasingly complex and dense with the passage of time. "'Black holes' are thought to be so densely packed that the curvature of space-time (which is always proportional to the mass in a given region) comes to equal the curvature of the surface."[16] Laszlo explains how light, according to the relativity theory, "travels along the shortest path, and the shortest path is determined by the geometry of space-time in any given region. In the neighborhood of a black hole, the shortest path is a circle around the star. Hence light—and mass energy in any form—would never escape from a black hole."[17] The black hole gets its name from the fact that a distant observer looking at it would see nothing at all. If we perceive the manifest universe as three-dimensional, then the etheric dimension, entered via the black hole, is the fourth dimensional space. If we were to conceive the black hole as the place where energy enters from the Feminine receptive side and from where it is then transformed to a Masculine creative force, we might recognize the older concept of "the neuter aspect of the holy place."

The image of the end-state of matter in the universe as a superintegrated state of energies, expressed in a highly ordered structure that eventually achieves a *status quo* at the end of a very long cycle, is a difficult image to grasp for one who is not at home in the field of astrophysics. The more philosophically oriented will find it interesting to note that there were alchemical images in the Middle Ages which intuitively expressed ideas that bear some striking similarities to this contemporary theme. The speculations of the human intellect tend to be repetitive in nature, even though they meet with different results because they have different sorts of data with which to work. The archetypal "forms" remain the same, but their "contents" differ from age to age.

The alchemists of old understood that in their opus they were dealing with complementary principles that had to undergo a continual serial process of unification and separation. One of the ways of imaging the crucial elements of the process in their interaction was to speak of Sol and Luna (Sun and Moon). Sol represented the gold, which in its turn was a symbol for light, for strength, for energy, for power, and for all the manifold elements and principles that were associated with these ideas. Luna, in her turn, was the dark, receptive one, the source of vitality and the refuge in times of difficulty or need. Sol was personified in the King figure and Luna in the Queen. Together these two formed the classical alchemical *syzygy* (a pair, the existence of which is maintained by its essential complementarity). The heavenly pair were sometimes described as Solomon and the Queen of Sheba, Solomon being the king whose name was associated with the Sun while the black Sheba is the Queen of darkness. The archetypal marriage of the Feminine and the Masculine occurs when the chaste, wise and rich Queen of Sheba was willing to give herself to none other than King Solomon. The symbolism is evident as Penotus, author of *Theatrum Chemicum*, writes:

> You have the virgin earth, give her a husband who is fitting for her. She is the Queen of Sheba, hence there is need of a king crowned with a diadem — where shall we find him? We see how the heavenly sun gives his splendor to all other bodies, and the earthly or mineral sun will do likewise, when he is set in his own heaven, which is named the "Queen of Sheba," who came from the ends of the earth to behold the glory of Solomon...[18]

The Masculine energy, which is associated with the light, has begun to fade; it is then met by the "chaste, wise, rich" Feminine, which corresponds to this dense superintegrated state characterized by blackness (the "black hole" theory). The Masculine then joins with, or enters into the Feminine, whereby it is returned again to the "womb," but now the energy is organized in a different way from the way it was when it first emerged at its own birth. What was born out of the *chaos confusum* has been subjugated to the principle of order. The old king, *Senex*, is represented as the status quo that precedes the new birth, the birth of the "young king" in alchemy; or, in our terms, the transformation of energy in a universe that goes on recreating itself.

We turn once more to the scientist's view of this cosmic evolution. With black holes, which have the fantastic density of upwards of $10^{15}$ grams per cubic centimeter, we reach the limits of the structural integration of masses and energies in the cosmos. "The very same forces, which ultimately attain a *status quo* at the end of the long cycle of evolution, act as organizing forces producing intricate structures in earlier phases. In the physical sector of evolution, they give rise to the many varieties of atoms which populate the vast reaches of the cosmos. The evolution of atoms takes place in an interacting process."[19]

And so, as Laszlo put it in one of his lighter moments, "the beat goes on." Over and over again the cycle is symbolically experienced. It can be viewed microcosmically or macrocosmically. Also, the cycle can be viewed rationally or mythologically. The pattern has a consistency about it, however we may look at it: the beginning is always beyond the furthest reaches of imagination, shrouded in darkness, in a confused state that is identified with chaos because everything is in it, or with the void because we cannot imagine anything that is unformed. The potentiality that is shrouded in mystery undergoes some kind of change, some energy exchange in which the nothingness or the totality is imagined to have coalesced into the spark or ray, the infinitesimal point or the explosion that brings the universe into being. It is all the same, because how can one speak of the size of the spark of creation when there was nothing to compare it with and no one to do the comparing in any case? Energy streams forth, and the source appears to us, in our solar system, to be the sun. If we break down this energy into its elementary components, the streaming forth is described as the nucleus of the atom or, in psychological terms, as the Masculine principle. The Masculine principle, going through the cycle, encounters the Feminine principle into which it is merged, and in the process the quality of the flow is altered. The positive charge becomes the negative charge; the corresponding elementary particles are electrons. In the closing of the circle, the energy that exploded as "sun" now has been gathered together and condensed until it reaches its limits in the ultimate condensation of the "black hole." Once more chaos, and once more the process repeats itself.

The miracle is that we human beings have become aware that such a process is taking place, and beyond that, we are aware of ourselves as part of the process.

# Chapter 18

## Energy and the Evolution of Consciousness

The question is "whether the whole of reality is an organism or a machine."
Weston Labarre

*Organism:* An entity having an existence independent of, or more fundamental than its elements and having distinct members or parts whose relations and powers or properties are determined by their function in the whole.
*Webster's International Unabridged Dictionary.*

In the view of evolutionary consciousness, the universe is an organism. The Tao is the Way in which all life moves through the living universe in alternating pulsations. Yang moves outward; Yin returns inward. Diastole and systole; the energy pulses through rhythmically, expanding the cavities of the heart contracts darkness until it is filled with chaos. Then the heart contracts and a ray of light is forced outward. The circulation of the light has begun; life is in process.

The child asks, "Where did I come from?" And, growing older and more curious, "How did the universe come into being?" Was there a cosmic explosion, the Big Bang as described by the contemporary creation myth? Was it as *bindu*, the minute drop, according to the Hindu tradition? Was it born of an infinitesimal ray that shone forth from the crown of *Kether*? Did it break forth from the Orphic egg, the world egg? In what vessel was the evolutionary energy contained? What vessel broke and set life free to evolve from myriads of scattered particles, to organize itself into systems and hierarchies of systems gradually increasing in their complexity?

It does not matter what names we assign to the mysterious process that gave birth to the universe before the beginning of time. The capacity for awareness of the process is an innate quality of the human psyche. It makes itself known when individuals experience the archetypal dimensions of their beings. It is the Way and the Word, the Light and the Tao. It is the breath of

179

God as it transformed a heap of dust into a living organism: it has been called *ch'i* and *prana*, *pneuma* and *ruach*, and the holy spirit. It is energy in all of its manifestations. Because it exists in the psyche as the generator of human consciousness, it does not seem necessary to search for proof of its reality or to accept it on "faith" either. The process of evolution manifests itself in the evolution of consciousness; the process is its own evidence for existence.

The universe appears purposive when viewed from an evolutionary perspective; that is, it appears to be moving from relative simplicity toward relative complexity. Furthermore, it appears to be moving from relative chaos to relative order. When viewed as a closed system — from the point of view of linear progression within a limited time span — complexity seems frequently to fall apart and order seems to collapse into confusion. But in the wider view of the universe as an open system where time is cyclic and space is open-ended, it is possible to recognize an ordering principle at work guiding the functioning of all creation. This principle obtains throughout the universe. Since human beings are members of the universe, the principle operates in us also. The principle operates in and of itself, as is clear from the fact that it is not necessary to inform the embryo how it should organize itself in the womb in order to emerge as a human being.

The principle also functions in letting people know how to grow, to dance, to play and to make love. Yet society seems to feel that it is necessary to inform human beings how to conduct the inner organizing process which leads to sexual behavior. This is what people have been doing all over the world, and especially in the Judeo-Christian culture where a vast artillery of sexual laws and sexual imperatives has been established — as though to guard human beings from the most dangerous enemy imaginable. The enemy, as it appears from a perusal of those many sexual theories that are grounded in religion and psychology, can only be unbridled sexuality, for sexuality has long been considered to be the most powerful generator of emotions and determinant of behavior. Those who would guard the public morals presume that protection from the power of sexuality is needed, and they have provided this protection through laws and strictures, conventions and punishment for infringement of the conventions. It is not that everyone today observes the "old morality." Complete disregard of it leads to amorality. Open rebellion against it leads to immorality. Attempts at creating a "new morality" remain rare in our time.

In areas of human life other than that of the direct expression of genital sexuality, it seems possible to function in far less moralistic and judgmental ways. There seems to be more objectivity in almost any other area as, for example, when we speak in general terms about human development. The biologist traces the growth of the embryo from the moment of conception until birth, as though energy-transformations came along as a matter of course according to a process that could be, and often is, described as logical. The Western rationalistic thinker adds causes and effects together and from those derives an explanation of phenomena. The mythological approach tends to be expressed more often in metaphysical and religious terminology, and is able to accept that some miracles do occur and some events cannot be explained except by analogy and symbolic reference. The new evolutionary approach to consciousness will go beyond both of these, yet it will not reject them either. It will synthesize the new insights of science (which incorporates previous insights) with the essential insights of mystical religion. The evolutionary approach will provide a basis for a new understanding of sexuality which goes beyond both rational and romantic notions. It is on such a foundation that any really new sexual theory will have to be constructed.

It is now possible to see that sexuality can be discussed in very different terms, depending upon whether one's views stem from a mechanistic-causalistic view of space and time — as in Freud and the early Jung — or from a symbolic view as exemplified in certain religions, or from a unified view that includes the two previously mentioned views but goes beyond them. The first view would be espoused by the rationalists, the second by the mythologists, and the third by those who are moving into tho new evolutionary consciousness. It is this third view with which we will be concerned as we turn our attention to the place of sexuality in the future.

Evolutionary consciousness heralds the new age. It accompanies the onset, and will help to design it. Evolution has been proceeding all these many millennia without human beings' having been aware of their active role in it. Today we are beginning to understand that how we live and what we do may have a profound effect upon forces that we formerly thought of as inexorable. We are not only the products of creation; we are also the co-creators. Our potentiality for affecting the course of the future derives from our ability to make conscious choices. To be able to make a choice, after a reflective process that allows us to weigh values and to consider long-term goals, is a distinguishing feature of human beings. Other organisms make choices, to be sure, but their choices are generally made in response to immediate stimuli. A dog runs to greet his master when the master appears down the street. Birds respond to the sight of ripe mulberries on the tree. Fish seek deeper waters when the surface waters are too warm for them. Plants are able to direct their roots when they sense the presence of moisture nearby. Only human beings are capable of the kind of reflective thinking in which the eventual consequences of their behavior are measured *in advance* and where impulses are held in check, not because of the expectation of immediate reward or punishment, but because of an underlying attitude toward themselves and toward their place in the world.

Attitudes are undergoing a continuing process of refinement in response to feedback from our perceptions of the external world and perceptions of our own bodily sensations. We tend to transpose the latter into psychological terms when we speak of thoughts and feelings and intuitions and regard these as mental processes. No matter how we choose to interpret our perceptions of ourselves, the experience is an experience of and by a total organism; namely, ourselves. What we experience, among other things, is that we are able to make choices and that we are, in fact, eternally at a fork in the road, deciding which path to take. Through these choices we participate actively in our personal evolution. To a considerable degree, these choices enable us also to participate in the designing of our world.

Suppose someone were to say to you: "You now have the capacity to remove from the face of the earth every living human being, and you may create in man's place a new race with all the characteristics needed to build a new society according to whatever plan you might devise." Furthermore, suppose all the money you might require were at your command, and also all the technical equipment devised by science were in your hands with instructions as to how to operate it. And also, suppose that you were empowered to discard any old, worn-out traditions or laws that would hamper your freedom to apply all the means at your disposal to create the kind of world you would decide to have. What would your world be like?

This is, of course, a metaphysical question, transcending the practical possibilities of the physical world. One lifetime would not be long enough to accomplish this task, even if we were able to conceive and plan the superproject. However, in a hundred years from now, when almost no one who is alive today will remain on earth, we know that collectively, if not individually, this metaphysical question will have its answer. Men and women will have chosen their partners and will have produced the children they wanted to populate the new world. By precept and example, people will have taught the succeeding generations how to operate this world of the future. The lessons as to how the new world should be operated will have proceeded according to the ideas of the former generation, whether the former generation was conscious of the nature of those ideas or unconscious of them. Also, the buildings we will have built, the land we will have replenished or exploited, the information systems we will have installed or will have allowed to be imposed, the politics we will have voted for and the morality we will have espoused, will all contribute to the equipment with which the children we have chosen to conceive and bear will continue to plan the life of the human system.

Like it or not, knowingly or not, we do design our future and the future of life on this planet. There is a grave responsibility in all this. Sexuality plays a significant role in this responsibility because how we exercise our sexuality, and with whom, and whether or not we choose to become parents are those homely old questions on which nothing less than the future of the world depends. Today's situation differs from that of the past in that today we have more control over our sexuality than we ever had before, and also in that *we are aware of how much we can control our sexuality and of the ramifications of all the ways in which we do control it*. The sexuality of the past was often preached about as a moral issue. Today it *is* a moral issue, but it cannot be preached about because of new factors — biological and genetic advances in science — and there are no conventions and no laws as yet that take these into account as well as the emerging consciousness of the Aquarian Age.

Nineteenth-century concepts of energy were appropriate when people were

thinking in the three-dimensional models of Newtonian physics and orthodox psychoanalysis. Freud and Jung, especially during the time Jung was working under the influence of Freud, borrowed their concepts of psychic energy
from the prevailing ideas about energy in the physics of their times. They
knew nothing about energy as it is conceived of today, but took their own
contemporary scientific models and tried to convert those metaphorically into
psychic systems. Freud's analogy for physical energy was psychic energy, which
he called *libido*. For Freud, *libido* was primarily sexual, and sexuality was seen
as the prime mover of the human psyche. Jung, in responding to this central
focus upon sexuality, found the concept too narrow to account for all the psychological phenomena he encountered. Schooled as he was in religion and
philosophy and with more than a little interest in the occult, Jung was unable
to accept unequivocally the limited view of energy that seemed to satisfy his
older erstwhile colleague, and so he broadened the concept of *libido* to include
*all* psychic energy, regardless of whether it was expressed in terms of sexual
feeling. Jung differentiated between the characteristic ways in which psychic
energy could be expressed, and showed how it could find many channels into
which to flow. Furthermore, Jung saw the alterative channels — for example,
creative imagination or religious experience — as *primary* motivating forces that
gave psychic energy, or *libido*, its specific quality. Jung did not see creativity
or religious feeling merely as sublimated sexual energy; these were experiences
in their own rights which provided valid channels into which the generalized
psychic energy could flow.

Both Freud and Jung were working out of a pre-Einsteinian framework,
although Jung was acquainted with Einstein and had some idea of the direction in which Einstein's speculations were leading. The models at the turn
of the century were closed-systems models. Freud had learned his physics from
Helmholz — that the sum total of all the energy in the universe was constant,
that it was a closed system, and that it is not regenerated. Energy, according
to this view, is never created or destroyed within a closed system. The system
could be the whole universe or it could be one human being. With respect
to psychic energy, this meant that if the energy were channeled in one direction, it could not at the same time flow in the opposite direction. Or, if it
did flow in two directions at once, whatever flowed in one way necessarily
diminished in volume or intensity the flow in the alternate direction.

That Jung agreed with Freud in this, especially in the early days, is evidence by Jung's concepts of psychological types, in which he characterized
individual attitudes as extraverted or introverted. To the degree that one was
an extravert, one could not be an introvert, and to the degree that one was
introverted, one could not exercise extraversion. Likewise with the psychological functions. Jung characterized as opposites "thinking" and "feeling" and
stated that a person who was a "thinking type" would necessarily have inferi-
or "feeling," and there would be little likelihood of his ever developing his feeling to a high level of functioning. Similarly, he posed as opposite functions
"intuition" and "sensation" and expressed the view that an individual who tend-

ed intuitively to perceive things holistically, as an "intuitive" does, would never be able to accomplish a high degree of mastery over detail, which is the province of the "sensation" type. Experience, however, does not necessarily bear out this thesis because it is based upon laws of physics that have been proven no more adequate to describe a wide range of physical phenomena than were its psychological correlates. I know from my own observations of the psychological typology of the people with whom I work that if I can disregard the objective test results, I find there are some people who can function on a superior level in two functions that would have been termed by Jung as "opposite" and therefore incompatible. In fact, I have found that those people who were best at intuiting what might be going to happen next would often be the very ones who did not let a single detail of sensory impression escape them. This combination of intuition and sensation is, of course, exactly what makes a good detective.

Jung, master of the paradox as he was, while operating out of a "closed system" model in many respects, nevertheless had a sort of intuitive foreknowledge about the possibility that there were other systems outside his own. Unlike Freud, he was always willing to admit that whatever conviction he might hold, there was always the possibility that he might be wrong. So Jung maintained a provisional attitude toward the mechanistic-causalistic psychological system of Freud. Jung acknowledged its value, but nevertheless left a way for other possibilities. Perhaps this was a result of his long-standing interest in anthropology and comparative religions, from which be learned that there were always other ways of looking at phenomena, and always other conclusions that could be drawn from a single set of data. His study of the primitive religions of Melanesia, for example, brought to his attention the idea of *mana*, something of psychic nature that is extraordinarily effective. While nothing "divine" attaches to *mana*, it imparts to individuals a greater intensity of energy and power. These emanate from a mysterious source outside of the individual, in a way that is not explainable by rational criteria. From such observations as this — and Jung sought them far and wide — he developed his "energic" point of view as a complementary position to that of Freud's "causalistic" viewpoint. Jung wrote in his essay, "On Psychic Energy":

> The almost universal incidence of the primitive concept of energy is a clear expression of the fact that even at an early level of human consciousness man felt the need to represent the sensed dynamism of psychic events in a concrete way. If, therefore, in our psychology we lay stress on the energic point of view, this is in accord with the psychic facts which have been graven on the mind of man since primordial times.[1]

Jung seems to have been aware that there were definite limitations in the concept of the human organism as a closed system. He apparently recognized the prevalence of open systems where the energy comes from outside the system and powers it. No system can operate unless it receives energy from outside itself, be that system a human cell, an airplane, or the universe itself. This is why it was necessary to posit something like the "anti-universe" in the previous chapter. The moment you close the system, the system begins to run down and die. That does not seem to be happening in the universe, as physicists today are observing.

Freud, however, was operating out of an earlier context. Not only was he dependent upon the scientific views of his day and the times immediately preceding him, but also upon the moral fabric of the entire Judeo-Christian civilization. He, and most of the psychologists who followed him, based their theories on a materialistic-mechanistic view which reached back into ancient times for its psychological and philosophical parallels. The feeling of *possessiveness* in human relationships that we have been programmed to experience stems from the idea that what I have is mine, and what I give away or what is taken from me is no longer mine to enjoy. The idea is so basic that it even is to be found in the Ten Commandments, which begins and ends with precepts founded on it. The first Commandment insists that all devotion shall be directed to the Lord who brought the Hebrews out of the Land of Egypt, "You shall have no other gods before me," lest energy be diverted from the "jealous God" with whom the covenant should be made. And the tenth Commandment concerns coveting one's neighbor's property, which is limited, and which serves as a symbol for the limited energy contained in it. So, too, all ideas about adultery, still the one universal ground for divorce; for the theory that when love (i.e., sexually directed energy) flows in one direction, it is not available to flow in any other direction. This is why the poet William Blake was so revolutionary when he put these words in the mouth of Oothoon, the embodiment of the freely loving woman:

> Father of Jealousy, be thou accursed from the earth!...
> Till beauty fades from off my shoulders, darken'd and cast out.
> A solitary shadow wailing on the margin of non-entity.
> I cry: Love! Love! Love! happy happy Love! free as the mountain wind!
> Can that be Love that drinks another as a sponge drinks water,
> That clouds with jealousy his nights, with weepings all the day,
> To spin a web of age around him, grey and hoary, dark,
> Till his eyes sicken at the fruit that hangs before his sight?
> Such is self-love that envies all, a creeping skeleton
> With lamplike eyes watching around the frozen marriage bed.[2]

Freud pioneered an original and daring theory of sexuality and presented it as a rational system in terms of the scientific thinking of his time. Jung was not so bound to rational considerations; he was able to hear voices outside of his system as well as those in it. Because of his commitment to religion and to the symbolic systems of all religions, he was able to escape the temporal network and see the universe in terms of an expression he liked to employ, *sub specie aeternitatis* (under the aspect of eternity). It is clear that here he was thinking of an open system, a system that no matter how vast it may be, allows something beyond it to be imagined. Jung enjoyed the possibility of speculation on unknowable matters; hence, he maintained an open mind despite the vigor with which he expressed his ideas. This applied, of course, to his views on sexuality, with the result that he never constructed a rigorous theory of sexuality.

Freud's sexual theory was based on the biological science of his time; consequently, it reflected some of the prejudices and misconceptions of the day. A critical example of this is his contention that *to begin with we were all bisexual*. This was a prevalent view, in fact the classical concept of the innate, embryonal bisexuality of all vertebrates has been challenged only in the past thirty years. Freud's theories were based on the "truism" of a bisexuality in the womb. Following him, most current sexual theorists have not taken into account recent discoveries to the contrary in the area of sexual differentiation in the embryo. I am now referring to physiological bisexuality, for it was a *biological* and not a psychological concept that provided a rationale for the psychosexual theories that were developed by Freud and his followers. Freud's basic premise grew out of the idea that the undifferentiated human embryo is innately bisexual, and that after differentiation occurs, male and female structures evolve unequally, with one or the other dominating. Hence, he concluded, everyone remains bisexual to some degree.[3] It was his understanding that the penis and the clitoris evolved from the same embryonic structure, but that the clitoris was more rudimentary. This led him to the interesting conclusion that women are sexually incomplete in comparison with men. It is remarkable that this conclusion was accepted for so long by so many men, in spite of the fact that only women are able to conceive, gestate, bear and nurse children. The insistence of Freud and his followers, not to mention his predecessors, on this point is but another example of the adage that just because an argument is convincing does not necessarily mean that it is right.

More recent comparative embryology has added some new biological information that makes obsolete the traditional psychoanalytic concepts that suggest the inferiority of female sexuality; yet these newer concepts have yet to be integrated into psychological theory. Even so, the growing awareness of the recent findings has come about more as a result of pressure from the Women's Movement than it has through any major change in attitude in the mainstream of psychiatry or psychoanalysis.

According to recent discoveries in the field of embryology, we do not begin life as bisexuals. The early embryo is not bisexual, as formerly thought; it is not undifferentiated, "it" is female. While genetic sex is established at conception, all human embryos develop as females until the fifth or sixth week of fetal life. At this time the sex genes begin to exert their influence. If the genetic sex is male, the primordial germ cells migrate to the future testes where they stimulate the production of a substance that, in turn, induces the development of fetal androgen, the male sex hormone. This androgen suppresses the growth of the female reproductive system and induces development along male lines. By the twelfth week the male reproductive system is firmly established and reversals of these tissues can no longer occur — although suppression of their growth and function can take place later in life. If the genetic sex is female, the germ cells arrive at the ovaries but no inductor substance is needed to stimulate the production of estrogen. The female simply develops along the lines of her innate genetically determined female structure, while the male differentiation must be acquired. Although biologists are aware that we were all female in the beginning, it will probably be a long time before the influence of these discoveries filters down to the level where theologians will be ready to consider an "Adam-out-of-Eve" version of Genesis.

If there is no evidence for a *structural bisexuality* in the embryo, the question arises as to the source of our *concept of bisexuality* as a basis for behavioral attitudes. While maleness and femaleness are genetically determined, masculinity and femininity are subject to hormonal modification. There is a continuous production of both estrogens and androgens by both sexes, although with a preponderance of one or the other. The particular mix in each individual seems to be related to the particular place on the continuum which ranges from the extreme of powerful muscular masculinity on one side to the most delicate version of femininity on the other. In comparison with other animals, however, the genetic code for humans calls for a certain proportion of each hormone, with the result that males and females are not very different. In other species the imbalance is so great that males and females seem hardly to belong to the same species.[4]

Given this information, it appears that there may be, after all, some biological basis for bisexuality, or for the variations in the sexual proclivities of individual men and women. If the balance of male and female hormones affects the masculine/feminine balance from one species to another, it seems reasonable to assume that lesser variations within species would produce individuals who would vary correspondingly from the sexual norms. Thus, we might expect to find in men a range of "masculinity"; some tending to be more and some to be less "masculine" by reason of hormonal distribution, with women also exhibiting the effects of their hormonal distribution in similar ways. And we would also expect to find some individuals in whom the balance between androgens and estrogens would be such as to predispose an individual to make an easier peace with his or her contrasexual element. It is not clear just how the hormonal balance affects sexual behavior, but there is reason to believe that there is an interrelationship. It might be conjectured, conversely, that behavior and attitudes are not without their effect upon hormonal production.

Jung did not get caught in the trap of "biological bisexuality" to the degree that Freud did, although in his concept of woman's role in society Jung was influenced to a considerable extent by his environment. Even here, however, he was aware of the exceptional potential of certain women, as evidenced by the unusually strong group of talented women who were his pupils and later his colleagues and the founders of the Jungian movement in the United States and elsewhere. There is no question but that Jung broke new ground when he separated the concepts of sex and gender and was able to see the Masculine as apart from maleness and the Feminine as apart from femaleness. The Masculine as apart from maleness he saw as the *animus* in woman; the Feminine apart from femaleness he saw as the *anima* in man.

Jung's descriptions of the annoying and irritating qualities of the *anima* and the *animus*, which evoke so much resistance from those who read them today, are those very personal qualities that are bound to emerge in a raw and unrefined state in an individual because they have been so long repressed and denied their natural development. When observing the unpleasant qualities of the negative animus in women, it is important to realize that until the last half of the twentieth century — despite the development of an industrial society that did not depend on the brute strength of men for its productivity — the tradition still obtained whereby the men were the ones who did the major physical, commercial and professional work in the world, while women were sheltered from all of that and did their own work about the home, rearing children, or working in the adjunctive, helping and nurturing professions. As secretaries, teachers and nurses, they functioned in an enabling or nurturing role. These areas were the nearly exclusive province of women, just as business, commerce, intellectual endeavor and government were the nearly exclusive province of men.

Small wonder then, that the *anima*, the Feminine in man, was oppressed and rejected equally as much as the *animus*, or Masculine element in woman. It was no more "appropriate" for a man to stay home from work and don an apron and prepare dinner for the family than it was for a woman to become an executive in a large corporation. So man's nurturing qualities, which abide in the *anima* aspect of his personality, had to be excluded from his daily functioning. A man would feel guilty even *desiring*, for example, to wear brightly colored clothing, or taking an opportunity to weep openly. One could almost see this as a recapitulation on a contemporary and personal level of the ancient and collective rejection of mother-goddess worship by the patriarchal tribes who entered the fruitful agricultural areas after their wanderings on the barren deserts. The *anima*, oppressed and denied expression as she was in man, acquired a kind of dammed-up energy that must eventually burst forth in a negative way when the tension of holding her in became too great. This is probably why Jung saw the *anima* in men primarily when she had broken through the boundaries of repression. Then she appeared as moodiness and petulance, lassitude and irrational argumentativeness. Likewise, the *animus* in women became most obvious when he appeared in his negative forms, as stubborn, pedantic and opinionated.

It is on account of this formulation, made in his early years, that Jung has received so much criticism from those who have been striving for an equalization of opportunity and status as human beings for the two sexes. People who have been attempting to break down the sexually based stereotypes have seen in Freud, and equally in Jung, specific characterizations of what is "masculine" and what is "feminine," and they see how these characterizations have become associated with societal expectations of how people ought to behave in their roles as women and their roles as men.

Because Freud did not go beyond these conceptual characterizations, his sexual theory is no longer so relevant to a society in which women are no longer *forced* into the traditional gender role. Since women have become able to achieve control over their own reproductive functions, there is no longer any biological reason for them to carry on the traditional role of woman in society. It is a viable option, to be sure; but as the growing competence of women in areas outside the home is being recognized more generally, one realizes that there are other viable options for women as well.

The unexpected dividend of the Women's Movement, a dividend that has not yet made its full impact, is the effect upon men of the broadening concept of woman's roles and woman's potentialities. As woman becomes more adept in the world outside the home and the "helping professions," through the acquisition and practice of an increasing variety of skills, she makes an increasingly large financial contribution to the family. The inevitable result, *if the family can be maintained long enough to allow this trend to mature*, is that man will be relieved of the crushing burden of spending most of his waking hours earning enough to support a dependent wife and children. This promises opportunities for men to exercise other aspects of their psychological constitutions besides the rational, the managerial, the competitive and all the other "manly virtues." At the same time, woman, formerly sheltered from the machinations of the higher echelons of business and politics and the constructive uses of the intellect, now begins to have the freedom, the time, the space and the money to develop these "animus" aspects of her nature along positive lines.

On the practical and rational level, Jung may have been a spokesman for the time and place in which he lived and did his major work, primarily the Switzerland of the first half of the twentieth century. But, as he himself had recognized before he was out of his teens, he possessed a "number one" and a "number two" personality. Number one was the rational and scientific one, the ego-personality bound to its milieu and speaking out for its traditions. It was number two, however, that made him truly great. This was his transpersonal aspect, the one that broke through temporal and spatial boundaries and found itself concerned with messages embedded in the symbols of other times, in secret accord with the Middle Ages, as personified by *Faust*, with the legacy of a past that had obviously stirred Goethe to the depths.[5] This personality explored Greek and Teutonic mythology, the lore of Gnosticism, the secret books of ancient Egypt, medieval alchemy; places far and wide: Japan and Zen, Tibet and *The Tibetan Book of the Dead*, China and the *I Ching* and *The Secret of the Golden Flower*; and he even went to India to learn about yoga, and to the Southwestern United States to speak of healing with an old Indian medicine man. The number two personality's excursions were not into distant landscapes alone, but into the inscapes of many peoples—where he was able to enter into the symbolic life of the soul and to hold it up to view.

In his later life, and especially in his works on alchemy and the alchemical analogues of psychological processes, Jung was able to see the psyche in a new way—as an open system. His concept of the unconscious was an open one, with space not only for the forgotten and the unknown, but also for the forever unknowable void that is the mother and father of the living universe. On one side, he found that the individual human psyche was rooted in the collective psyche of the culture. We are not only the children of our parents, we are the children of our age. On the other side, he found that the unconscious of the individual is rooted in the collective unconscious. We carry with us not only the drives and repressions of our personal histories, but also the weight of centuries of tradition, of belief, of fears and of expectations. He saw that behavior and attitudes are conditioned not only by our parents and the members of our generation, but by the archetypal parents, who make themselves known in myths as the kings and queens, gods and goddesses, the sun and the moon, the demons and muses.

Alchemy with its ongoing processes of separation and fusion became a leitmotiv of his life; consequently much of what he has to say about it has its bearing on concepts concerning human sexuality.[6] Alchemy seeks to make a precious compound by working with substances that are, in their original form, incompatible opposites. Through an appreciation of what these substances are and how they function under a variety of circumstances, it would be theoretically possible to fuse their qualities in such a way as to produce a magical medicine, an elixir that would cure all human ills, to extend the life span and even, ideally, to bring about immortality. In any case, it would produce offspring of a new sort. The opposites, when finally distilled, would contain the essence of the Feminine (*anima*) and the essence of the Masculine (*animus*). Each element in the dyad, whether a real human being or a symbolic representation as chemical substance, would first be joined to its inner opposite and then to its external partner in the *mystical marriage*. The offspring of this would be the spiritual child, who would be called the *filius philosophorum*, or the son of the philosopher, and the child would be an androgyne, unlike any child that might be born of the flesh.

The end of the alchemical opus, the child of the philosophers, corresponds to the elixir, the lapis, the pearl of great price, the diamond body, the goal of spiritual perfection. As *perfection*, it remains an ideal which is never reached; but the path toward this goal loads to *wholeness*, which involves the meeting of the opposites—the dark and the light, the pleasure and the pain that come along with openness and sensitivity. It has the same meaning as the tiny golden pill which was the object of the Yoga of Dual Cultivation in Taoism. Alchemy was, in its own way, such a Yoga, in that the opus was performed by a pair absolutely equal as to their importance to the task, adept and soror, linked together in common purpose. Their task, as Jung describes it, was first the differentiation and then the union of the Masculine and the Feminine principles, through working on their analogies in matter.

The exploration of alchemical symbolism was the great opus of Jung's life, for it set the spiritual foundations for a different way of looking at the Masculine and the Feminine. It is true that Jung was bound by his times and his society with respect to his views about men and women and their sex-linked qualities. But his genius was that he soared above these stereotypes in his search for the archetypal Masculine and Feminine. He was able to see the principles intuitively long before any practical applications for them in human relationships had been conceived. In this sense, he was like Democritus, who was talking about the atom in ancient Greece — when few were listening. Jung, who had long been undervalued as a scientist and a philosopher, is now at last beginning to be heard. He offers a way of looking at human sexuality that is congruent to an open-systems approach. He recognized early in his life that sexuality is only *one* way of expressing, bodily and spiritually, that universal energy that is incarnated in the living flesh of every human being. This energy is subject to an infinite number of potentialities for transformation. But nothing works without the dynamics of the interaction of the opposites, and this is what androgyny is: the rhythmic interplay of Masculine and Feminine within the psyche of one individual. If the problem of the opposites is solved within the individual, a step will be made toward the better understanding of all warring opposites — between individuals, and between the wider systems to which they belong.

# Chapter 19

## Toward a New Theory of Human Sexuality

A new sexual theory is in order, because of the obvious dissolution of the old order and the old conventions. The psychologies that perpetuated the old order by attempting to keep sexuality under moral or rational paradigms are rapidly falling into disuse. The newer psychologies offer sexual freedom and release from the inhibiting forces that maintained controls in years past. They bombard us incessantly with experiments in sensory awareness and alternative life styles and every sort of gadgetry, until we grow weary and jaded. Sexuality becomes more and more important as to pleasure, and less and less significant as to value. All too often, despite the hawking of new delights by the sex-merchants, even the pleasure falls away. People have gained almost total control over their own reproductive processes, and sexuality is no longer necessarily attached to marriage and family. The ingredient of commitment is not required when persons engage each other sexually. The old laws have been repealed, and no adequate substitutes have been found. Most people are either detached from the total process of the emotional experience of sexuality, or are into a sexual nihilism in which everything is experimental and anything goes.

Our jadedness is the outcome of thinking in the old ways, in terms of closed systems with entropy setting in as the result of too much discharge of (sexual) energy. Ahead lies the prophecy of William Blake, "If the doors of perception were cleansed, every thing would appear as it is, infinite"— for truly the doors that once were slightly parted by the esoteric religious disciplines have now been flung wide by contemporary physics and molecular biology and other sciences. Yet our attitudes toward sexuality, aided and abetted by most of contemporary psychology, have remained behind, as Blake also foresaw when he wrote, "For man has closed himself up till he sees all things through the narrow chinks of his cavern."[1]

Our generation is still suffering from the excesses of the Age of Pisces in which the rationalists kept the Masculine principle in the position of dominance and the Feminine principle subordinated to it. Men who functioned

193

primarily out of their verbal cognitive sides, who were extraverted in their thinking and aggressive in their behavior, exercised control in important places; and women who were successful in the world were well-endowed with the so-called "masculine" qualities. In those areas of life in which the mythological approaches were still permissible — music, drama, creative writing, fantasy activity of all kinds, the media with their strong emotional appeal — the Feminine principle prevailed. But the Feminine was either fearful, awesome and incomprehensible, or else it was light, inconsequential and fit only for the less serious aspects of living.

A well-functioning interdependent relationship between a man and a woman became ever more rare in our society; still less frequently were the Masculine principle and the Feminine principle likely to be seen working together harmoniously within an individual. People had been taught that it was important to maintain a conscious attitude that was in keeping with the expectations for one's own sex: sex and gender roles were not differentiated from one another. This attitude in traditional "straight" society necessitated the suppression of the contrasexual element, or at least the channeling of that element into restricted and socially approved areas. Therefore, many people, although innately androgynous in nature, were unable to fulfill many of their potentials because this would have been seen as inappropriate in the circles in which they moved.

It followed then, that in choosing a partner one would be attracted to a person through whom one could experience, vicariously at least, those aspects of one's own being that one could not live out conveniently in the world. This person would generally be of the opposite sex, although not necessarily. Unfortunately, all too often the expectations that the other person would fill the void in one's own personality were frequently not met, because people rarely behave as we imagine they will or as we need them to behave. Many relationships foundered because they were based on illusion and wishful thinking. There were no longer the old bonds to hold them together, and a romantic attachment was not durable enough to last.

No theory of sexuality is ever formulated, nor can it be, without that theory's being tested in intimate relationship to human lives. It is not my intention to attempt to formulate a new sexual theory, for I believe this ought to be the work of many minds, bringing together experience and wisdom and interacting with one another in open exchange. Yet in dealing with the pain and dysfunction and concern and curiosity of the people with whom I work, when it comes to sexual questions I have had to discover for myself a viewpoint that could have some theoretical implications. My own experience, sitting in the chair of the analyst in a room where secrets are shared and hidden feelings and thoughts exposed to view, has provided me with a good deal of information about how people think about sexuality and all its amplifications of meaning. I appreciate why Jung is so often quoted as having said that when people brought sexual questions to him they invariably turned out to be religious questions, and when they brought him religious questions they invariably turned out to be sexual. If, then, my responses to the archetypal questions surrounding such familiar issues as heterosexuality, homosexuality, bisexuality, celibacy, widowhood, masturbation and creativity seem to point toward a theory of sexuality, I can only say that my views as presented here are extremely tentative and are offered more as a stimulus for the reader's own thinking than as a position statement.

Nevertheless, I feel that if I am to express my own androgyny through my willingness to react with every part of my being to all that is said to me, I must also be willing to make some statements of a theoretical nature. I must dare to give outward expression to what I receive and assimilate. All the while, I am reminded of the dangers of saying too much too soon when I reflect on the consequences of Freud's error in assuming the biological bisexual origin of human beings, and of Jung's unconscious incorporation of the sexual stereotypes of his day into his first *anima-animus* concepts. Yet if one does not venture to make statements and express opinions, however tentative and provisional, that do not accord with current popular ideas, one cannot hope to move forward in the vanguard of the new consciousness.

It seems to me that any new sexual theory developed for the years ahead must place sexuality in a far wider context than it has been seen in the Western world in modern times. The new era we are entering will require a shift from the exclusively personal viewpoint to one that includes the transpersonal, a shift from an egocentric position toward a universal orientation. The new consciousness is founded in a deeply felt awareness that our being in and of the universe means that the universe is in and of ourselves. If we recognize ourselves as being whole and indivisible organisms, yet essential elements within a larger system, then our inwardness is related to our outwardness as convex is to concave. Inwardness, called "psyche," and outwardness, called "world," may *appear* to be in opposition to one another. From a more encompassing viewpoint they may be seen simply as two systems, one subsystem contained within another larger system.

The new model of sexual consciousness will need to be inward-turning for, paradoxical as it may seem, in order to be aware of oneself as a cosmic being, one needs to discover the nature of one's own essence. In the view of individual as microcosm within the macrocosm, the idea loses its strangeness; it is like putting a drop of blood under a microscope to find out what the blood in the whole body is like.

Whenever sexuality has been seen purely as a form of interpersonal relationship, theorists have concerned themselves primarily with the nature of the communication between people. This is an outward-turning model. The communications may be of many sorts—verbal communication is only one form. Even within the area of verbal communication there are many levels of meaning, and still more levels of concealment or subversion of meaning. In the realm of sexuality there are, in addition, those non-verbal behaviors that can also be called communication, ranging from contact, confrontation, conflict and cooperation in the setting of work or play—all the way to the battleground of the body, or the paradise of the body, as the case may be, in sexual inter-course. As therapists treat sexual problems, the question usually asked is, "Who does what to whom, and why?" One reason why it has always seemed so reasonable and attractive to treat sexuality as a simplistic subject-object rela-tionship is that there is always a ready scapegoat on whom to load the failures of one's own efforts to hold onto relationships.

Most therapists claim to expose this "scapegoating" or "projecting onto the other" when they deal with people who have sexual problems. But even if the partner ceases to be blamed, and even if the unfinished business with the par-ents or with parental ideas or parental images is resolved, the aim of most psychotherapy is as conservative as it ever was. It is to help the identified pa-tient or patients to gain the ability to achieve and maintain a "right" relation-ship with a partner. From this achievement a sense of well-being is expected to emerge. Freed from sexual conflicts, the individual will supposedly have at his or her disposal the libidinal energy that was formerly bound up; now it can be directed into more "constructive" channels. The ego will have gained a sense of autonomy according to this line of thinking, and the individual will consequently become more effective in the management of relationships in the future. This ego-centered psychology is essentially adaptive, providing the means by which an individual may learn to make peace with society through the process of learning to relate peaceably with another human be-ing. If one's essential personality does not quite conform to the requirements of the society in which one lives, then the prescription has often been that one go through a "reconstructive analysis" or, if time is too short, a "behavior modification." The troubled psyche is treated as a maladapted organism that needs to be persuaded or shocked into a normality acceptable to the world.

There is little need to reiterate the basic premises of those psychologies of sexuality that have as their goals the development toward mature, stable and non-exploitative heterosexual relations. These presuppose an explicit norm that corresponds to a collective standard. The developmental process involves the building up of enough ego-strength, courage, and self-sufficiency in the child or young person to make it possible to break out of an incestuous family circle. It is recognized as necessary for the developing individual, in symbolic terms, to kill the mother or the father, or both, in order to overcome the pow-er of the parental image as the controlling force in his or her life. Only having accomplished this does it became possible for the young person to venture out of the safe haven of home and family into a problematic world, there to establish relationships based on one's own way of being rather than on the basis of consanguinity.

The culmination of this development is experienced in the achievement of what is considered by the collective to be a "normal" sex life, and the more closely it adheres to the monogamous heterosexual ideal, the better. In this view, Freud's "polymorphous perversity" properly belongs to infancy and ear-ly childhood. Later on it is called "promiscuity" and it is looked at askance, especially if it is practiced by middle-class women; homosexuality and bisexuality after puberty are considered to be pathological, and masturbation is thought to be, at best, a necessary evil. Group sex and unsanctioned pairings are seen as vestiges of an extended adolescence. And there is hardly any place for a legitimate celibacy in this model.

The Freudian model of consciousness was extraverted in that it sought the key to the sources of neurosis, anxiety and pain in traumas inflicted upon the organism from the outside. Freud's view has pervaded almost all of depth psychology, and its popularized versions surround us with images of helpless infants and growing children being wounded by the people around them until they develop ways of defending themselves by concealing their real natures from everyone, including themselves.

The thread running through the learning-theory model, from its beginnings early in this century with J.B. Watson to the more sophisticated formulations of B.F. Skinner and his followers, was also extraverted. The child and the adult are always and ever victims of what they learn from society. They are trained into patterns of behavior imposed from outside; these patterns are assimilated and they condition people to behave in certain ways until someone wiser and more powerful is able to modify their behavior by extinguishing the old patterns and substituting new ones.

One might make the superficial observation that Jung's model of psychological functioning was not especially radical in its departure from Freud's. Like the older man, Jung saw the ego as mediator between the unconscious elements of the psyche and the demands and expectations of the world. For Freud, however, the greater value was in the world "out there," and in removing the obstructions that had risen like dinosaurs out of the past, blocking the road to the future. His ideal for growth would be characterized by improved human relations. The image of an outward-turning psychology is parabolic, curving outward from a state of lower or more primitive consciousness, reaching toward maturity and sexual fulfillment, then with diminished energy returning in the direction from which it started, toward lesser consciousness, old age and death. Once the apex is passed, the individual's struggle for increasing consciousness tends to attract less and less interest from the psychoanalyst. It is similar with behavior-oriented psychologists who deal more symptomatically with their clients. Once the objective is reached, the symptoms relieved or the illness cured, the clients are sent forth to confront the world outside in whatever way it is their business to do it.

The ego in Jung's thought is engaged in the same struggle, but its valence is different. The emphasis is placed on the enormous, even unfathomable, depths of the unconscious. This image of psychological process can be better described in terms of a helix. The ego turns round an ascending helix, and sometimes it retraces steps in descending turns as it retraces the circle of time and space and events and interactions, as well as that other world of depth and darkness and timeless expanse. The ego revolves about the central axis, which is experienced as something other than one's own being—as a guiding principle. It is not only one's own guiding principle, it is the *axis mundi*, the gyre of the world. Jung has called this guiding principle the "Self," and it is not only a personal reference point, but an orientation of the individual to all the surroundings to the furthermost extent.

Jung recognized that any psychological approach that did not posit a center that was stronger than the ego would not hold up when the ego faced a struggle it could not possibly win. The classic example of such a struggle is the inevitable capitulation to death, but there are smaller capitulations all through life. For the ego-centered psychology, Jung substituted a psychology in which the ego circumambulates the Self. The way was analogous to the shift with which the astrologers had to contend when Copernicus offered his new notions, and the old geocentric view of the universe was confronted with a heliocentric view. The dynamism of the ego was guided by its relationship to the Self as the earth's motion was guided by its relationship to the sun. It was possible to rely upon this Self as a kind of nebulous Absolute, "a circle whose center was everywhere and whose circumference was nowhere." This paradoxical "center" in and of infinite space was acceptable as long as people could put their faith in God or in Science or in the hope of Peace or the triumph of Power. But today it appears that a universe with a "sun" as its center is no more tenable than one with the "earth" as its center.

> Turning and turning in the widening gyre
> The falcon cannot hear the falconer;
> Things fall apart; the centre cannot hold;
> Mere anarchy is loosed upon the world,
> The blood-dimmed tide is loosed, and everywhere
> The ceremony of innocence is drowned;
> The best lack all conviction, while the worst
> Are full of passionate intensity.
>
> W. B. Yeats[2]

These lines from Yeats describe the situation at the end of Pisces. There is no center "out there" in the world powerful enough to provide the model for the strength the individual needs to confront the mysteries of the unconscious. There is no center "out there" to provide the sustenance the individual requires in order to develop the capacity to love, to be exquisitely sensitive to the needs of the other and to those of one's own being. The Self, as it is symbolized in the *axis mundi*, is intellectual and impersonal. Or, if it is seen in religious terms, it is likely to be so numinous that its white light becomes a cold fire. A more personal, more human experience of the Self in its wholeness is needed.

In this new Aquarian Age, people are turning away from the old psychological constructs that are either too egocentric or too abstract to deal with the human condition that is in danger of losing its sense of humanness. We must look toward a whole new way of being where we are concerned not so much with the doctoring of symptoms, either in individuals or in society, as we are with energic relationships among people and between people and their global environment. The key to the new consciousness is the capacity to feel oneself in the flow, in process; and to focus on the dynamic interchange of energy that goes on continuously in the open system to which we belong. In an open-system approach people are regarded as total organisms—each one of unique quality—and individuals are seen as process factors, generating the energy by means of which society evolves. We need to think of ourselves no longer as exclusively "masculine" or exclusively "feminine" but rather as whole beings in whom the opposite qualities are ever-present. This is not merely a hypothesis, but an important guiding principle that affects all aspects of living.

The androgyne is a symbol of the Self par excellence. But more than that the androgyne is a *representation in human form* of the principle of wholeness. Each person, as androgyne, has his or her unique combination of qualities, the person's own assortment programmed into the genetic code of the DNA molecules. It is a program that is present at birth, a program by which the individual is armed to meet the exigencies of experience in a specific way. The intercalation of the double helix of endowment with experience in the world structures the evolutionary development of the individual both as to growth patterns and as to responses made to the events of life. But to say that the androgyne is only a certain type of person is to miss the point entirely. *Androgyny is the outcome of a dynamism based on the application of energy in an organic system that is open-ended and that interfaces with an open-ended universe.*

The long mythological excursions I have taken into the ubiquitous background of androgyny show how important an aspect of human nature this principle is, and how it has been present throughout the history of human consciousness. To be sure, the androgynous potential of the individual has often been overlooked and even more frequently repressed, especially in the Western world. But it is not incumbent upon the individual to create it or to assimilate it; it is not even necessary to work on it. It is present in each individual, and its expression will vary within the framework of his or her own particular personality.

The androgyne is here. The androgyne is present in each person. How shall I describe the androgyne? It is hard to describe a feeling that is so much of the essence of one's being that one is scarcely aware of it. It is as if the molecules of one's being were dancing together without touching. To some this may come as a new idea; to others it is as old as the mystical dance of the Man-Woman-Lord, Siva, who moved in the fiery circle of process as Destroyer of what was old and had been presented too long, toward the primordial chaos from which new creation springs.

One may ask, how do we become androgynous? The answer to this question is that we do not become androgynous; we already are. It is necessary only to let ourselves be ourselves. It is not necessary to *learn* how. This may sound like the easiest thing in the world, but for a society that has become expert at manipulating and forcing and conditioning the psyche to function in an adaptive way in a world that appears to require adaptation, there may be much to *unlearn* in the process.

Once energies cease to be dammed up or forced into "appropriate" channels, the androgynous core that all human beings possess will be able to manifest itself on the surface and produce a new ease of being-in-the-world and
being-with-ourselves. The shifting back and forth from the constellated opposites, be they the rational and the mythological, the ego and *animus*-or-*anima*,
Yin and Yang, or whatever designation we give to the Feminine and the Masculine energies, this shifting of energies once thought to be separate will occur so rapidly, so smoothly, that the oscillation will be practically undiscernible.
We will have the situation of a dynamism in the microcosm, with the energies
actively powering the human organism; but looked at from the point of view
of the human being as macrocosm, there will be an appearance of equilibrium. Without a sense of disjunction, the person will become at once tender
and firm, flexible and strong, ambiguous and precise, focused in thinking and
diffused in awareness, nurturing and guiding, giving and receiving. It will
be like listening to a duet skillfully played by a pianist and a violinist, when
one does not hear the two separate instruments so much as the harmonious
interplay between them. Androgyny is to be experienced as a conversation
where every sentence builds on the totality of what has gone before, and not
as a succession of alternating brief speeches. In an androgynous interaction,
an individual knows the simultaneous working of that intuitive aspect by which
he is able to encompass wholes, with the sensate aspect wherein each minute
element of a situation is seen and felt in its relationship to the totality.

This is a description not of a state that is often realized today, but rather
of the ideal of *fusion* toward which the new consciousness may be moving. In
the present reality, faced with the disintegration of the old mores, many people find themselves in a state less of fusion than of *confusion*. With the breakdown of traditional sexual patterns, people are free to experiment, and often,
finding themselves in great difficulties, they seek guidance through the tangled labyrinth of sex and soul. Many who still pretend to be are no longer
comfortably situated in the conventional heterosexual roles. There is much
confusion about who belongs where in the sexual categories.

One of the most crucial issues with which any new theory of sexuality must
come to grips is how to regard the labels that are commonly applied to
sexuality — heterosexuality, homosexuality and bisexuality — and the relative
meaning of these terms. I pose this as a single issue and not as three issues
because in my own analytic practice it comes to me frequently as a single,
though complicated issue. Most people are convinced that they "belong" in
one of those three categories, that they are, by nature, heterosexuals, homosexuals or bisexuals and they must accept being what they are. Or, if they cannot accept themselves as a member of a fixed category, then they conceive
it their task to attempt to change themselves so they can fit. Toward this end
they are willing try any means, from aversive conditioning to cutting all at-
tachments with the parent supposedly responsible for their being something
which they do not want to be. It is my belief that these sexual categories, when

ly fluid. We are only encapsulated in a category when we allow it to happen
to us.

One would not expect this to be so much a problem with people who reached
their sexual maturity in the '60s when the contraceptive revolution had already taken place. Still less would these labels have been expected to remain
at issue in the '70s with the advent of women's liberation, gay liberation, a
strong feminist movement, legalized abortion, and an increasing trend toward
greater social and economic parity between the sexes. Yet in my analytic practice I find the problem of "sexual identity" to be a deeply ingrained concern
even for the post-World War II generation. Their sexual attitudes were formed
largely while they were still infants, unknowingly incorporating their parents'
views. So it is just this generation, which has been conditioned on an *unconscious* level by the old moral standards and which on a *conscious* level is practicing the new, that finds itself so often in a deep internal conflict. Their parents,
knowing in what ethos they were grounded, may be able to view the "new
morality" with more objectivity. Still, when it comes to introducing changes
into their own lives, the pre-war generation receives less support from peers —
for their peers were never trained in group therapy and "encounters" to place
their feeling and fears out for public view. These people still confront their
individual situations with a sense of terrible aloneness. So many of them come
into psychotherapy with aching problems of trying to face what sort of people
they really are and how they may be permitted to give their reality expression. They may feel isolated and strange, unknowing that many of the people
with whom they move socially and with whom they would not think of discussing either their sexual or their spiritual dilemmas, are secret sharers in
the same questions, the same confusions.

Since archetypes are innate potentials for human functioning in certain specific ways, they remain largely unconscious, and what we know of archetypal
issues comes to us through thoughts and feelings and bodily experiences. There
is no thought without the human brain, although what we know of the structure and function of the brain is insufficient to explain the nature of all thought.
There is no emotion, there is no feeling, there is no sensation without the
involvement of the entire body, including the brain of course — although what
we know of the structure and function of the body is also insufficient to explain all emotion and feeling and sensation. Archetypes are not to be found
by examining the brain, nor are any thoughts, as such. This fact has been
testified to by brain physiologists, among them the eminent neurosurgeon
Wilder Penfield, who first explored with electrodes every part of the cerebral
cortex of a conscious person. Penfield writes of "the mystery of the mind," and
here seems to be the entity that accounts for the phenomena of consciousness
and for the archetypes of the unconscious. After forty years of exploration
of the intricacies of the brain, Penfield writes:

Physicians, whose task it is to deal with the whole man, take a unique view of him. They have long been aware of the unexplained dichotomy (the functional split) between mind and body. Indeed, they have learned, as the saying goes, to "treat the mind as well as the body." They are well aware that body, brain, and mind make up the child. They develop together and yet they seem to remain apart as the years pass. These three, in a sort of ontogenetic symbiosis, go through life together. Each is useless without the other two. Mind takes the initiative in exploring the environment.[3]

It is necessary, then, to consider the principle of androgyny outside of the archetypal realm, the realm of mind, and see how it is manifested in human experience, which includes the total human being, with his body and his brain as well as his reflections upon his own life processes. Therefore, I will speak now in terms of individuals in order to show some of the patterns into which questions of sexual identity are falling today and the ways in which androgyny is manifesting itself in these patterns.

# Chapter 20

## Androgyny Experienced in Homosexuality, Bisexuality and Heterosexuality

Androgyny is innate in each individual, but it is often the environmental circumstances that trigger homosexual or bisexual behavior. Sometimes, but not always, these types of behavior represent the resolution of a conflict between the psyche's urgings toward androgynous functioning and the demands of a sexist society in which people's sexual differences remain more significant than their human commonalities.

In order to understand the interplay of the psychological constitution and the impact of environmental forces on it, it will be helpful to consider individual situations and experiences. The "individuals" I will discuss will be presented as illustrations of fairly common experiences. Descriptions of the persons have been altered to preserve their anonymity, but the events described have been real experiences.

The case of Mr. A will show how a man's unlived inner androgynous nature led him into psychotherapy, although he was not aware of the archetypal element in his difficulties. He was torn between polarities which he knew no way to reconcile. The sexual problem which lay just below the surface did not present itself as an initial complaint. Mr. A entered therapy because of his concern about a long-standing depression that had lately become more serious for no apparent reason. To complicate matters, he had been using more than a moderate amount of alcohol in an attempt to overcome the depressive feelings, and this, too, had begun to worry him. He usually took several cocktails when he arrived home from work, and would frequently continue drinking into the evening. To all outward appearances he was a successful corporation executive. He was slim and attractive, active in church and community, was married and had two children in high school. A casual observer would not have judged him to be a troubled man. But Mr. A had deep concerns about his sexuality. He found himself obsessed with an attraction to younger men, a feeling that didn't seem to him in any way compatible with his conventional and proper life style. Nor did the attraction appear to be related to any special unhappiness he was aware of in his marriage.

Mr. A's history showed a close relationship with an older brother, with whom he had shared a bed until he was twelve, and who had led him into sexual exploration and mutual masturbation that also recurred occasionally after puberty. The parents either were unaware or did not notice; in any case they appeared unconcerned about sexual matters. When anything came up in family discussions, the parental attitude was to change the subject. Mr. A grew up with the impression that sexual relations between his parents (his model for heterosexual relations) were at best a grim business. He discovered, independently of any parental influence to the contrary, that with someone of one's own sex it was possible to enjoy a stolen pleasure. While in high school, and even more in college, he found himself in struggles between the prospect of moving toward the expected role of husband and family man, or succumbing to what he thought of as the "weakness" of homosexual encounters. At this time in his life the latter were mostly in his fantasy, although on a few occasions they were lived out briefly, and with attendant guilt feelings. In the long run, he adapted himself to the heterosexual world. When I first saw him he had all but forgotten that he had engaged in homosexual relations from time to time; the only residue of that memory being his current and persistent interest in looking at younger men.

As we talked of his drinking pattern, we noted that every evening as he approached his home, he began to feel a little uneasy. A first he said that he did not know why, but he soon recognized the conflict in him between a desire for the kind of satisfaction he had formerly received in youthful homosexual relationships and a growing feeling that he was masquerading as a heterosexual with his wife. He was convinced that were she to find out what his true nature was, she would not want to live with him. The more he became aware of what the issue was, the more his anxiety increased, and with it his consumption of alcohol. At one point I said that perhaps it would make more sense for him to risk exploring the reality of his obsession with his idea of possible homosexuality, than to continue down the path toward alcoholism.

It was then that the nature of his confusion began to be clarified. He had become obsessed with the feeling that were he to give way to his desire for sex with a man, that he would somehow cross over into the land of no return. He would no longer be a heterosexual; he would become a homosexual. He would no longer be acceptable to his wife; nor would he, if he were still married, be acceptable to men with whom he wanted to engage sexually. He imagined his wife leaving him, his children losing respect for him, the family being destroyed by scandal, his being fired from his job. Life could only become a series of catastrophes. He cursed his brother, whom he blamed as the cause of it all.

As we began to speak of the meaning of the terms "heterosexuality" and "homosexuality," I had to rely on my own theoretical background in order to frame my own responses. I do not mean some theory that I had been taught, but rather the outcome of information gathered from a variety of sources, but primarily from the people with whom I had been working and from recent research findings. I realized that these terms have been defined and described in many ways. It had not been long since the American Psychiatric Association had reversed its official view of homosexuality as "pathological," and that in spite of the protest from a large and vocal minority of its membership. It was clear that any definition one might come to would have to be flexible in view of the variety of individual situations. It seemed clear that homosexuality was not a genetically determined trait. Increased production of opposite-sex hormones might have some effect on the masculinity or femininity of body structure in general, but homosexual behavior was not limited to persons of specific bodily configurations. In the case of Mr. A there was no trace of effeminacy either in physique or manner. As with all of us, there were personality characteristics that might be associated with either sex, but the total effect of Mr. A's appearance and personality was that of a normal well-adjusted male.

The propensity of energy to move about in an endless variety of ways and directions had some important implications with regard to Mr A's sexual concerns. He needed to know that *every* individual is subject to the ongoing oscillation between Masculine and Feminine types of energic flow. Having experienced successful sexual relations with members of both sexes, Mr. A was able to see that he could function with either type of energy in the leading position. His own experience showed him that he had the potential for an androgynous way of being, but he was not *psychologically* prepared for this. His rearing had not provided a model of freedom from the prison of gender, and this was equally true for his wife and her background. She expected him routinely to initiate sexual relations and to be the more active partner, while she was content with an almost entirely passive-receptive role. Because of his male-oriented fantasies, Mr. A more often than not felt uncomfortable in the role his wife required of him, and in compensation he felt doubly obligated to act the part of the dominant controlling male. But partly because of his early experiences in being passive and being made love to, and partly because his working days demanded behavior of a dominant and controlling sort, he wanted and needed a different kind of sexual experience from the kind he was having. More or less unconsciously, he yearned to be embraced in the way he remembered the carefree youthful sexual escapades with the male. A few drinks before and after dinner had helped to take the edge off the conflict for him, but now it was clear that alcohol not only failed to solve anything, but was becoming an even more serious problem than the sexual one.

I inquired into the way Mr. A was conceiving of his own energic flow. In his mind energy was sexual by its very nature. It followed that sexual energy was to be categorized as either heterosexual or homosexual. If, as a man, your energy flowed toward women, you were a heterosexual; if toward a man, you were a homosexual. If it appeared to be available for both the male and the female, you were bound to be paralyzed because there was only so much energy and it could go only one way or the other. Furthermore, Mr. A was convinced that when you cast your lot in with the heterosexual community you necessarily excluded yourself from the company of homosexuals, and vice versa. This summarizes Mr. A's attitude as he verbalized it to me. But his feelings were quite different. His feelings, which were carried by his energy, were equally capable of being stirred by men as by women. His sexual energies could flow in either direction, if he were only able to discover a way to suspend his inhibitions in the direction of intimacy with men.

It appeared to me that Mr. A thought of himself as being boxed into a closed system. He had to discover that energy is not a limited commodity that diminishes in exact relationship to amount expended, but that under favorable circumstances energy is capable of regenerating itself. As many people are aware, the more one loves, the more one is able to love—while the more one inhibits loving, the more incapable of loving one becomes. The fear of loving is perhaps one of the most destructive influences one can encounter. In discussing Mr. A's feeling with him, I did not consider that in his situation it was necessary to make a distinction between loving and its sexual expression, because what we were talking about was neither a desire for hedonistic gratification nor for the exploitation of another individual. We were dealing with the expression of a human desire for being on the receptive side in finding warmth, understanding and companionship. This desire can, of course, take sexual form, but "loving" seems to be the better term here, and sexuality is one context in which the energies generated in loving can be experienced. Of course, sexuality is not the only way of expressing the energy generated through love— other possibilities can be acted upon which have their own value and meaning. These may be experienced in place of love's sexual expression, or in addition to it.

If Mr. A could accept the idea that energy can be expressed sexually or non-sexually, or that it can be expressed both sexually and through other channels, it would become easier to take the next step. The possibility exists that this free-flowing energy may be expressed wherever it is attracted; that is, in intimacy with members of one's own sex, with members of the opposite sex or, a third alternative, with members of both. At this point it was necessary to consider the bisexuality potential. Bisexuality is no stranger to those who experience their sexuality as polyvalent and who enjoy a variety of sexual experimentation for its own sake. But bisexuality as a possible form of enduring relationships, to be taken seriously in the context of love and to be the basis of serious commitment, has yet to find many outspoken supporters. Whether one finds bisexual behavior acceptable for his or her life style is beside the point; it seems that bisexuality as a psychological attitude merits consideration by anyone who seeks an increase in consciousness and self-awareness. I raised the question of bisexuality with Mr. A.

In the context of androgyny, bisexuality would seem to be a perfectly natural alternative through which some people might express their sexuality. This is not to say that either of the other two alternatives would not as well provide the potential for fulfilling the interpersonal aspect of the drive toward wholeness. Mr. A, who was probably more disposed than most people to identify with the perspective of the androgynous male at this point, began to entertain the idea that bisexuality might be more in harmony with the natural tendency of his energic flow, or at least as that flow had been directed — given his background and his current situation. Freed of the feeling that any homosexual experience at this time would make a "homosexual" out of him, he considered risking an exploration of this aspect of his nature. Responding to his need for assurance, I reminded him that he would not lose his identity as a person if he were to undertake the experiment he contemplated.

It is not necessary to detail what followed, but only to state that there were some sexual fantasies with men which, at first, had the obsessional quality one might have expected, but soon lost the compelling quality that was initially present. It was not long before he discovered that what he needed was not so much the experience of homosexual relations *per se* as it was to be able to express, through his sexuality, the tender receptivity in himself which he had denied sufficient outlet. His own Feminine aspect needed to respond to the active sexuality of a person who would allow him at times just to be, in a passive way, while the other took the more active role. The problem had appeared as sexual in nature, but sexuality was, in fact, a symptom of a condition that had causes extending far beyond that area.

Mr. A lived his days too much on the "sun" side, with little opportunity to retreat into shadow. There was almost no opportunity to give his feeling side freedom of expression. This aspect was constantly being suppressed. In his working day he was forced to conform in his dress, in standards of organization, in accuracy in technical matters. In his position *he* felt unimportant; it had been impressed on him that all that counted was what he could do for the company. His position as supervisor required that more often than not he deny human feeling.

Returning home at evening, the *rite de passage* called forth the "spirits," the sacrament needed to pass from the light world into darkness. But, rather than meeting with the Feminine directly and openly, he drowned himself in her. Rejecting now his rational side, he would embrace the non-rational; he *became* the feminine side of his nature. It was as though he had entered into the mythic world, the wild forested mountains near Thebes which had once harbored the fabled Maenads, companions of Dionysus. Those women had left their homes for a season of worship of the half-man half-woman god, for revelry and joy, and sometimes for destruction. So, too, was Mr. A enchanted by the god of bisexuality and the bisexuality of the god. He felt his own bisexuality the more because he saw his life as demanding only the masculine functioning, at work and at home. He saw his wife as a woman who filled all the feminine stereotypes, and who demanded that he take the masculine role. He felt he could not do this. The idea of sexual relations with her became more and more repugnant to him, as he longed to rest and live out his own grace and beauty, and especially his passivity, in the arms of a man.

He had gotten stuck in a purely masculine-conscious system, and his suffering psyche produced a bitter conflict by demanding enough time for the feminine side, which he refused to allow. So he was under constant psychic stress, and because he did not know how to resolve it, he used alcohol to deaden the pain and the nameless feelings of loss and alienation.

One important way in which Mr. A was able to deal with this complex inner and outer situation was to recognize that he had identified himself with his *role* in the world. This means that he was unconscious of his *persona*, that masklike aspect of the psyche with which one faces the world in order to meet the world's expectations. The *persona* was an intolerable coat of nettles he wore, which he felt unable to remove. It was as though it were part of him. He was unable to admit any warmth or softness into his workday world. The main thing was that the figures on the profit and loss sheet had to be approved. The same coldness and heartlessness that he felt within himself, he saw all around him wherever he went. The internal anguish was projected onto the environment.

To have said that he was in a "homosexual panic" when he feared and desired a particular sort of relationship, would have been simplistic and reductionistic. It would not have been helpful to refer his condition to the supposed inception of the problems in his early relationship with his brother. Healing began for Mr. A when he realized that he did not need to think of himself necessarily as the victim of a world that forced him into a one-sided role. He, himself, could make the necessary space for the other side, once he assumed the responsibility for cultivating it. He began to relinquish his desire to be authoritative and controlling. He discovered where the hiatus in his sexual experience with his wife had been and found that he was able to alter the pattern significantly. He did not even require words to let her know what shifts in their manner of relating would relieve the tension in him and enrich the ways they were with each other. The quality of energic flow underwent a gradual change. Mr. A seemed more relaxed, more at peace with himself. When the question of what label to put on his sexuality became less important to him, he was able to discuss the whole matter with his wife, including his feelings and his insights. Without any special effort, his drinking lost its compulsive quality. He seemed more able to make autonomous choices in this area, when he had become able to do so in terms of his sexuality.

It would be an exaggeration to say that Mr. A came to a peaceful solution of his sexual identity without further difficulty. In many ways, through his ideological development he was able to put those problems into a reasonable perspective. He gained a far wider view of his energic potential. He became more conscious of the ebb and flow of energies, the need for experiencing both kinds of movement: that which was active, progressive, and tended toward order; and that which was passive, regressive, and tended in the direction of creative chaos. Both are necessary to the dynamic of living.

It is also necessary to recognize that there are inhibitory forces which seem to block the dynamics of energy. Whenever there is a psychological block that prevents one from doing what one intends to do, the inhibitory forces are functioning. Natural desires have always had to be inhibited. This we learn early in life from parents who act as the promoters and conservators of the old values. These are, of course, the parental values. We internalize these old values before we are old enough to know what has happened to us. This inner inflexibility, which Freud labeled the "superego," functions in us as Mephistopheles in *Faust*, as "father of all hindrance." It seeks to interrupt and interfere with our progress, but ends by pushing us in the direction of progress. It seeks to do evil, but in a strange and incalculable way it ends by doing good.

The second case I will discuss concerns the creative problem in a woman who withdrew from a traditional and sexist society to find a freer existence for herself in a love relationship with another woman. Here, too, the question of energies is important, because when these are not allowed to find their natural gradients, the individual either functions on a level far below his or her potential or else some radical change in life pattern must be made. Many women have moved from the center of the Women's Liberation Movement, which sought equality with men, to a nearly segregated feminist society. The following is the experience of a young woman who, like so many women in their twenties, has made some radical decisions about her life.

Ms. B is an attractive young woman who today presents an appearance of softness and gentleness coupled with a high level of vitality. This is in contrast to her appearance the first time I met her, when she was tense and nervous, her brow furrowed, her eyes dull. She has recently left her husband after some five years of an apparently good marriage, and is now living in a lesbian relationship. This woman, who needed time and space at home to pursue her career as a free-lance artist, was mated to an exceptionally supportive man. He placed her needs ahead of his own on most occasions, and made minimal demands for himself. Despite the efforts of her cooperative husband to make her feel better, she was often depressed, and she related this to a blocking of her creative energies. She could not bring together the spontaneity of flowing ideas with the discipline needed to communicate them, to meet her schedules and to satisfy her clients. She said that all in all she had little to complain about, her life was secure enough. But there was no spark in her marriage, she could feel very little for her husband, she was not particularly interested in having sexual relations with him, and when she did there was very little sensation on her part. She would often be cross or out of sorts with her husband, and this stirred neither reaction on his part nor responsiveness on hers.

She related that previous to her marriage and also on several occasions in the course of her marriage she had had sexual relations with two types of men, those who were exceptionally mild and gentle in nature, and those of rather erratic disposition, at times seeming to be extremely soft, at other times exhibiting bizarre behavior verging on the paranoid, and occasionally becoming violent and physically abusive. She was the younger child of two in her family. Her brother, two years older, provided a model for her to develop in tomboy fashion. By the age of eight she could climb trees and play baseball well enough to be included on the playing field with her brother and his friends. Often she had to struggle to keep pace with the boys, but she would conceal her weariness and manage to tag along.

A critical event occurred when she was eleven. The group of boys with whom her brother played had used her in what apparently amounted to a gang-rape, while her brother stood by. Her memory of this was hazy; there was some confusion as to whether she had resisted from the start or only later, but she finally fled in panic from the scene. She recalls vividly the misery of having been betrayed by her brother. After this, there was a long period in which she stayed away from all boys. Nor had she any special friendships with girls, but spent much time alone. She only began going out on dates when she went away to college. She invariably selected men whom she thought she could manage, but occasionally she formed a liaison with someone unpredictable. With the milder men she rarely entered into sexual relations, and when she did she was usually non-orgasmic. With the others, when they would become threatening or bizarre she would fill a masochistic role and then she could achieve orgasm.

She married a warm-hearted but passive man and settled into an apparently stable relationship, though not an exciting one. It was not long before she was feeling internally lifeless, and there was almost nothing that her husband could do to engage her emotions. Nor was she any more successful in her painting. She began frequent use of marijuana, and she believed that the creative work she did while in an altered state of consciousness was of superior quality. Her opinion was not shared by anyone else and as a consequence she found herself receiving fewer and fewer assignments. During this period she started considering the possibility that she should not be married at all because she was more than likely "naturally homosexual."

As this notion assumed greater proportions, she withdrew even more from her husband than she had done previously. She moved from their common bedroom to sleep in her studio, but even there she felt constricted. At this point, she temporarily suspended therapy. Several months later she returned and brought me up to date on the events in her life. She had started going to meetings of a group of radical feminists, and some of the women in the group supported her growing desire to leave her husband. She moved out altogether and took an apartment of her own. A short time later she had met and formed a liaison with a lesbian woman. It was after the two women had been living together for a short time that I saw Ms. B again. Whatever reservations I might have had about her summary withdrawal from the marriage and about the sudden strong relationship that had developed with the woman, I could not deny that Ms. B had undergone a remarkable change in appearance. Her features had become softer, more relaxed. Her hair had been cut in a flattering style, quite unlike the long and shapeless look it had presented before. Her eyes were bright, her posture erect, her bearing energetic and self-confident. I hardly needed to hear a word from her to know that she was happy, loving, and enjoying a kind of freedom that she had never known before in her life.

She told me how relieved she felt since she no longer had to deal sexually with men, whom she had long regarded as, at best, problematic. Interestingly, she had discovered in her female lover all the well-disciplined, self-activating qualities that women as a rule expect from men. In addition, this woman had a perception of Ms. B's longing to be able to be sexual in the traditional feminine way, without fear of being taken advantage of as men had taken advantage of her in the past. Therefore, the woman as lover could bring her to ecstatic heights of sexual pleasure such as she had never imagined would be possible to achieve with a man.

I had to ask myself the question, was Ms. B really a homosexual? There were no doubts about it in Ms. B's own mind; she happily identified herself as such. I was not so sure, despite her assertions that she had achieved her first truly satisfying sexual experiences with a woman. It seems to me that the polyvalent energy, which at times takes sexual form, carries the potentiality of expression with either sex until early experiences in life deflect it from one to the other. When Ms. B was a young child, with little access to girls of her own age, her natural sexuality flowed toward the little boys with whom she played. Even her traumatic rape experience did not block entirely her capacity late sexually to men later on.

Here we may reflect on the interesting parallel between the way Ms. B tried to live out her adult sexuality and the practices of the Amazons of ancient legend. Ms. B, like those women of the fabled past who proclaimed their independence from the world of men, had grown up with an early distrust of men and a belief in her innate weakness of the sex that in the rest of the world was invested with the greater power. Like her forebears in spirit, she had engaged in sexual episodes with men of the wildest kind, primarily to serve her own ends; but of course all this was fully unconscious to her. The main purpose was to prove that she could find her own independent way as well as any man, that she could wrest the control of her life from the restrictions of a home and husband, and live a life strictly on her own terms. Instead of the ancient passion for the hunt as enjoyed by those daughters of Artemis, Ms. B enjoyed the excitement of the creative and the competitive world, which she combined in her career of commercial art. Her rejection of her conventional life, her marriage, however, only served to intensify the available energies, and, being a highly sexual person, she was able to give vent to that aspect of her being in a way that was safe and secure for her, that is, with another woman. The alterative would have been isolation, and in light of what has been said about closed systems, it is understandable why Ms. B took the more dynamic route.

In my own mind, I could not respond with the expected and perhaps obvious answer when I reflected as to whether Ms. B could properly be categorized as "homosexual." In the light of her history, I could not be sure that her way of functioning with the other woman involved that abandonment of her natural feminine manner in a way that is so often associated with the rejection of traditional gender roles. Perhaps now, for the first time, Ms. B was beginning to experience her sexuality *as a woman*. In the past, the men to whom she had related had in many ways fulfilled the feminine image. They were either soft and compliant, or emotional and irrational, and some were essentially passive but prone to hysterical behavior when aroused. She had been unable to tolerate relationships with men possibly because, in an inverse way, her functioning with them was closer to what we might imagine as homosexual. That is to say that the quality of their sexuality was so much like her own, that relationship with them could not be called "heterosexual" on any but the purely phallic level.

On the other hand, Ms. B's relationship with her female companion was clearly a relationship with someone who was different in kind from herself. Ms. B's feminine nature was engaged by the masculine element in the other woman. This masculine, this *animus*, was expressed in the wider aspects of her way of relating to Ms. B. This woman was the more active in the "courting" when the relationship first began, and in their sexual relations she was the initiator, taking Ms. B gently, as though she were a young virgin (which in a psychological way, she was). The woman was also active in her intellectual pushing and probing. She gave constructive criticism to Ms. B about her work. She made the suggestion that the two live together, and she volunteered to assume considerable financial responsibility for the household.

Surely the stereotypical concepts that are commonly associated with the words "homosexuality" and "heterosexuality" must fall before the experiences of real people such as these. If human beings are released, or can release themselves, from the boundaries of sex and gender, there can be a far wider reaching-out in love to people *as people* on the basis of individual needs and desires. But the reluctance to let go of the old conventions remains strong, and one senses the tenacity of the overwhelming view: every man must have a woman, and every woman her man, otherwise they are wrong, sinful or sick. These conventions arose in societies that needed to perpetuate themselves through the production of numerous offspring. To waste semen was a crime against God and mankind. But now, in a day of vasectomies and once-a-year birth-control implantation and legal abortion, the old arguments no longer have any social reason for being. Nevertheless, we go on thinking in the same old ways, and when the reasons for such thinking are no longer valid, we substitute rationalizations.

One more example will serve to show how necessary it is that in the age of androgyny we eliminate the categorization of people on the basis of their preferences for sexual partners at some given moment in time. Mr. C is a young man who has recently graduated from college and is now in his first job. He came to a large university from a small southern town, where he was conventionally reared. His parents had been extremely ambitious for him to get into a good college. They had successfully pressured him to concentrate on his studies in high school, with the result that he had very little dating experience and no sexual intercourse before beginning college. He arrived at the university and soon found himself nearly overwhelmed with its bigness and sophistication. It was during a period when gay liberation was becoming particularly vocal on the campus. Before Mr. C could muster up the courage to initiate friendships on his own, he found himself being coaxed into attending meetings and parties given by men who openly and cheerfully identified themselves as homosexual. Before long, Mr. C joined in with this crowd and was soon participating in their activities and feeling very much at home with them. He was convinced that he had always been homosexual, and that he was fortunate in finding himself in an environment where he was encouraged to "come out" and "be himself." He had a series of sexual relationships with various men, and he developed an intense, nearly compulsive fascination with black men as sexual partners. How much of this activity, especially that with the blacks, was in the nature of rebellion against the parental values he had experienced as so limiting is a fair subject for conjecture.

The problem that arose after graduation, when Mr. C was employed at his first job, was that of feeling isolated and insulated in his "homosexuality." Most of the men with whom he worked were married or were going out with women. He was hesitant about establishing relationships, being fully convinced that if he saw any of them socially after work his homosexuality would be discovered and that he would be ostracized. At the same time he longed to be able to be as comfortable with women as his working colleagues appeared to be, at least as he judged from conversations around the office. But, according to the rules of the game, you are either gay or straight. He continued to pick up men in the gay bars and to associate with the college gay-liberation crowd, even though he was no longer actively part of that milieu and was beginning to feel like an overaged alumnus at homecoming. In these settings he firmly believed the credo that to attempt to establish relationships with the straight world would be an act of capitulation to the values of the Establishment. The fact that these were also the values of his parents undoubtedly reinforced this conviction.

Nevertheless, the longing persisted to cross the very visible barrier between homosexual and heterosexual society and to live a life that was more consonant with his childhood and growing years, and from which he had little psychological cause to stray. It erupted in a curious and unexpected way. While he was on a business trip to a distant city, he happened to come across one of his college friends who had proclaimed himself to be an active homosexual. The friend suggested that they go to a private club where "anything goes." Mr. C accepted, and found himself in a fantastic carnival atmosphere. People were in all kinds of costume and undress, and couples and groups of all sizes were engaging in every possible form of stimulation and copulation. There were no sexual boundaries; men related to other men and to women at the same time, women did the same, and there were male couples and groups, female couples and groups, and people moving freely from one group to another like drunken dancers in a ballet composed by a mad choreographer.

The shocking nature of this experience annihilated all constrictions of thought about narrow sex roles which Mr. C had ever entertained. He realized that his past behavior in the homosexual community had been hardly less circumscribed by convention, within its own context, than had been the lives of his parents. The homosexual stereotype he had experienced earlier had been different from the heterosexual stereotype of his family background, but in neither situation had there been much room for deviation from the "norm." After observing and participating in the orgiastic night in question, Mr. C found himself entertaining the idea that if *this* could occur, anything could happen if one were sufficiently open to it. Even the possibility of a committed sexual relationship with a woman, of marriage and a family, were not as impossible as he had imagined. He no longer felt that he had no options. It, naturally, took some courage on his part to act on the new feelings, and there were some false starts; but in not too long a time this young man made the transition from homosexual to heterosexual behavior. In his case, his excursion into homosexuality had been a step in his psychological and sexual development. This is not to say that homosexuality is necessarily to be equated with immaturity, or heterosexuality with maturity. But in Mr. C's case, the progression was a developmental one.

While this kind of situation sounds particularly contemporary, it also has an archetypal association. It brings to mind an ancient ritual that is still practiced today on the streets of Old Delhi. Miguel Serrano has described the procession along the phantasmagoric street of Chandni Chowk, in honor of the androgynous god of Elephanta, who by some is referred to as a hermaphrodite.

> Suddenly the fire dance begins. This dance is performed by young boys wearing artificial breasts, who are known as the hermaphrodite dancers. Their dance begins slowly and insinuatingly as they swing their breasts and their hips, but gradually, as the rhythm of the great drams increases, they reach a state of frenzy. Their eyes sparkle, their naked feet hit the dusty asphalt and their metal bracelets tinkle. In their hands they have been carrying lighted torches, and when they enter their trance they push the fire into their mouths, they jump over it, they step on it, they embrace it, and they eat it — all before the serene and quiet eyes of the spectators. These hermaphrodites have performed this dance since childhood, and so they have long been accustomed to fire. Trained by their fellow tribesmen, they have earned a good deal of respect and prestige from their dancing. But there is also something disturbing and sad about this spectacle, for these boys have not attained peace. The external fire they brandish is not capable of melting the opposites they represent. There is a great difference between the hermaphrodite god of Elephanta and the hermaphrodite boys of Chandni Chowk. Whereas the first has overcome his manhood, the latter have negated theirs.[1]

# Chapter 21

## Androgyny Experienced in Masturbation, Celibacy and Marriage

As we continue to reflect on the impact of androgyny upon any new theory of human sexuality, it is necessary to take into account the degree of extraversion or introversion in each individual, for this determines to a large extent the person's approach to self and others. The androgyne is poised between two dynamics: on the one side there is the internal development that takes place within the individual; on the other, his awareness of his own being in relation to everything in the universe that is outside of his own body. To the introverted sides of one's nature come the problems of dealing with that energy which finds channels that are other than interpersonal; for example, the issues and dilemmas surrounding masturbation, creativity, widowhood and old age. To the extraverted side come the questions about loneliness within a marriage, or a sense of alienation in the midst of a group or organization. I will comment on each of these areas of concern.

If androgyny has remained submerged over the centuries, then masturbation has been similarly ubiquitous and nearly as secret. Since the practice is so widespread as to be unmistakably "normal," some logical questions arise: why was there so widespread an inhibition within the individual about masturbating? Why have there always been so many prohibitions against masturbation in conventional societies? It is well known that masturbation is not only a natural part of childhood, but is also part of the sexual repertoire of adults. It does not matter whether they are engaging in other types of sexual activity or not — masturbation continues to enjoy universal popularity. If, as enlightened people say, it is perfectly natural and everybody does it, why has it been the subject of so much moralizing and frustration and guilt feelings? What is the nature of the powerful urge toward masturbation that has led children to defy their parents and the pious to deny the authority of the Church, for the sheer pleasure and excitement of it?

It seems to me that the physical pleasure and the release from tension that masturbation can bring about is only a minor part of what is involved. The fact that masturbation is so prevalent and that it is able to bring about an unfailing sensation of delight, or at least relief, proves that some important human need is being met by it. The shame that so often surrounds masturbation comes not from the act itself as much as from awareness of guilt for having transgressed the prohibitions around it.[1] The connection with the problem of androgyny must be apparent: from earliest childhood on into youth and maturity, masturbation is an act of self-assertion, the object of which is a movement in the direction of independence.

The urge toward masturbation begins in infancy. At first the infant knows no object except the mother. She is the first love object. Even before there is love, the mother is the source of warmth and food and caring. Only in her absence is the discovery made that the mother is something separate, not a part of the baby's own being or body. Mother, the infant soon learns, must be called, persuaded, propitiated. When mothers are not at hand and the babies are left alone in the crib, they have ample time for self-exploration. They learn the limits of their own bodies. Their parts become real to them. Hands can reach out and grasp. There is a mouth into which food can be put, and there is a warm feeling in the stomach when the food goes down. The genitals are found and the pleasant sensations that can evoke from them are discovered.

Masturbation and the prohibitions against it can be viewed in connection with the legends that are told about the Tree of Knowledge. Here, also, the issue is the potential independence of the individual from the more powerful Other. There is the prohibition against eating the fruit of that tree because if Adam and Eve do eat of it, they will learn the secrets of carnal life, which are allied with the secrets of generativity and creativity. This knowledge would make them like the gods; that is, powerful and independent. The God of Genesis is not supposed to want this. But God, in his darker aspect — that is, as Satan — does want people to be powerful and free, even if it means taking the risk of losing Paradise. The God who prohibits eating the fruit of the tree which enables humans to know good and evil may be afraid they will begin to believe that they can become self-sufficient if they can meet their own sexual needs through self-manipulation. Fulfilled within themselves, people would have less incentive to move out into the world in order to establish relationships with other people and so establish societies.

This is not to say that through masturbation people can meet all their own sexual needs, or that they would even want to do so if it were possible. In most cases, this is a far from satisfactory way of meeting those needs, people being the social creatures that they are and having a need for human relationship. Still, there are times when it is necessary for an individual to relieve pressures and tensions; and if this is accomplished through masturbation, it may be possible to avoid an emotional explosion. One need not be afraid. One may not want to relieve oneself in this way; one may prefer sexual expression in participation with another person, but one is not obliged to sacrifice one's independence — if it comes to that — simply for the sake of having a partner in sex. One is free to do his own choosing when masturbation is an option.

Why then is the transgression of the masturbation prohibition the occasion for so much guilt and shame? The taboos that have long surrounded this act account for them in part. The biblical injunction against the spilling of semen is also found in varying forms in other cultures. These prohibitions are not explicitly directed against masturbation. The sin of onanism, as related in Genesis 38:8-10, is actually coitus-interruptus, but the separation of sexuality from procreation seems to be the common element here and is probably the reason that this sin of Onan is associated with masturbation also. The wasting of semen was also proscribed in the practices of Kundalini Yoga, the Tantric ritual of Maithuna and the Taoist Yoga of Dual Cultivation. All warned against the ejaculation of semen because it was thought that the sexual fluids carried the essence of the life force. The widely held concept of a channel from the testicles upward, through or around the spinal column to the brain, gave force to the idea that if sexual energies were dissipated there would be a deleterious effect on the brain; that is, upon consciousness. That this idea, which has no basis in human anatomy, should have been so much a part of common knowledge in many places around the world suggests that it is based on archetypal material. The interpretation can, of course, be made in symbolic terms, and this is what happens in the certain esoteric practices.

But, if we are to attempt to understand the masturbatory experience of the individual, it is important to consider the manifestations of the archetypal models in the personal life of the individual. The inner motivations of the parents cannot be overlooked inasmuch as the parents are the ones most likely to enforce the widespread prohibitions against masturbation. Where there is no parental prohibition, there is usually little if any internal inhibition on the part of the child. Can it be that the imposition of frustration by the parents onto the children might be the expression of the parents' own frustrations which they cannot adequately express elsewhere? Can it be that parents, who are themselves locked into less than satisfying sexual relationships with each other, secretly long to possess the very key to self-fulfillment which they deny their children? That kind of need, and that way of attempting to respond to it, must be denied by the parent who is unprepared to take the risks involved in his own meeting with the issue of unfulfilled sexuality. At stake, for parent and child alike, is the risk of being thrown out of paradise, the place where what one requires is provided and where one is in good repute with one's gods. The challenge to be self-sufficient is tempting, but it entails the risk of loneliness. Still, Satan is always lurking nearby, offering his alluring blandishments.

The experience of a man in his thirties with an obsession of an archetypal nature will describe how one individual experienced this issue in an intensely personal way. Mr. D had a persistent masturbation fantasy. He would imagine that he was standing naked at a window of his apartment watching a girl of high-school age in her room across the courtyard. He would observe her every movement with growing excitement as she slowly undressed. As he watched, he would masturbate until he reached climax. It was not so much this particular girl who fascinated him; it was her age. He was able to tell me why. He had felt himself to be a highly sexual person when he was in high school. He had stimulated himself frequently during those years, years which, in retrospect, seemed to be the time he had felt most vital sexually.

He described his first experience of sexual intercourse. "Some older boys invited me to join them for a 'party' where there was a girl of about fifteen who would take on any number of fellows. I was a little nervous. They asked me to watch once and see, so I would know what to do. I watched awhile, feeling very uncomfortable, then decided not to watch. I would rather try it for myself. I knew I wouldn't climax, and I didn't. It was just lying on top of her and nothing happening. But then, not long after that, I picked up a girl and was fondling her breasts, getting stimulated. I didn't do anything more then, but went home and masturbated. That was the first time I remember that I ever masturbated to orgasm. It was a great feeling. For the first time *I was feeling in control of my sexuality.*"

Mr. D later went to prostitutes for his early sexual experiences. He would drive to a neighboring town for about five minutes of sex, and then for a week or so he would masturbate with fantasies of the prostitute. He married several years later and had a reasonably adequate but not particularly involving relationship to his wife. This applied to all aspects of their intimacy, including the sexual. He remained in the marriage despite the tensions that arose and found outlets which, he said, made his marriage tenable. These outlets included one or two affairs with women with whom he was able to enjoy emotional closeness, but there were also many prostitutes and street pick-ups with whom he could engage in uncommitted sexual activity. Of this ongoing practice, he said, "I still imagine sex with young innocent girls, even though I am with prostitutes. I fantasize that I am teaching them about sex. I have more of a sense of security when I believe that they won't be comparing me with anybody else. I don't mean just to compare my sexual performance, but also the quality of emotion, of trust."

I understood his masturbation fantasies about the very young girls to be regressive in the sense that they returned him to a point at the beginnings of his awareness of his own sexuality. Given his history of abandonment at the age of ten by his father, and his being reared by a mother upon whom he was excessively dependent and who made demands on him to assume an adult role early, there were obstacles at that time to his feeling able to go through the normal adolescent probing into the world of active sexuality. He had no image before him of an effective male; on the contrary, his mother was always making deprecating remarks about his father. Nor did he get support from anyone toward developing the ability to assert himself against his mother's unreasonable demands. For him the mature female was formidable, but the innocent girl in her early teens might be one with whom he could have some hope of success.

And yet, he could never be sure. If he could only experience the feelings of both the lover and the girl to be loved. If he could only be sure of her sexual feelings, and she could only be sure of his, then a perfect sexual encounter could take place. But how could he be *sure* that the partner would be utterly sensitive to his tenderest needs, and that he could be equally sensitive to hers, unless he were able to be both the male and the female? The archetype of the androgyne now emerges from the forgotten depths beyond consciousness to respond to this need for security and self-sufficiency. This archetype, buried deep in the unconscious, gives evidence of its existence through the images of the masturbation fantasy.

In the reality of this man's life, however, the experience of a truly free and loving relationship did not exist. His sexual relations with his wife were fraught with doubt — would he be able to meet her demands; would he find out what would bring her to orgasm? If he did, or even if he did not, would she be able to help him find the release that comes from giving up the attachment to ego in this most intimate human situation, when his trust in her was incomplete?

Mr. D's casual sexual relationships with other women were the cause of much guilt. Had he to admit that he was failing with his wife, and did he require the other relationships in order to establish his own potency? Actually, the extra-marital sexual relationships he had been having were only moderately successful from the standpoint of emotional release, and they were disastrous as to fulfilling any sort of spiritual need. The masturbation and the accompanying fantasies in which Mr. D indulged had their positive aspect. They provided a chance to bring together the two adolescent sides of this man: the wounded youth, and the innocent virgin. This is an example in which masturbation responded to a need to return to the sense of nascent wholeness that was lost somewhere in childhood — the inner union of the Masculine and the Feminine response that is implicit in the archetype of androgyny. Whether that need would be fulfilled would depend in great measure upon the degree of consciousness that was brought to the act.

Masturbation is not and probably never will be the ideal form of sexual expression, but there are times when it is better than a wrong relationship. There are times also when it serves as a regressive transition phase from an unsatisfactory expression of sexuality to an earlier stage of development in which mistakes were made or opportunities lost. Going back in masturbatory fantasy can help one to reorganize the distorted masculine development, as in this case, or a distorted feminine development which might follow a similar pattern in a woman. Back then at the point where the one-sided masculine or feminine development went askew, there is an opportunity to live out in fantasy some alternative ways in which the problematic situation might have been resolved. This activity can supply closure to an issue that had never been resolved. This is most effective when the contents of the fantasy are noticed and reflected upon, for it is then that the individual discovers that he can become aware of his unconscious processes by observing their action through masturbatory fantasies and, furthermore, that he can guide his own development by conscious attention to his fantasy life.

Masturbation can provide a person with the intensely felt experience of being the lover and the beloved at the same time. The experience can be a total one if accompanied by fantasies that are healing; that is, "making whole." It provides also a stimulus for creativity, reminding us of the Egyptian creation mythology in which creation proceeds from a masturbatory act.[2] Here giving and receiving, activity and receptivity are combined.

Masturbation can serve to further a sense of personal autonomy under many different conditions: first, in adolescence it is a way of coming to know one's own capacity for sexual response, as preparatory to initiation into a full sexual experience; second, in adulthood in a person who is not able to achieve orgasm due to what is experienced as anxiety over loss of control; third, in mature sexual relationships when for some reason sexual intercourse is impossible or must be inadequate to the needs of one partner or the other; and fourth, in periods of sexual isolation, either by design or by necessity, when it is important to maintain a sense of completeness and responsiveness to the twin demands of physical tension and psychological need for union.

There is great freedom in knowing that one can be whole in one's inner life, and that this wholeness need not depend absolutely upon a relationship with another person. This is not to say that we should prefer masturbation to sexual relations. What is most important is that if one is open to the possibility of masturbation and to the value of masturbation, then a sexual relationship with another person becomes a matter of choice rather than a matter of necessity. When the sexual relationship with another person does occur, it has the character of strength coming from the union of two independently potent individuals. The alternative is a relationship that is less free because the need of each for the other is so crucial.

Masturbation is an inner resource that may be drawn upon only rarely, yet this remains as a part of the sexual repertoire of the androgyne. How is this different, one may ask, from the masturbation in which we all indulge, now and then, and more or less? The difference is that the masturbation that belongs to the androgyne's experience is performed *consciously*; the reason for it is understood and accepted; and it is entered into with the fantasy which allows the soul to participate in the experience of the body without guilt or shame. Nor is there any trace of the compulsive quality that so often accompanies masturbation. The androgyne knows that "being one's own person" includes the freedom of doing many things — not the least of which is being one's own lover.

If masturbation can be seen as the expression of an urge toward the independence of an individual from other people, as well as from an authoritarian God-image, then celibacy can be seen as a form of giving expression to one's sexuality in a way that testifies to a sense of deep spiritual commitment to a transcendent God. There is a great difference between these two ways of being "alone," yet in each experience the androgynous nature of the individual may come into play.

Celibacy is a commitment to abstention from sexual intercourse, or abstention by vow from marriage. I have asked several Roman Catholic priests what they thought celibacy meant. While they agreed that it meant living in an unmarried state, one felt that celibacy implied that there was to be no truly close relationship with another person, male or female. Another felt that loving relationships should be permissible within celibacy, even with the possibility of some sexual expression, as long as personal relationships did not interfere with the primary commitment to the religious work. I found myself with the impression that most people under vows of celibacy today would find themselves somewhere between these two positions, and more or less willing to entertain warm and significant relationships which were not explicitly sexual.

If Father E's commitment to the celibate ideal can be understood in terms of his inner relationship to the Feminine, we may be able to understand how it is possible for a priest to live as androgyne. Father E was devoted to his work as a college professor and a scholar. His interest in a studious way of life stood in the way of his progression in the church hierarchy because of certain "political" considerations to which he was unwilling to attend. Although he was a man of considerable intellect and generally well-respected in his field, he was unable to expend the amount of time he would have wished in formulating his ideas and writing them out. He told me sadly, "My creativity has been frustrated by authority." I understood this to mean that his superiors demanded that he fulfill a certain role model, one that left him insufficient time or freedom to pursue his own interests. Yet his understanding of what he needed to attain in terms of personal fulfillment within the celibate framework indicated his recognition of the role of the inner Feminine or, in Jung's term, the *anima*. In his own words, "If the anima is not differentiated as the womb of creativity, it cannot be fructified and become productive. Priests and other men of religion must be open to the Feminine in themselves in order to be mystagogues. The Spirit in man is the Masculine principle coming from God, and it is this that is able to fructify the *anima*. With his Masculinity, the man has to protect and foster the child of his spirit, and he must also understand and support the Mother that produced it." Jung believed that women are naturally more receptive to the Spirit of God through their Femininity, and that the male mystic relates to the Spirit through his *anima*. Father E was keenly aware of the two energic qualities within himself, and he could live their relationship as inner harmony, even while feeling frustrated in his exterior life because so little space was allotted for his intellectual work. Only recently is he coming to understand that in his celibate life as androgyne, his contribution comes not so much from what he is doing, as from his way of being. Androgyny does not depend on what you do, but on what you are.

Mrs. F is a married woman with three daughters, yet in her spiritual life she comes very close to the celibate ideal. There is still a virginal quality about her, as though she were untouched by life's difficulties even though she willingly fulfills the regular obligations that occupy a woman with a family. She commented to me that until recently women had only two choices: either they could enter the monastic life, or they could be in the world as wives and mothers. She believes that even today, when a woman is able to engage in a demanding profession, it is expected that she will push it aside when she is at home with her family. And yet, Mrs. F had found a place for herself, a small corner in the house where, she said, "I can feel whole, complete; where my entire being functions at once, and harmoniously." She takes time for herself each day for contemplation and meditation. She hesitated to speak much about these times — she said that they were so intense, so detached from the rest of her life. She said that she disliked the term "mystic," as one that is over-used and misused. Yet she confessed to having understood and felt kinship with St. John of the Cross and St. Theresa of Avila. She was different from the women she knew and she had faced this truth about herself, accepting the reality of her involvement with the Spirit. All this belonged to a separate life for her, and to a deep inner relationship. Yet all the while she had what she called my "kitchen friends" as a woman, and also family friends. These relationships were based on common tasks and the shared experiences of be-ing what, in her circles, a woman is: housekeeper, wife and mother.

On a different level of existence she lived a life that was the complementary opposite of Father E's. Like him, she had admitted into consciousness the liv-ing presence of the contrasexual element of the soul, through which she could also become aware of her inner androgyny. Both she and Father E had ar-rived at a sense of fulfillment apart from any sexual attachment, which attest-ed to an inner wholeness and freedom. Both of them had arrived at this stage of development after having lived through a period in their lives in which they had conformed in an outward way to the usual gender definitions. This had not basically changed, but now both had made progress in their internal de-velopment, and this extended beyond and was independent of society' s view of them. One was a priest and one a married woman, yet both found their androgyny through a form of spiritual celibacy.

In a marriage where husband and wife divide the tasks and responsibilities along the traditional lines, where each fills the "appropriate" roles in society, one would not necessarily expect the issue of androgyny to arise with shock-ing pain. And yet, just because this issue has been so utterly unconscious, its subterranean effects on the personality sometimes erupt in most unexpected ways. This is what happened to Mr. G, a man who was extremely successful in the world in a conventional way, and who was considered a "perfectionist" in the way he conducted his work and his personal life. If he made demands upon others, he was even more exacting when it came to what he required of himself. He was extremely intellectual, highly competent in technical mat-ters and a thorough-going rationalist, as almost anyone who knew him would have agreed. Mr. G was married and had three exemplary children. He was in analysis, having come into treatment to understand and deal with his fre-quent headaches, for which no organic cause could be found.

An important episode occurred while the analyst was away on vacation, and was related upon her return. Mr. G was going through a stage in the analysis which required that he face some qualities in himself that did not conform to his image of what he wanted himself to be. In the process he quite naturally developed some negative feelings toward the analyst which, quite unconsciously, had become mingled with some negative feelings about his wife and about his mother — none of which he had recognized in anything approaching their true intensity. The absence of the analyst just at a time when he wanted to speak with her brought all these hidden feelings to the surface, although the nature of them was not apparent. Mr. G wakened in the middle of one night next to his sleeping wife, and found himself feeling bitterly lonely. It was an extremely painful loneliness, a man's loneliness, characterized by the feeling that "no woman can possibly understand what I feel." He was certain that women experienced life in a totally different way from men, and that the possibility of communication between men and women was only slight and superficial. As overstatement is characteristic of depression, Mr. G's personal feelings about the three major women in his life had been generalized to include all women, and he was experiencing the great and universal burden of being a man. He felt that back in his childhood he had been cut off from something that women know. He imagined woman as connected with earth, he envisioned her as crawling along the ground, while he had to walk upright — in every sense of the word. He felt that he had been cut off from the material, physical world in which women are so much at home, in a way analogous to woman's isolation from the intellectual world. He could not stay any longer in bed next to his wife, and so got up. He felt a need to take a shower, went into the bathroom and began to feel such intense hatred for his mother that he wanted either to vomit in the shower or to kill his mother. His very thoughts turned and twisted in his stomach.

He went downstairs, helped himself to a glass of milk and wept over the kitchen table. "I felt that life is not about life — that life is about death. Until we recognize that death is always at hand, nothing important can happen to one." He wanted to talk to the analyst, but could not even do that. He thought he would never survive until her return. Yet he could not deal with it himself. So, in desperation, he decided that the only thing he could do was to talk to his wife. He went upstairs and wakened her. He told her how he felt taken advantage of by her. He admitted that she did most of what he required of her, but often she would spend money on things she did not need without asking him, and while she kept the house in order, she rarely washed the scuff marks off the baseboards or cleaned out the closets. He said that he felt manipulated by her — that he had always felt manipulated by women — "if they are nice to me, they get what they want." He told his wife that she always managed to get what she wanted out of him. To his great surprise, his wife responded that she had been feeling manipulated by *him*! She told him that he earned the money and was able to decide how it should be spent, while she had to figure out just how to please him if she wanted to have anything for herself.

This provided a sudden insight for Mr. G. It had never occurred to him that he could possibly be guilty of the very act he had ascribed to women, namely, manipulation. He looked back on his past and remarked that no sooner had he moved out from under the thumb of his mother than he had fallen under the thumb of another woman, his wife. Now he realized that there was another side to the situation. He was willing to discuss it with his wife, who for once had faced an issue directly with him. They centered on their way of handling money. He had always felt that since he earned it, it was his to spend, and that he gave his wife whatever she needed almost as a benevolent gesture. She stated that she felt her work in the home was equally valuable. After many hours the discussion ended with a decision to split the income that he earned in half, that each of them would pay one-half of the household and family expenses out of his or her half, and that each would have the balance to use according to his or her own discretion. If he wanted to use his share to go on a trip and she wanted to use her share to entertain friends (such decisions had always been matters for contention), then each would have the privilege of doing what he or she desired.

In relating this episode to the analyst, Mr. G gave some relevant background material. He said that he had not wanted to turn to his wife with his troubles, probably because he had never felt that his mother had listened to him, and he did not trust women to pay attention to what is on a man's mind. He said, "The time I hate my wife most is when I see my mother coming through her." He recalled his mother having told him that he had been toilet-trained at nine months. He understood this to mean that she had moved in too soon to split the ego from the Self instead of allowing the ego to languish in the Self. He realized that this probably accounted for his perfectionism — there was no other way he could get what he wanted from his mother. He spoke with sadness, "You never 'float' when you're a perfectionist; you're always swimming as hard as you can."

He was nearly apologetic when he said, "I know that we came to an understanding over money, but I know that money isn't the real issue between us." It was as though he felt that important insights had to be far more intellectual in their nature. But the analyst told him that indeed, money *was* the heart of the issue because of what it symbolized in him. In his agreement with his wife he was, for the first time, giving the Feminine equal value. He had heard of the proverb, "ever since the Phoenicians invented it, money is the sincerest form of indicating value." So what he had done in simple, concrete terms — first, by listening to the woman and giving her the opportunity to truly hear him; and secondly, by acting upon the results of the verbal intercourse — was to come into a relationship with the woman in his wife and the Feminine in himself at one and the same time. Out of his loneliness, caused by his alienation from the Feminine, came the insight that brought a reunion with the Feminine and the beginning of the recognition of his androgyny.

# Chapter 22

## Androgyny Experienced in Widowhood, the Creative Life and Old Age

Widows and widowers often have a very specific problem in adjusting to an aloneness they did not choose and which in many cases has come upon them suddenly, with very little preparation. Although each must suffer in her or his own particular way, I want to speak specifically of the woman who finds herself alone following the death of her mate, and who may need to face the challenge of developing the androgynous potential within her. I have had far less experience with speaking to widowers, probably because there are fewer of them to begin with, and also because any widower who wishes to remarry seems to be besieged with eligible women of all ages. This is not true of the widow, especially when she is no longer young, given the statistical proportion of older women to older men.

The woman who has defined herself and her personality in terms of her relationship to a man suffers most when she is faced with widowhood. Unlike the divorcée, she has not deliberately chosen the path of self-determination — she has not prepared herself for being without the man who has been her partner, through a period of questioning the validity of the relationship, through dissatisfaction with her status as wife, and through the conscious growth toward that independence that is necessary to decide to terminate a crucial relationship and to stand alone. The widow is faced with the disturbance of an equilibrium that, for better or for worse, was working for her.

The termination of a relationship through death often robs the woman of the conscious choice to prepare for her singleness. Faced suddenly with the necessity to assume the role of completeness, of androgyny, that was formerly split between herself and her husband, she finds that she has not gone through the necessary steps to bring her to this change with any sense of security. She discovers that though she has not changed much inwardly, her status in the world has changed drastically. For one thing, she has probably been used to functioning in a "couples-society." Suddenly she does not belong there any more. She begins to feel like a pariah. There were, of course, the solicitous visits after the funeral, and the condolence calls in the weeks following. And she is invited out, at first to the kind of parties she went to before. She is acutely aware that *he* is missing. She does not fit, alone, and it is strange to be paired off with a person who means nothing to her. If it is hard for her to be both host and hostess, or if life makes so many other demands that she does not feel up to entertaining, her invitations soon diminish. She then becomes the guest of her closer friends, especially at odd times when they are not having anyone else. She realizes that she must be careful on these occasions. If she is too charming or attractive or vivacious or intelligent, she fears that the wife will be annoyed with her and accuse her of taking advantage of the proffered hospitality. If the widow plays herself down, she may be considered boring, or worse, pitiful. If she could only be herself—but she cannot, because half of that self has been ripped away and the bleeding wound is all too apparent.

In the traditional wedding ceremony people used to promise to love, honor, and cherish one another "until death do us part." I have heard many wedding sermons which dealt with the nature of love, what it means for two people to honor each other, and with the importance of cherishing the beloved. I do not believe I have ever heard a clergyman use as his theme for the wedding the implicit imminence of death, and the importance of living each day, each moment, of a marital relationship with the awareness that each party to it must be whole in herself and himself so that, when the inevitable parting comes, tomorrow or in fifty years, preparation will have been made. *Alone I came into the world and alone I shall depart from it. Blessed be the name of the Lord*. These words should be in every marriage service.

It is not only the beloved that one must cherish when one enters into and sustains a relationship. One must also cherish his or her aloneness. One must cherish it and preserve it—and the latter may be the most difficult aspect of marriage. It will be necessary to make endless compromises in order to adapt to the needs of the other person and to the new social unit. It will be necessary to relinquish a certain amount of autonomy because when two people are close together the boundaries of the individual personalities become mutually limiting. Still, a beautiful aloneness can exist and must exist through all the changes in status. Sometimes the only way it can exist is as inner process. Time and space must be made for it.

How does it work? How is the androgynous core preserved in the midst of marriage, of child rearing, and of living a life in which the major decisions are shared decisions? A wife becomes accustomed in her marriage to confronting many problems with the question, "What will *he* think of it?" Too often the equally important question is overlooked, "What do I feel about it?" The woman who fails to preserve her individuality does not place a sufficiently high value upon her own feelings. She does not regard them to be as important as the approval she may get from her husband. Then, too, there is always the issue of "peace" in the family.

When I was a young wife I had a favorite biblical proverb: "Better a dry morsel and quiet therewith, than a house full of feasting, with strife." After I came to terms with myself as an individual, I discovered that this was no longer the way I felt. I found myself drawn more to one of William Blake's *Proverbs of Hell*: "Sooner murder an infant in its cradle than nurse unacted desires." Brutal? It sounds so if one were to take it literally, but Blake characteristically overstates to make his points. The "infant" is symbolic of the emerging personality which is often strangled by the cord of self-depreciation. One must cherish not only those aspects of oneself that are acceptable to the partner, one must cherish also those aspects that arise autonomously from the deepest level of being.

Unless the inner child, the man-child, is cherished by a woman through all her days and years of wifehood and motherhood, she will not have the inner Masculine principle available to provide, in a cultivated way, the counterpoint to her Feminine side. The quiet authority provided by the *conscious* presence of the inner opposite makes it possible for a woman to know that however much she may receive from her man in terms of love and support and companionship — or how little of these — she has nevertheless with herself the basis for standing alone. She will be ready when the time comes, and that time does come sooner or later to most women. She will have dwelt upon her own needs and interests as well as those of her family. She will have explored her talents and discovered ways of using them creatively to gain pleasure from them and to make them work for her. She will experience loss and grief and there will be a huge empty space in her life. It will not, however, be a bottomless abyss if she has prepared for it. Rather, it will be just empty space, which her new freedom allows her to fill with the carefully nurtured essence of her own being.

It is practical and necessary in a marriage for the tasks and responsibilities to be divided between husband and wife. When this division of activity is carried over into the inner being of either partner, then the results in case of the death of one can be catastrophic. When one person does the thinking for the pair and the partner lives out the tender emotional side for both, when one is the decisionmaker and the other the peacemaker, a situation is created whereby a good wife becomes a bad widow. It were better that she were more concerned with her own personhood and less with her wifehood, for her personhood will accompany her until her last day on earth. If she has done this, she will prepare herself for *the day of judgment*, which is a metaphor for every day in which we examine ourselves and determine whether we have followed the paths that were our own.

A widow finds herself in a position in which she is nearly forced to develop her own creative powers in order to fill the missing part of her own existence with something to make her feel whole again. If she succeeds in this, she reaches a new level of conscious development.

But there are many women who are seeking the realization of their own potential within the structure of a loving relationship with a husband or another person. Here the path is less clear than it is for the widow, for the woman who is in love may have to face a specific kind of conflict when she weighs her own productivity as an independently creative person against her sensitivity to the needs of a man who relies upon her to be his lover, his muse and his support.

The dilemma of the creative woman in a love relationship has been poignantly expressed by Anais Nin in the third volume of her *Diary*. She wrote this at a time when she was with Henry Miller, and also in analysis with Martha Jaeger:

> Jaeger...has caught a truth not known to any male analyst: the guilt for creating which is strong in a woman. Creation linked with femininity and a threat to it. A threat to relation with man.
>
> In a woman who loves man as much as I do, it becomes paralyzing. The feminine and the maternal having developed protection and nourishment, not warm destruction, or revolution for the sake of new worlds. I had guilt for writing about those I loved, exposing the character of the father. Henry never weighed the consequences of his portraits. I feel them as a danger to love....
>
> I considered Henry's work far more important than my own. I tried to efface my creation with a sponge, to drown my creation because my concept of devotion and the roles I had to play clashed with my creative self.
>
> I opposed creation, its sincerity and revelation, to the disguised self. Creation and revelation threaten my loves; threatened the roles my love forced me to play. In love I played a role to give each man whatever he needed or wanted at the cost of my life. In creation I would reveal what I am, or all the truth....
>
> But Jaeger smiles. Guilt. Guilt everywhere....
>
> I did not want to steal man's creation, his thunder. Creation and femininity seemed incompatible. The *aggressive* act of creation....
>
> To create seemed to me such an assertion of the strongest part of me that I would no longer be able to give all those I love the feeling of being stronger, and they would love me less....
>
> Men fear woman's strength. I have been deeply aware of men's weakness, the need to guard them from myself....
>
> I have crippled myself....
>
> I have bound myself spiritually.[1]

Nin was writing as an extremely feminine woman, trusting insufficiently the other side of her being. Yet despite all her reluctance in the early years to take her stand as a fully autonomous person in her creativity, her daimon forced his way through to expression in this lament for the unrealized aspect of her being, and so brought that aspect into consciousness. One might well ask whether her secret communication over the years in her *Diary*, as part of her inner life, was not a confession of her infidelity to that god who implanted within her the creative spirit. If this were so, then the publication of the *Diary* would be a public proclamation of an act of faith in the creative spirit and a union with that spirit. The publication could be seen as evidence of the surfacing of her own androgyny, after her long period of floating through the darkness on that subterranean river.

Today, Nin has captured the imagination of an emerging generation of women. Born in an age subsequent to her own, the new women have shaken their spiritual bondage with less than Nin's gentleness. The creative woman of today apparently needs to go through a period of anger, of rebellion, against the men who, she believes, have oppressed her. She needs to make a stand against them, and often does so vociferously.

It was against similar but earlier raucous protests that Jung had raised his voice in criticism of the *negative animus* in woman. Yet, in the process of asserting herself and of saying no for the first time, a woman may learn a great deal. If she is sufficiently committed to the task of increasing her level of consciousness, she may discover that not all of the oppression is outside, not all is coming from men, not all is coming from the world. Much of it is internal. Woman is bound, at least to some degree, because she has allowed herself to be bound, and often in the name of love. It is a stage that many creative women have to go through. Somewhere along the path they have to learn that they cannot live in a way that makes them feel that most of their energies are expended on behalf of another person. This results in the despair that one woman revealed to me when she said, "Everything in me seems to go toward filling up his image of what I should be, and there is never enough to fill his need; and no matter how hard I try, inevitably I will do something that will be wrong in his eyes." Another woman, having taken a further step, said, "As a woman becoming independent, you don't ask for help. You struggle through on your own; you insist on your own space. Finally, you find that there were others who would have helped you, who would have worked things out with you, recognized your needs if you had expressed them. You begin to see yourself in more of a human context, with other human beings. You find out that you do not need *always* to be the assertive doer." So, after the first anger, the sense of balance takes over.

Coming to terms with the innate androgyny of one's being can be as well the problem of a creative and productive man, but the form it takes will be different from that in woman. There was a very successful businessman and a leader in community affairs, who always used the latest methods and techniques to persuade and influence people to cooperate with his plans. He managed a very large organization, and everything in it expressed his vigorous personality. Although in recent years he had received some criticism for being too demanding of people and too much of a power seeker, he had ascribed this to the jealousy of his less-effective associates. However, external pressures to produce had been building up, and the criticism from others, as well as self-criticism, had increased to the point where he was developing an agitated depression. At this point he came into therapy. In his introspective hours, aided by his therapy, he began to see how manipulative he had been, and how he had always insisted on being the person to make the decisions as to what others ought to do. He had expected that his subordinates would follow him automatically, and he was having a difficult time recognizing that the others also had their own needs, their own individuality. When he did confront this realization, the despair deepened. Then he had this dream: "I am falling into a deep dark well, whirling down, down, down, through the blackness. Finally, I come to a soft place and the color around me is a dark maroon."

I immediately saw this as a psychological correlate of the movement of a dying star which, after consolidating all its energies into an unbelievably dense state of organized complexity, finally is swallowed into the black hole of the universe, into the chaos. I did not put forth my impression, but asked him what he felt about the dream. He said, "I am very tired. I came to persuade people to do things my way. To give them a point of view. I have been too busy with an impossible task. I'm coming to the place where I want out. I want to face the void within myself for the first time, I want to own up to it, to acknowledge it, my own chaos." I asked him what that meant in terms of his way of life. "I need to put myself in a position where the people around me have a choice to do what they want to do. The feeling is so new that I don't know exactly what it means. I came to my work to tell others what to do. I see that I haven't been able to listen. I have to begin to encourage them to be themselves and to find their own expressions of themselves." In the next weeks he discovered that instead of expending so much energy to change others that he could withdraw, to a degree and begin to reflect — to take time to grapple with his own problems and to allow himself to grow from within. He had to deal with his compulsiveness and his tendency to overload himself with tasks that he believed only he could do. He realized that unless this endless work load was cleared out to a reasonable degree, unless the huge mass was diminished, there would be no space for anything new to grow. He said, "In my mind I'd always thought I didn't have the capacity to grapple with concepts and ideas, that when God poured me into the mold, he left that out. I was only good for being a man of action. Now I feel there are other options. I want to make space for them. I want to deal with that mass, first. I'm going to need a lot of support from others, because I am not going to carry the whole load any more. I'm not going to be afraid to show weakness, to show that I'm not omnipotent. I'm going to express myself just like everyone else does. And I will also listen. I need to take time — to allow what is within me to take its own shape and grow in its own way and in its own time." As he spoke I could imagine the new being that was taking form within him as an embryo in the maroon-colored womb at the bottom of the well.

Early in our lives we grow out of the undifferentiated and confused union with the mother, and we find our sexual identity as male or female, a development away from the "psychological hermaphroditism" of the infant. In the course of ego development there arises the tendency to polarize the sexes and to develop a differentiated femininity on the part of the female and a differentiated masculinity on the part of the male. This tendency as a rule supersedes the tendency toward androgyny. Nevertheless, androgyny exerts so profound an inertia effect that, despite all efforts to develop a concept of mature sexuality based on polarizing behavior around sexual norms, creative and imaginative people of every age have crossed the boundaries of gender roles.

In old age, when people have already proved their identity and established their position in the world, there is no longer so much necessity to live by collective standards. It is a time when those who have fulfilled the objective purposes for which they have striven are ready to turn inward and let themselves be more what they truly are and less what the world expects. This is true, of course, for both men and women.

The older woman, living alone, has a special potentiality to live out her true androgynous nature. For one thing, she is able to carry the image of the Sophia-wisdom, the companion of the soul — if she has prepared herself for this during her lifetime. This means that along the way to growing old she will have performed the necessary rites of passage: splitting off a part of her masculine element at puberty, along with the awkwardness of adolescence as she strives to find a new balance; the feminine development that brings her into early adulthood; the maturity that involves the recognition of the *animus* and its power; the feminine individuation that needs the harmonious relatedness within the circle of Yin and Yang; and finally, in old age, being able to dissolve all limits and to live in the way of the androgyne.

A lithe and lovely woman occupies much of her time with writing and with coaxing into bloom and fruitfulness a most beautiful garden on a California hillside. She is perhaps typical of such old, wise women, in that she is fully and uniquely herself. She is old in years only. The quality of her experience, which brought her to a state of health and vibrancy in her seventies, is expressed in her own words:

> If you have attained the perspective of a high place during a mountain climb, you find that the rough terrain below presents a gentler scene. What seemed bridgeless canyons look like brooks; the depressions, the declivities level out and show their serene aspect. You can pick out the places of desperate crisis where all that fed body and soul gave out — or so you thought — or you were robbed by death of a long-loved companion (*can* I make it alone?). Off there is the bog of struggle and sweat; but now you remember the iris blooming in it and the crimson and blue dragonflies which your tear-blinded eyes barely acknowledged although your heart murmured to them thank you between its laborings. The mountain itself lowered even as it lured. Why were you climbing it, you a woman alone, when even the doctors warned: your heart is not strong enough. (They were wrong: strength grows from need and the demand for it.)[2]

She concludes her reflections with a thought that may well provide an image for meditation on the wisdom of androgyny as it is being lived in our time:

> If you ask what philosophy I have lived and do live by I can only say it is close to what the Chinese know as Taoism. To ever be aware of and responsive to fluidity and change both within and without this transitory entity known as Elsa Gidlow. To feel my oneness with the natural world and trust it as I know and trust my own being. To accept the Mystery, the unknowable Source without needing to "fix" or name it. To act always from my center while giving and responding to

others and to circumstance, not needing to force or push them around. To be cognizant of the (arbitrarily named) "male" and "female" elements of myself in their dancelike interactions, neither the one nor the other in dominance. To love life while being ready to surrender it. To move on.[3]

# Chapter 23

## The Way of the Flowing Stream

A secret knowledge belongs to the androgyne. It is secret because the very nature of it is that it cannot be shared or taught or even spoken about. It is the knowledge that comes of working with oneself toward levels of consciousness in which the opposites within one's own being become apparent. One learns to recognize the inner oscillation between Masculine and Feminine modalities of being and to hear with the inner ear the music of their interplay. One can only hear this music in silence, while the noise of the world is stilled for a time and the reflecting surface faces inward.

The differentiation of the Masculine and the Feminine within the individual makes possible the flow of dynamic energy, the lightning leap between the positive and negative poles of being. Conscious awareness of these forces within, of their continuing separation and reunion, is an essential part of the inner development of the androgyne. One comes to it essentially alone. First of all the inner-marriage must have taken place. Although esoteric traditions have provided the models for this *hieros gamos*, it can be accomplished without the models. One must accept oneself as a total and complete being, else each will be looking for another person who will fill out the inner empty places. This must make the individual the victim of his own emotional dependence.

An individual who has come to terms with herself or himself, who is able to view the personal life as a tiny particle, whole in itself yet interfacing with the totality beyond, can enter into relationships without fear of being lost in them or dependent upon them. This person has experienced the continuing process of separation and reunion within, as necessary steps in the life process that leads to androgyny. Frances Wickes has described the inner isolation that exists when the journey toward androgyny is *not* undertaken:

> ...without separation and discrimination unity is only unconscious, and without interplay and reunion there is only opposition and warfare, or the dull content, or discontent, of a half life where the mind ignores the heart or the heart is unconscious of meaning, even the meaning of love itself.[1]

It is strange that Frances Wickes' words come to mind just now, as I am coming to the close of this writing. I picked up her last book, *The Inner World of Choice*, to copy the citation. It was a book I had not looked into for several years, but for some reason I could not fathom, I now found the book in my hands. Just as I was putting it down, the volume fell open to the flyleaf. In Mrs. Wickes' hand were inscribed these words: "For Dr. and Mrs. Richard E. Singer. With greetings and every warm wish for their success and happiness in their life in Chicago. Frances G. Wickes." I realized that this must have been written during the last few months preceding the death of that wise old woman who had continued her writing into her ninetieth year, who lived alone, yet who even in her last illness ministered to people who came to visit her. I was one of them. Her good wishes had arrived in the few months preceding the death of my husband, a loss that was to propel me into my personal search for the inner marriage. Mrs. Wickes' text seemed uncannily synchronistic in its appearance in my life when it was first received, and again now. The years between spanned the period in which the growing awareness of androgyny came upon me. I faced it quite literally, first of all in the change in identity from "Mrs. Richard E. Singer" to "June Singer." I faced it symbolically, as I searched the faces of everyone I knew for clues as to where I would find the resources to heal the wound that had been torn open in me. There were offers of help and expressions of love from people close to me, and not inconsiderable support. Nevertheless, I soon realized that I had my own solitary voyage to make, and that the land of discovery was within, where all the knowledge I could ever possess was already present, waiting to be recognized. Like the airplane at the end of the journey across the continent that has arched upward, soared swiftly over the miles and at last returned to earth, the body of an individual returns also at last to earth, to the Mother who gave it birth. Out of the darkness we come, alone; and we return to it, one by one. From a living, pulsing organism that functions as a whole, the body suddenly becomes a heap of chemicals that no longer functions in the sublime harmony of the motion it once knew. Something was which no longer is. That something is the dynamic process that characterizes an individual life.

What makes it all different, after the breathing has ceased and the heart has stilled its beating, is the cessation of our reciprocal conscious and unconscious interchange with the world around us. When a child emerges from the dark womb and draws its first breath, it re-enacts in a personal way the primordial mythologem: *God formed the original man-woman out of clay, and a clod of clay it remained until God breathed his breath into it — whereupon it began to respire and become a living being.* So each individual life begins with the exchange of energy with the surrounding atmosphere. Were one closed up in the cavern of the body, he would putrefy and decay. In the rhythmical inhalation and exhalation each person performs a continuing yoga, a union with Spirit, with the Divine, with Nature, with the Universe. Each finite creature takes its form in formless infinity for a brief interval in the cycle of time. This happens through the process of breathing, which can be understood as a symbolic act, an act that we can contemplate and meditate upon, so that we know to what we are yoked.

Breathing is more than a symbolic act, it is a bodily process as well. It proceeds as a visible, palpable, measurable process. When consciousness sleeps, one is scarcely aware of breathing, except when it is interfered with. If at some time we find ourselves gasping for breath, then breath becomes the most important thing for us, a matter of life and death. So we know that the body is a vessel for consciousness. It is through the sense organs in the body that we are able to know what is happening to us and what is happening in the world about us. When these sense organs are finely developed — through extraordinary gifts of nature, through arduous training in attentive awareness, or both — we speak of "paranormal experience" or "higher consciousness." Whatever else is involved, and I do not pretend to be able to fathom this mystery, the fact remains that it is in the body that consciousness arises, and it is from the body that consciousness moves out to extend the awareness from its base in the individual ego to its potential range in the universal Self. This is not to say that consciousness is limited to the body — but it is not possible for me here to speculate on what lies beyond those boundaries.

The quality of androgyny is experienced as much in the body as in consciousness, since consciousness is after all centered in the body during the sentient life of the individual. Therefore, we may ask, how is androgyny expressed in and through the body? Is the bodily experience of the androgyne somehow different?

The body, in and of itself, we know is either male or female; but the way a person moves, the way a person functions in and through the body, defines the androgyne. This movement derives from the inner experience of the individual, which is hidden and mysterious. The capacity to shift from the actively probing mode to the openly receptive mode is expressed in body language far more than it is in words. If, for example, we could imagine a conversation in which a man and a woman were attempting to come to some understanding, we would see how — if the two were functioning in the manner of the androgyne — first one would move forward with an idea, and the other would take it in. This would actually be visible in the bodily attitude of the first. leaning into the assertion, putting power behind it, the hands used as indication of intent, direct eye contact boring in, firmness of stance, perhaps even momentary rigidity. The attitude of the second would be more relaxed, open to the other, listening, rephrasing, checking out what he or she was hearing. Then, in a naturally occurring shift, the roles would reverse and the formerly active one would now become receptive while the partner responded and carried the process along. The flow would move back and forth.

The bodily experience of androgyny can find its ultimate expression through sexual intercourse, when this is experienced in the spirit of evolutionary consciousness. In this act are combined the potencies inherent in the union of the cosmic Masculine and Feminine, with those generated in the union between two human beings, in each of whom the "mystical marriage" has come to pass. Androgyny expresses itself through coitus in a dissolution of gender

identity. This breaking of the boundaries gives each woman and man the freedom to be her or his most natural self. It is akin to a counterpoint in which
two independent melodies combine into a single harmonic texture in which
each retains its individual character. The Masculine seeks, probes, thrusts,
and storms the jasper gates; the Feminine yields to him, and then a moment
later, she gently slides out from beneath him and begins to stroke him into
a tension-filled quiescence. And so they play together or dance together in
an ever-increasing intensity of swirling motion. Who leads and who follows
is inconsequential and fluid and of the moment. This sexual expression is
designed from within, a kaleidoscope of feeling guides the partners through
the shifting spectrum of the sensual mandala. There is nothing done that is
either good or bad, either right or wrong; there is only a series of infinite variations of the theme of interplay of diverse opposites in such swift alternation
that the sense of it is ultimately smooth. Nor is it the smoothness of torpor,
quite the opposite; it is the supple and powerful smoothness of the undulating
snake, moving slowly at times but containing the power of lightning speed —
with the small tongue that flickers and darts, expressing the volatility of which
the whole consists.

Because the Masculine and the Feminine energies in the androgyne are
combined, but not confused, each person realizes her or his unique individuality
through androgyny. The work that has been done by the individual in differentiating the various ways in which an experience can be approached, the subtle blending of the different energies into the most desirable mix for the
situation at hand, makes it possible for the person to emerge many-faceted,
flowing from within, and reflecting what is without, in a multitude of ways.
This is the image of the androgyne, evolved from its inception in the hermaphrodite figure after the many-staged process of inner meditation and practice in the world. The hermaphrodite, symbolized in alchemy as "Mercurius"
and fashioned of the prima materia, has been transformed into the "Philosopher's
Son," the philosophical "gold," or the "diamond body." As archetype, the androgyne exists as a potential of being for every human being who undertakes
the quest of bringing it into realization. In the life of the individual, androgyny
is a goal of the person' s individuation. In the relation between individuals
who have consciously internalized their own androgyny, sexual or sublimated (that is, "made sublime") love can be electrifying in its excitement. It
produces unbounded energy which can be turned inward and upward, or fed
out in a controlled streaming; it can burst through in galactic orgasm. Or
it can swell to a certain height, then find an oceanic rhythm, and then slowly
subside like the rolling sound that drifts away from one who falls asleep on
the seashore listening to the waves.

In the androgyne, the Two do not get lost in the One. It is rather as Nicho-
las Berdyaev has seen:

> The union of the sexes is four-membered rather than two-membered: it always
> means the complex union of the male element of the one with the female element

of the other, and of the female element of the first with the male element of the second. The mystical life of the androgyne is realized not in one bisexual being but rather in the quadripartite union of two beings.[2]

The power of androgynous sexuality is heightened because within its functioning is couched the seed of its opposite: silence, aloneness, withdrawal, asexuality. Even though, or even *because* two human beings are physically locked together, each movement of one or of the other becomes a moment in a total experience. As in the image of the T'ai Chi, while the two elements are in reality one, a whole, a circle — each half nested in the other is also whole, containing the seed of its opposite. The seed is quiescent, hardly noticed, waiting for the mystery of germination to take place. What brings it to life is the activation of the life force, *ch'i*, the breath, in the essence of Yin within the Yang force of the man, and in the essence of Yang within the Yin force of the woman. That which the Taoists call the Yin-fluid and the Yang-fluid is manufactured within each of us independently, and it is possible for each to keep these within and to feed from them, alone. But the precious substances only become fruitful as they find an outlet, a way of offering up to the part of the universe that is outside oneself that which is inner, belonging to the individual. The androgyne may at times feel complete, fulfilled within himself or herself. This is the asexual aspect of it. There is peace in this, but unless it finds some expression in work or relationship, in prayer or in art, it tends toward entropy, as a closed system does.

Individuals discover the alternatives in their own ways of living to express the life energy that flows in and through each one. Woman experiences her Yin as pregnancy with the seed of Yang stirring within; man experiences his Yang as pregnant also, with the seed of Yin. Sooner or later parturition occurs and the new energy manifests itself. Often, when the inner psychic process is unconscious, its expression becomes sexual in nature on a purely personal level. This means that the experience of loving is felt almost as something autonomous: people "fall in love," something "happens" to them, and suddenly they are caught in a web of emotions that envelop the self and the other person. The attention is on the individuals and the magical interaction between them. This is "romantic love," about which novels, plays, operas and movies are written. It is engaging, enchanting, ennobling, inspiring and exhausting. Although it has also the capacity to bring about a sense of peace and well-being, romantic love also tends inevitably toward entropy because the energy in it is discharged little by little until the passion dissipates itself. This is because romantic love becomes a closed system when the two involved in it merge their psychological reality into one, bound closely in a relationship that revolves about its own center. Love must progress beyond romance.

*Androgynous love is essentially transpersonal in nature.* This is its distinguishing feature, whatever else it may include. The transpersonal dimension of the so completely human experience to which we refer as "love" is the intimate knowledge, made conscious in every cell of our bodies and beings, that we are nourished into life by the "stream of androgyny." While the experience of androgynous love includes the inward reflectivity that helps to gain self-knowledge, it goes beyond the self-enclosed. It also extends beyond the interpersonal relationship we called "romantic love," although it may very well include the most tender and deep feelings toward a particular person.

The androgyne does not try to submerge differences. Polarities are recognized as existing in linear time, but they are seen also as illusory when time is conceived as cyclic and eternal. The androgyne accepts paradoxes and lives them, knowing that as a finite creature one often cannot see beyond the *apparent* contradictions that beset the individual at every turn. The androgyne can live, therefore, in the immediate present without losing the sense of eternity. The androgyne can also be centered in a particular place, and yet know that the place is a mere speck of dust on a planet whirling in space.

The androgyne sees the overriding principle of *union*, acting continually to overcome *separation*, and knows that the separation is as essential to life as the union. The old myths are remembered. When the primordial androgynous parents lay together in an endless embrace, the eternal eons rolled by and little changed; but when the "one-body" was dismembered, the world of Creation came into being. Then the forces of Love and Strife were born, the forces that still meet and part, conceiving offspring that perpetuate the qualities of both. The androgyne recognizes the presence of these two inner opposites and is equally capable of intimacy with Love and with Strife. Androgyny demands the freedom to function out of one side of our nature or the other as a dominant way of being; yet androgyny recognizes the responsibility to be aware of the other side as well, which needs to be taken into account in the long-range movement toward union.

The androgyne is in touch with the enormity of energy that exists and moves within and all about us. The androgyne knows how frightening it is to let energy flow in its own way, without trying to direct it into a preset channel; without knowing if the energy will take spiritual or sexual form as one reaches out to another, without knowing its limits or direction, how strong it is or how weak. How much easier it would be to think of energy as something that is limited, as if when one uses it here one cannot use it there! But that would be the product of thinking in terms of *closed systems*, and a human being is not a closed system. Organisms are interfacing on both sides—with the cosmos and with the atom. The energy flows not only within the system, but also between systems.

The androgyne is aware that every event within the human body affects every other aspect of the individual, whether viewed from a physiological or from a psychological perspective. This means that whatever people do with their bodies, what they put into them by way of nourishment, how they exercise, what kinds of stimulation they expose themselves to, how and with whom they engage sexually, every event has a profound significance on the whole because the energy of the totality respects no boundaries. Likewise, whatever individuals do is not isolated within the limitations of their physical structure, but affects in the widest imaginable degree all other events that are in process anywhere on earth. This may seem like an extravagant statement, but once one accepts the proposition of the systematic interrelationship of all things, it is impossible to exempt any facet of one's life from its effect on the totality. If this is true, then every individual is directly responsible to some degree for the fate of the world and the course of the future. This is an awesome responsibility, to be sure, but nonetheless real.

To bring this into a more personal frame, I often think of how significantly my own life has been affected by the thoughts, communications and behavior of other people; and it occurs to me that what is apparent to me is only a minute fragment of the totality of influences to which I have been subjected unconsciously over the years. I consider myself fortunate in that there have been strong positive influences in my life from many sources, and I also realize that all the pain and suffering that seemed to have been rained upon me by "circumstance," is, in reality, the outcome of the interrelatedness of all existence.

In the acceptance of androgyny as a guiding principle there are dangers. We live, most of us, utilizing only a small fraction of the energy that would be available to us were we not conflicted much of the time between the needs of the unconscious and the desires and wants that taunt our conscious hours. When the energy that was formerly bound up in the unconscious becomes released by an awakening to the presence in us of a powerful archetype, the individual feels a tremendous sense of power surging within. Jung described the dangers that may result from this in his essay, "The Relations Between the Ego and the Unconscious."[3] On the one side there is the accentuation of ego consciousness, a growing self-confidence, a feeling that one knows everything and that he is completely in tune with the unconscious. He tends to assume responsibilities for which he is ill-prepared, and goes about promoting his viewpoint to others who may not at all be prepared to listen to it. When exuberant self-confidence goes beyond all reasonable bounds, analytic scrutiny may disclose that behind the optimism lies far deeper helplessness, for which the optimism acts as an unsuccessful compensation. The danger on the other side is just the opposite. In the face of the powerful contents of the unconscious material that comes to light, the individual feels powerless and insignificant. Self-confidence dwindles, and the person becomes resigned to being utterly passive in face of the forces of nature and of society. But this pessimistic reaction to the awareness of unconscious material may mask a defiant will to control, and an impetuous bravado.

These are the two possible extremes of reaction in a person to whom an archetype has revealed itself as a living experience. When the archetype of androgyny is experienced as an unconscious tendency that has become conscious, the individual typically finds himself between the twin dangers of hopeful enthusiasm and frightened reticence. It is as though he were on a tiny boat, trying to make his way through the rapids that boil in a narrow strait. He tries to steer his craft, avoiding the rocks on one side and the shoals on the other. As a man, he is wary of going too far in the direction of the Masculine, yet is careful also not to move too far toward the Feminine. The woman will stay closer to the Feminine side, yet will want to be somewhere near midpoint. Both will be intent upon keeping their balance, and both will avoid at all costs the possibility of falling into the water. Obviously, these ways must be filled with tension and the fear of loss of balance. There is no way to maintain continuous control when one is confronting an archetypal force. The solution does not lie in steering a course between the opposites.

What then? Androgyny is not trying to manage the relationship between the opposites; it is simply flowing between them. One does not need to ride the rapids, one can *become* the rapids. One does not need to do anything but flow between the Masculine and the Feminine, touching both, yielding to all obstacles and thereby overcoming them, the energy building upon itself as it follows its natural tendency. The person who has become the androgyne, the hidden river that has risen to the surface, finds his or her own level and makes an impression on the world without any special effort to do so. Water is gentle, yet it wears away rock. It is strong because it is not opposed by nature; nor does nature go against it. And so it can be with the person who chooses the way of the androgyne.

Curiously enough, the concomitant of knowing one's limitations and flowing with them is knowing the capacities and talents with which one is able to participate in the designing of evolution. As it is important to flow with one's natural limitations, so is it necessary to flow with one's capacities to think, to plan and to act in the interest of the future. The androgyne participates consciously in the evolutionary process, redesigning the individual, redesigning society, and redesigning the planet, through a process of making ongoing choices. The available choices may be divided into two essential kinds, which I will call *hard choices* and *soft choices*. The *hard choices* are choosing to alter events from the standpoint of ego and power, to alter things to suit one's own wants, and to utilize one's powers to the maximum in order to reach the top. This is the ego-centered way of the *individualist*. The individualist's battle cry is, "What about me?" and the rest of the world can fend for itself. It is the way of competition and power-politics, of striving to be recognized and to be known.

The *soft choice* is the way of the androgyne. This choice comes out of the perspective in which the *individual* (in contrast to the *individualist*) sees himself or herself as only one element in a totality that is ordered by the principle that has been called *Self*, and many other names, but is essentially nameless. The *soft choice* is the choice that comes from being sensitive to the aims of that *Self*, as expressed in the rhythms of nature and the sense of inner harmony that comes from being in tune with them. If inner peace is to be found, it is to be found in moving as the stream, the Tao, over, around and through any obstructions, "the watercourse way."

Human beings cannot really go against nature. When they try to do so they become weary, frustrated and discouraged in the process. They can only twist and turn and tie themselves into knots by refusing to accept the reality of themselves as a combination of limitations and potentialities. They can only grow sluggish through refusing to make the choices that engender the life-giving possibilities. They can only diminish their potency by trying to avoid participating in the creation of the design for evolution. Nevertheless, the evolutionary development of human consciousness will proceed onward, spurred by mutation, metamorphosis, risk-taking and planning, whether or not specific individuals are willing participants in it. To the degree that people are conscious of their wholeness, they can rejoice in the exercise of it. To the degree that they conceive of themselves as fragmented and isolated beings on a stormy sea, they experience life storm-tossed.

Life is process; process is life. People either commit themselves to participating in life as consciously as possible, or else they are dragged along by it, kicking and screaming and feeling victimized. In the latter case they live in existential despair or else find ways to fill their days with so many items of business and trivia as to scarcely notice that they are dying by the minute. In the former case, people attach themselves to a vital and flowing consciousness, perceiving their intimate involvement with the entire universe. However, these people, too, are dying by the minute; the difference being that they are aware of it and accept it with a knowing calm. And so, they are not afraid to fly.

Death is taken as a matter of course as one of many events in the recurring cycle of emergence from darkness and chaos, of movement back and forth between positive and negative charges of energy, of growing strong and gaining power, of later relinquishing power and growing wise, and of returning at last to the birth-giving chaos. All the while, however slowly, evolutionary consciousness is increasing in the world. And if life is really cyclical, as some perceive it to be, who knows but what the energies that coalesced and formed the human beings that we once became may not collect again in some other living configuration—which will have no remembrance of the past?

Those who have embraced the evolutionary consciousness are forming centers of energy all over the world. They belong to an emerging network of individuals and groups who support the creative potentials that arise as a consequence of the eternal flux between the Masculine and Feminine in each person. Those who live each day in consonance with this awareness are the New Androgynes.

The New Androgynes are but the latest to have joined a straggly band of pilgrims. Since the beginning of mythic time, these travelers have been making their way toward the East. They follow *Sol niger*, the black sun, in its Night-sea journey, as it moves through mysterious places invisible to people of the Day. The wanderers tread a well-worn way; before them have gone the Orphic bards, the Chaldean astrologers, the worshippers of the Serpent-power, the Kabbalists seeking the Tree of Life, the Tantricists, and the old Chinese philosopher carrying a bundle of yarrow stalks. Some faces may be recognized: Christ, Mary, Solomon, the Queen of Sheba, Siva—Lord of the Dance—and Sakti, Copernicus and Galileo, Einstein, Max Planck and Carl Jung. Besides the well-known travelers there have been an unimaginable number of people who achieved neither fame nor fortune, but nevertheless persisted in the way. They must have had their reasons, reasons of the mind and of the heart.

# EPILOGUE

## A Dream of the Writer

After the manuscript of *Androgyny* was completed, I made a trip to New York to discuss the future of the book with my editor. The night following our meeting, I had this dream: I have been walking the streets of New York for days and nights, marveling at the contrasts — the glass and steel structural Babels rising defiantly into the sky, and huge plastic bags of garbage piled before the most and the least elegant of buildings; the modish shoppers on Fifth Avenue looking into the dazzling windows of stores, and on Broadway after the show the pressing crowds of whores and pimps and hawkers of cheap pictures and fleamarket gaudies — and a huge sign on the *Times* Building, a mural in red, white and blue lights glaring down on the throng and proclaiming over all, *Pres. Ford says New York will* SURVIVE!

I walk into a drugstore. It is of an old-fashioned kind, lighted with hanging lamps of the art-nouveau era. I go to the prescription-filling department. There is a druggist of uncertain age, a youngish Doctor Faustus, mixing various powders and measuring them onto balancing scales. There are glass flasks and bottles about, holding different colored substances. I approach this pharmacist who seems rather preoccupied with his work, and I say to him, "Have you got some androgyny?" He looks up at me a little surprised, excuses himself a moment, and goes into the back to look over his shelves. He peers into drawers and pigeon-holes, looks at the labels of several bottles, and then returns to say, "I'm afraid not. We seem to be out of it. I'm not sure if we ever carried it, but if we did we've been out of it for a long time."

I awoke — or was I still asleep — when I felt this vague sense of disappointment, even pain. I knew it would be fruitless for me to look for it in other stores, even in this huge city where every kind of goods imaginable and every service imaginable could be purchased for a price. I reflected, where would I get it? Where in the world would I find it?

I remembered the old Chinese tales of the Secret Alchemy, which was another name for the Yoga of Dual Cultivation. This was the art reputed to have been practiced by the Taoist adepts of ancient times in order to distill within the adept's body a golden liquid from which the elixir leading to longevity, possible immortality, and union with the Tao could be produced. As can be imagined, the purpose of the Sexual Yoga was often misunderstood by those not acquainted with the fact that chastity was as important for the adept who practices this Yoga as it was for the monk who practiced celibacy. Indeed, even greater chastity was required of the former, for a monk may think lustful thoughts although in practice he may be chaste; but the adept of Dual Cultivation may not proceed in the art without first having completely rooted out lust from his mind. Nevertheless the state authorities did not appreciate the true intentions of the adepts, and they often treated communities of sexual alchemists as depraved criminals.

I recalled a legend that illustrates the greed and blindness of some of the highest authorities.[1] A long time ago, a noted physician persuaded a certain judge to release a wandering peddlar who had been arrested and was being cruelly tortured to extract a confession from him. A short time later the peddlar visited the physician and, in his gratitude, bestowed upon him the secret formula for distilling the elixir of immortality. The physician realized that he was fated to become a recluse, and so went to live on a mountain where he gradually achieved fame as the "Pine-kernel Fairy." He gathered a flock of disciples about him, and instructed them in the healing arts. Those whom he found most gifted and most devoted to their calling received from him the secret formula, for which in exchange they gave the promise to transmit it only to certain appropriate persons. Eventually the authorities heard of the Pine-kernel Fairy's activities and had him arrested, alleging that he practiced medicine chiefly as a means of achieving lecherous intimacy with female pilgrims who came to the sacred places on the mountain. Because of his influence, the Pine-kernel Fairy was quickly released, but the record of the incident came to the attention of the emperor.

One day a eunuch came from the imperial palace and demanded that the Pine-kernel Fairy appear before the emperor forthwith for an audience. He was brought to the palace and treated with honor and deference. The emperor ordered that he receive a handsome dwelling with every comfort, a retinue of servants, and whatever else he might require. In return for this, he was ordered to compound the elixir of immortality for the personal use of the emperor. In vain the Fairy pleaded that the was not something that could be passed from hand to hand. The emperor could not believe this, and told the Fairy, "You are either too modest or terribly selfish." He then presented the Fairy with a vessel he thought suitable for the elixir; it was fashioned of flawless green jade. He insisted that the Pine-kernel Fairy produce the perfected elixir in time for his birthday, and gave orders that whatever ingredients the Fairy needed be provided immediately.

The Pine-kernel Fairy was in a state of despair, knowing that were he to disclose the true secret the charges against him would be sustained and he would again be imprisoned, but if he did not do so he would be penalized severely for incurring the emperor's displeasure. He retreated into his quarters. The servants were dubious of his sanity as they observed his books and alchemical equipment gathering dust while the Pine-kernel Fairy spent his days and nights behind closed doors with a number of young ladies he had discreetly added to his household shortly after his arrival at the palace.

When the emperor's birthday arrived, the Pine-kernel Fairy took to his bed as if in severe pain, and sent a note to the emperor stating that the substance requested by the emperor was now bubbling in the crucible of the four elements, but it required still more time to perfect — however, the golden pill was slowly taking form. The Fairy was granted a reprieve, and the servants expected him to hasten to the laboratory. The Fairy, however, only acquired more female companions, and his door remained closed to all others, no matter what their rank, while he proceeded to gather Yin-force in anticipation of the day scheduled for his final audience with the emperor.

On this day he approached the court with a carefree gait and smiling face. When the emperor demanded the vial, the Fairy responded with a joyful countenance, "Your Majesty, I bring with me the golden pill in perfected form. The crucible of the four elements about which I wrote to you is none other than my own body, but as I have told you from the beginning, the elixir cannot be passed from hand to hand. Nevertheless, I can acquaint you with the formula and it is to be expected that Your Majesty will compound the pill more swiftly than I was able to do, being a hundred times better prepared as to the ingredients." The emperor said he would not accept the excuses, and demanded of the Fairy to know what were the ingredients of which he spoke, with which he was better supplied than the Fairy. "I was referring," said the Fairy, "to the ah — relatively insignificant number of my wives." The emperor, mistaking the Pine-kernel Fairy's statement for a crude allusion to his many concubines, ordered him banished from the kingdom. Just as the guards rushed forward to take him, the Fairy, having perfected the golden pill only the night before and thus achieved immortality, rose from the ground, and saluting the emperor in a grave farewell, sailed through the doorway and upward to the higher realms where the cloud-riding immortals pass their time in contemplation of the Tao.

The emperor remained below, gazing through the doorway in utter amazement, never knowing that by being overhasty and foolish he had lost the opportunity to acquire knowledge of great value. Because he believed *literally* what he had been told about—the possibility of grasping the magical substance through the efforts of someone else, he would never understand the truth, which is *symbolic* in its essence.

In the quiet hour before dawn, I suddenly realized that my dream was telling me in its own symbolic language what those early alchemists, the Taoist sages, knew long ago. As dreams do, they, too, had veiled their secrets behind a confusion of language. Those who were unable to penetrate beyond words into meaning could not steal and misuse the secret knowledge. The precious golden pill that was the secret of longevity, if not of immortality, was not to be purchased or gotten by theft or trickery. Everyone who desired it would have to manufacture it through his or her own efforts. I knew that I would have to manufacture my "androgyny" within myself; that is, within my total organism which is both body and psyche, both Feminine and Masculine. As the adepts of old had distilled the *Yin* and *Yang* substances over and over, using their flasks and jars and their fires as allegories through which they might give visible form to *inner processes*—so do I, through words, give *apparent* substance to evanescent thoughts and feelings which can never be adequately conveyed so as to be *literally* understood. The real flask is the physical body, and the real mixture that is held in that vessel is the "subtle body"—which is formed by distillation and refinement, by separation and by fusion, of all that a person has ever been and all that the person is. The fire that effects the transformation is the passion that a human being brings to life when there is an embrace between the inner-Masculine and the inner-Feminine. Of this union is born the willingness to transmute experience into meaning, relationship into love, and egotism into the worship of the Spirit embodied in matter.

There is no easy way. There is no book of instructions. Though many "panaceas" were offered, no one can produce the true elixir for anyone else. There is no need to seek it out in the Cosmic Drugstore, because androgyny is not for sale.

Look within.

# Reference

Chapter 1 *Androgyny as Guiding Principle of the New Age*

[1]William Blake, "The Marriage of Heaven and Hell," *The Complete Writings of William Blake*, p.151.
[2]C. G. Jung, "Archetypes of the Collective Unconscious," *The Archetypes and the Collective Unconscious*, *C.W. 9,i*, para.5-6.
[3]Carolyn Heilbrun's term in *Towards Androgyny*.
[4] R. Buckminster Fuller, "Time Present," *Synergetics, Explorations in the Geometry of Thinking*, (extract), *Harper's*, March, 1975.

Chapter 2 *Hermaphrodites, Bisexuals, Androgynes and the Uncarved Block*

[1]S. Freud, "Analysis Terminable and Interminable," *Complete Psychological Works, 23*, p.252.
[2]Susan Sontag, *Partisan Review*, XXXI, 4, pp.518-19.
[3]Mario Praz, *The Romantic Agony*, p.301 ff.
[4]Mircea Eliade, *Mephistopheles and the Androgyne*, p.100
[5]Arthur Waley, *The Way and Its Power, A Study of the Tao Tê Ching and Its Place in Chinese Thought*, p.178.
[6]Alan Watts, *The Watercourse Way*.

Chapter 3 *The Two in the One: Pathology or Mythology?*

[1]C. G. Jung, *Two Essays in Analytical Psychology, C.W. 7*, para.437.
[2]S. Freud, "The Psychogenesis of a Case of Homosexuality in a Woman," (1920) *Complete Psychological Works, 18*, cited in Robert J. Stoller, "Facts and Fancies: An Examination of Freud's Concept of Bisexuality" in *Woman & Analysis*, Jean Strouse, ed., p.343.
[3]S. Freud, *op. cit.*, cited in *Women & Analysis*, p.343.
[4]*Ibid.*
[5]For a fuller treatment of Jung's views on bisexuality and homosexuality, cf. C. G. Jung, "The Love Problem of a Student," in *Civilization in Transition, C.W. 10*.
[6]Mircea Eliade, *Rites and Symbols of Initiation*, p.26. (The hardbound-edition is titled: *The Mysteries of Birth and Rebirth*).
[7]*Ibid.*

Chapter 4 *Becoming Liberated from Sex and Gender: Risks and Challenges*

[1]C. G. Jung, *Two-Essays in Analytical Psychology, C.W. 7, para.330*.
[2]Ibid, para.331.
[3]*Ibid.*
[4]*Ibid.*, para.336.
[5]*Ibid.*

[6]S. Freud, "Some Psychological Consequences of the Anatomical Distinction Between Sexes," *Collected Papers, 5, cited in Phyllis Chesler, Women and Madness,* p.76.

[7]S. Freud, *New Introductory Lectures in Psychoanalysis,* cited in Chesler, *ibid.*, p.76.

[8]*Science News,* 102, December 16, 1972.

[9]Bruno Bettelheim, "The Commitment Required of a Woman Entering a Scientific Profession in Present Day American Society," in *Woman and the Scientific Professions,* Massachusetts Institute of Technology Symposium on American Women in Science and Engineering, cited in Chesler, *op. cit.*, p.77.

[10]C. G. Jung, *Contributions to Analytical Psychology,* cited in Chesler, *ibid.*

[11]M. Esther Heading, *The Way of All Women,* p.69.

[12]From "The Plays of Aeschylus," G. M. Cookson, trans., in *Great Books of the Western World, 5,* p.88.

[13]C. G. Jung, "The Stages of Life," *The Structure and Dynamics of the Psyche, C.W. 8.*

[14]Paul B. Baltes and K. Warner Schale, "Aging and I.Q.: The Myth of the Twilight Years," *Psychology Today, 7, 10.*

[15]Jan Morris, *Conundrum.*

[16]C. G. Jung, *Two Essays in Analytical Psychology, C.W. 7,* para.336.


Chapter 5 *In the Midst of Chaos the Woman Danced*

[1]Robert Graves, *The Greek Myths,* p.27.

[2]William Blake, "Vala or The Four Zoas," *Complete Writings, p.335.*

[3]Heinrich Zimmer, *Myths and Symbols in Indian Art and Civilization,* p.152.

[4]Graves, *op.cit.*, p.30.

[5]*Ibid.*

[6]*Ibid.*, p.32.

[7]*Ibid.*, pp.39-40.

[8]Elizabeth Gould Davis, *The First Sex,* pp.63-64.

[9]Quoted in Graves, *op. cit.*, p.36.

[10]Erich Fromm, *The Art of Loving,* p.55.

[11]George Boas, "Preface," to J. J. Bachofen, *Myth, Religion and Mother Right,* p.xiii.

[12]J. J. Bachofen, "Introduction to 'Mother Right,'" in *Myth, Religion and Mother Right,* p.75.

[13]Cf. Robert Graves, *Adam's Rib and Other Anomalous Elements in the Hebrew Creation Myth*; also Erich Neumann, *The Great Mother and The Origins and History of Consciousness,*

[14]Bachofen, *op. cit.*, p.73.

[15]Joseph Campbell, "Introduction" to Bachofen, *Myth, Religion and Mother Right,* pp.liv-lv.

[16]James Mellaart, *Çatal Hüyük,* p.70.

[17]*Ibid.*, p.60.

[18]*Ibid.*, p.136.


Chapter 6 *The Golden Age of the Mother and the Rebellion of her Sons*

[1]René Malamud, "The Amazon Problem," *Spring,* p.5.

[2]*Ibid.*, p.10.

Chapter 7 *Monotheism in a Patriarchal System: Its Disintegration into Polytheism*

[1]Fabra d'Olivet, "Histoire Philosophique du Genre Humain," in Eduard Schuré, *The Great Initiates*, I, pp.26-52

[2]J. J. Bachofen, *Myth, Religion and Mother Right*, p.81.

[3]Erich Neumann, *The Great Mother and The Origins and History of Consciousness*.

[4]Euhemeristic tradition dating from fourth century B.C., in Greece; cf. J. Seznec, *The Survival of the Pagan Gods*, p.13.

[5]C. G. Jung, "The Sign of the Fishes," in *Aion, C.W. 9, ii*, para.147.

[6]Robert Graves, *Adam's Rib*, p.16.

[7]*Ibid.*

[8]*Ibid.*

[9]Alexander Heidel, *The Babylonian Genesis*, a complete translation of all the published cuneiform tablets of the various Babylonian creation stories, with discussion, p.97.

[10]*Ibid.*, p.18.

[11]*Ibid.*, p.3.

[12]Yehezkel Kaufmann, *The Babylonian Captivity and Deutero-Isaiah*, C.W. Efroymson, trans., pp.30-32.

[13]James Hillman, *The Myth of Analysis*, p.217.

[14]*Ibid.*, p.238.

[15]*Ibid.*, p.248.

[16]C. G. Jung, *Psychology and Religion: West and East, C.W. 11*, Part One: Western Religion.

[17]H. Richard Niebuhr, *Radical Monotheism and Western Culture*, p.24.

[18]*Ibid.*, p.32.

[19]*Ibid.*, p.118.

Chapter 8 *Eden Revisited: The Divine "Us" Who Created Persons*

[1]James Hillman, *The Myth of Analysis*, P.275.

[2]Charles Poncé, "An Alchemical Allegory: Notes Toward an Understanding of Genesis," *Maitreya* 5, p.26."

[3]S. L. MacGregor Mathers, *The Kabbalah Unveiled*, pp.21-22.

[4]*The Zohar*, I, Harry Sperling and Maurice Simon, trans., p.90 ff.

[5]Mircea Eliade, "Mephistopheles and the Androgyne," *The Two and the One*, pp.104-5.

[6]Poncé, *op. cit.*, pp.21-22.

Chapter 9 *Zodiacal Man as Macrocosm: The Astrological Model for the Psyche*

[1]Idries Shah, *The Way of the Sufi*, p.74.

[2]*Jewish Encyclopedia*, II, "Astrology." p.241.

[3]*Ibid.*, pp.242-43.

[4]Keith Thomas, *Religion and the Decline of Magic*, pp.283-335.

[5]Warren Kenton, *Astrology, The Celestial Mirror*, pp.12-13.

[6]Charles Poncé, *The Game of Wizards*, p.27.

[7]Thomas, *op. cit.*, pp.249-52.

[8]C. G. Jung, "Synchronicity: An Acausal Connecting Principle," *The Structure and Dynamics of the Psyche, C.W. 8*, para.901.

[9]Zodiacal Man, page from ms. *Les Très Riches Heures du Duc de Berry*, French, early fifteenth century, as reproduced in Warren Kenton, *Astrology, The Celestial Mirror*, plate 43.

[10]*The Five Books of M. Manilius*, cited in Poncé, *op. cit.* p.67.

[11]William Blake, "Auguries of Innocence," *Complete Writings*, p.431.

[12]Poncé, *op. cit.*, pp.59-60.

[13]G. S. Kirk and J. E. Raven, *The Pre-Socratic Philosophers*, pp.329-30, cited in Poncé, *op. cit.*, p.61.

Chapter 10 *Plato's Androgyne: Origins of Heterosexuality and Homosexuality*

[1]Abridged from Plato, "Symposium." Benjamin Jowet, trans., *Great Books of the Western World*, 7, p.157.

[2]Arthur Waley, *The Way and Its Power*, p.141.

[3]S. L. MacGregor Mathers, *The Kabbalah Unveiled*, p.16 f.

[4]William Blake, "The Book of Urizen," *Complete Writings*, p.222.

Chapter 11 *Monad, Jot and Tittle: The Gnostic Vision of the Fall*

[1]G. R. S. Mead, *Fragments of a Faith Forgotten*, p.4.

[2]"Hymn of the Soul," attributed to the Naassene Gnostics in the *Philosophumena, V, 10, 2*, as cited in Jean Doresse, *The Secret Books of the Egyptian Gnostics*, p.ix.

[3]Titus Burckhardt, *Alchemy, Science of the Cosmos, Science of the Soul*, William Stoddart, trans., p.17 ff.

[4]C. G. Jung, *Aion, C.W. 9, ii*, para.14.

[5]*Ibid.*, para.19.

[6]*Ibid.*, para.298.

[7]*Ibid.*, para 340, citing Monoimus, in the writings of Hippolytus.

[8]*Ibid.*, para.340.

[9]*Ibid.*, para.345.

[10]*Ibid.*, para.322, citing E. A. Wallis Budge, *The Gods of the Egyptian*, I, p.301 ff.

[11]William Blake, "The Marriage of Heaven and Hell," *Complete Writings*, p.155.

[12]Jean Doresse, *The Secret Books of the Egyptian Gnostics*, Philip Mairet, trans,. pp.203-4.

[13]G. R. S. Mead. *Pistis Sophia (A Gnostic miscellany: being for the most part extracts from the books of the Saviour, to which are added excerpts from a cognate literature)*, pp.1-95.

[14]Jung, *op. cit.*, para.307.

[15]Mircea Eliade, "Mephistopheles and the Androgyne," *The Two and the One*, pp.104-5.

[16]*Ibid.*, p.34.

[17]Jung, *op. cit.*, para.368.

[18]Theodore Thass-Thienemann, *The Interpretation of Language, Volume II: Understanding the Unconscious Meaning of Language*, p.329.

[19]Eliade, *op. cit.*, p.105.

[20]Jung *op. cit.*, para.314, citing Epiphanes.

[21]*Ibid.*, para 316.

[22]*Ibid.*, para.320.

[23]*The Gospel According to Thomas*, Coptic Text (established and trans. by A. Guillaumont, H.-Ch. Puech, G. Quispel, W. Till and Yassah 'Abd Al Masih), p.17.

24*Ibid.*, p.57.

Chapter 12 *The Philosopher's Stone in Alchemy: The Androgyne Imprisoned in Matter*

1Cited in John Read, Prelude to Chemistry, p.54.
2Cited by C. G. Jung *Mysterium Coniunctionis, C.W. 14*, para.2.
3Jung, *Aion, C.W. 9, ii*, para.248.
4*Ibid.*, para.249.
5Ralph Metzner, *Maps of Consciousness*, p.87.
6Cited in Jung, *Psychology and Alchemy, C.W. 12*, para. 438.
7Mircea Eliade, *the Two and the One*, pp.107-8, citing *Corpus Hermeticum, II, 20, 21*.
8William Blake, "The Four Zoas," *Complete Writings*, p.265.
9*Ibid.*, p.264.
10Cited by Jung in *Mysterium Coniunctionis*, para.137.
11*Ibid.*, para.329.
12Jung, *Aion*, para.268.

Chapter 13 *Adam Kadmon in Kabbalah: The Tree of Life as Androgyne*

1Timothy Ferris, "The Universe as an Ocean of Thought: A Speculation of the Possibility of Interstellar Communication," *Harper's*, July, 1975, p.40.
2Gershom G. Scholem, ed., *Zohar, The Book of Splendor, Basic Readings from the Kabbalah*, pp.27-28.
3Ferris, *op. cit.*, p.38.
4Charles Poncé, *Kabbalah, an Introduction and Illumination for the World Today*, p.34 ff.
5Poncé, *op. cit.*, p.39. Poncé notes also first publication of the seminal work, *Sefer Yetsirah*, was in the Latin of Gulielmus Postellus, Paris, 1552. The first publication was in Mantua, 1565, in which edition the text was accompanied by five commentaries purported to have been written by Moses Nahmanides, Abraham, B. David, Eleazer of Worms, Moses Botarel and Saadia Gaon.
6These questions are raised today by Herbert Weiner in *9 1/2 Mystics: The Kabbala Today* (a warm study of Kabbala as experienced by a group of initiates who still carry on the tradition today), p.40.
7*En Sof, Ain Sof, Eyn Sof*, and *Ayin Sof* are all transliterations of the Hebrew and are all equally correct. *En Sof* is used here following the Sperling and Simon translation of the *Zohar*, published by the Soncino Press.
8*The Zohar, I*, Sperling and Simon, trans., p.70.
9Poncé, *op. cit.*, p.80 ff.
10Weiner, *op. cit.*, p.33.
11This description follows the formulation of Ponce in *Kaballah*, p.134 ff.
12Weiner, *op. cit.*, p.109.
13Siegmund Hurwitz, "Psychological Aspects in Early Hasidic Literature," *Timeless Documents of the Soul*, pp.202-3.
14*The Zohar, III*, 296a, cited in Hurwitz, *op. cit.*, p.203.
15Gershom G. Scholem, *Major Trends in Jewish Mysticism*, p.227.

[16]From the recording by the New York Philharmonic Orchestra of the *Kaddish Symphony*, which had its premiere in Tel Aviv by the request of the composer, Leonard Bernstein, on December 10, 1963.

Chapter 14, *Purusha-Prakriti, Siva-Sakti, Yab-Yum and Other Manifestations in the East*

[1]Heinrich Zimmer, *Myths and Symbols in Indian Art and Civilization*, p.123.
[2]*Ibid.*
[3]From the "Kena Upanishads" in *The Upanishads*, Swami Nikhilananda, trans. and ed., pp.99-100.
[4]*Ibid.*, p.113.
[5]*Ibid.*
[6]Philip Rawson, *The Art of Tantra*, p.207.
[7]Gopi Krishna, *Kundalini, The Evolutionary Energy in Man*, pp.7-10.
[8]Agehananda Bharati, *The Tantric Tradition*, p.202.
[9]Carl Friedrich von Weizsäcker, "Introduction" to Gopi Krishna, *The Biological Basis of Religion and Genius*.
[10]Bharati, *op. cit.*, p.200.
[11]Rawson, *op. cit.*, pp.9-10.
[12]Mircea Eliade, "Mephistopheles and the Androgyne," *The Two and the One*, pp.117-18.
[13]*Ibid.*, p.118.
[14]Eliade, *Yoga: Immortality and Freedom*, p.254.
[15]*Ibid.*, p.271.

Chapter 15 *Dynamic Union in Tao*

[1]Chuang Tsu, *Inner Chapters*, p.38.
[2]*Leonardo Da Vinci*, a memorial edition, p.60.
[3]*The Secret of the Golden Flower, A Chinese Book of Life*, Richard Willhelm, trans., p.12.
[4]John Blofeld, *The Secret and Sublime, Taoist Mysteries and Magic*, pp.20-21.
[5]Arthur Waley, *The Way and Its Power*, p.227.
[6]*The I Ching or Book of Changes*, Richard Willhelm, trans., pp.1-3.
[7]*Ibid.*, pp.9-10.
[8]James Hillman in *The Myth of Analysis* and Irene Claremont de Castillejo in *Knowing Woman*, also Richard Wilhelm in his "Discussion of the Text" of *The Secret of the Golden Flower*, to name a few examples of where this "fuzziness" has taken place.
[9]*I Ching*, p.10.
[10]Blofeld, *op. cit.*, p.132 ff.
[11]*Ibid.*, p.132.

Chapter 16 *Androgyny in Motion: T'ai Chi and the Hollow Brush*

[1]Al Chung-liang Huang, *Embrace Tiger, Return to Mountain*, pp.125-26.
[2]Arthur J. Deikman, "Bimodal Consciousness," *Archives of General Psychiatry, 25*, pp.481-89.
[3]Michael S. Gazzaniga, "The Split Brain in Man," *Scientific American, 217, 2*, pp.24-29.
[4]Joseph E. Bogen. "The Other Side of the Brain: an Appositional Mind," *Bulletin of the Los Angeles Neurological Societies, 34, 3*, pp.135-62.

[5]G. William Domhoff, "But Why Did They Sit on the King's Right in the First Place?" *Psychoanalytic Review, 56.*

[6]Bogen, *op. cit.*

[7]Robert E. Ornstein, *The Psychology of Consciousness.*

[8]Ornstein, ed., *The Nature of Human Consciousness.*

[9]Ornstein, *The Psychology of Consciousness*, p.67.

[10]*Ibid.*, pp.62-63.


Chapter 17 *Dynamics of Androgyny: The Systems View*

[1]Hugh Kenner, "Bucky Fuller and the Final Exam," *The New York Times Magazine*, July 6, 1975, pp.10-12.

[2]*Ibid.*

[3]Ervin Laszlo, *The Systems View of the World*, P.5.

[4]Marcel Granet, "Le depôt de l'enfant sur le sol: Rites anciens et ordalies mythiques," cited in Mircea Eliade, *Myths, Dreams and Mysteries*, pp.179, 167.

[5]Eliade, *Myths, Dreams and Mysteries*, p.179.

[6]Laszlo, *op. cit.*, p.19.

[7]*Ibid. passim.*

[8]*Ibid.*, p.79.

[9]William Blake "The Marriage of Heaven and Hell," *Complete Writings*, p.15.

[10]Chuang Tsu, *Inner Chapters*, p.123.

[11]T. S. Eliot "East Coker," *Four Quartets.*

[12]Heinrich Zimmer, *Myths and Symbols in Indian Art and Civilization*, p.131.

[13]George Gamow, *The Creation of the Universe*, the classic popular defense of the "Big Bang" Hypothesis.

[14]William Blake, "Milton," *Complete Writings*, p.16.

[15]Lao Tsu, *Tao Tê Ching.*

[16]Laszlo, *op. cit.*, pp.56-57.

[17]*Ibid.*

[18]C. G. Jung, *Mysterium Coniunctionis, C.W. 14*, para.533.

[19]Laszlo, *op. cit.*, pp.67-68.


Chapter 18 *Energy and the Evolution of Consciousness*

[1]C. G. Jung, *The Structure and Dynamics of the Psyche, C.W. 8*, para.130.

[2]William Blake, "Visions of the Daughters of Albion," *Complete Writings*, p.194.

[3]Mary Jane Sherfey, M.D., *The Nature and Evolution of Human Sexuality*, pp.30-31.

[4]*Ibid.*, pp.42-43.

[5]C. G. Jung, *Memories, Dreams, Reflections*, p.87.

[6]The major works in which Jung deals with alchemy are *Psychology and Alchemy, C.W. 12, Alchemical Studies, C.W. 13, Mysterium Coniunctionis, C.W. 14*, "Psychology of the Transference" in *The Practice of Psychotherapy, C.W. 16*, and his "Commentary" on *The Secret of the Golden Flower.*

Chapter 19 *Toward a New Theory of Human Sexuality*

[1]William Blake, "The Marriage of Heaven and Hell," *Complete Writings*, p.154.
[2]W. B. Yeats, "The Second Coming," *Selected Poems and Two Plays*, p.91.
[3]Wilder Penfield, *The Mystery of the Mind*, p.86.

Chapter 20 *Androgyny Experienced in Homosexuality, Bisexuality and Heterosexuality*

[1]Miguel Serrano, *The Serpent of Paradise: The Story of an Indian Pilgrimage*, pp.19-20.

Chapter 21 *Androgyny Experienced in Masturbation, Celibacy and Marriage*

[1]James Hillman, "Toward the Archetypal Model of the Masturbation Inhibition," *Loose Ends*, pp.105-25."
[2]"The Latin term *masturbo, -are*, which is not very transparent in its first part (and can be found also in *mas-culinus*), has a synonym parallel in the noun *mas -carpio, -ionis*, "masturbator." The second part of this latter word belongs to *carpo, -ere*, 'to pull out' (as *carpet*, from *carpita*, means something 'pulled out'), and it denotes also "to pluck." In the Greek *karpos* means 'something plucked,' and 'fruit plucked from the tree,' which *fruit*, from *fructus*, from *fruor, -ere*, means also primarily something 'enjoyed.' The 'plucking' of the fruit from the tree seems to be symbolic of the autoerotic pleasure, just as in the case of the Biblical plucking of the apple from the tree of knowledge." From Theodore Thass-Thienemann, *The Interpretation of Language, Volume II: Understanding the Unconscious Meaning of Language*, p.52.

Chapter 22 *Androgyny Experienced in Widowhood, the Creative Life and Old Age*

[1]*The Diary of Anais Nin, V. 3*, 1939-44, pp.256-60.
[2]Elsa Gidlow, "Seventy Plus Has Many Plusses," *Country Women, 11*, July 1974.
[3]*Ibid.*

Chapter 23 *The Way of The Flowing Stream*

[1]Frances G. Wickes, *The Inner World of Choice*, p.162.
[2]Nicholas Berdyaev, cited by Charles Poncé in "Women, the Feminine and Alchemy: Notes from an Alchemical Journal," *Maitreya 4*, p.32."
[3]C. G. Jung, *Two Essays in Analytical Psychology*, *C.W. 7*, para.221-22.

Epilogue *A Dream of the Writer*

[1]Adapted from John Blofeld, *The Secret and Sublime*, p.137 ff.

# Bibliography

Aeschylus. *The Plays of Aeschylus.* G. M. Cookson, trans., and reprinted in *Great Books of the Western World,* 5, Chicago: Encyclopedia Britannica, 1952

Avakib, Arthur. (Sir John Woodroffe). *The Serpent Power.* Madras, India: Ganesh and Company, 1958.

Baltes, Paul B., and Schale, K. Warner. "Aging and I.Q.: The Myth of the Twilight Years," *Psychology Today, 7, 10,* March 1974.

Bettelheim, Bruno. "The Commitment Required of a Woman Entering a Scientific Profession in Present Day American Society," *Woman and the Scientific Professions.* Massachusetts Institute of Technology Symposium on American Women in Science and Engineeering, Cambridge, Mass, 1965.

Bharati, Agehananda. *The Tantric Tradition. New York: Doubleday Anchor, 1970.*

*Blake, William. The Complete Writings of William Blake, with all the Variant Readings,* ed. Geoffrey Keynes. London: The Nonesuch Press, 1957.

Blofeld, John. *The Secret and Sublime: Taoist Mysteries and Magic. New York: E. P. Dutton, 1973.*

——. *the Tantric Mysticism of Tibet.* New York: E. P. Dutton, 1970.

Bogen, Joseph E. "The Other Side of the Brain: Am Appositional Mind." *Bulletin of the Los Angeles Neurological Societies, 34,* July, 1969.

Budge, E. A. Wallis. *The Gods of the Egyptians, I,* London, 1904.

Burckhardt, Titus. *Alchemy, Science of the Cosmos, Science of the Soul.* William Stoddart, trans. Baltimore: Penguin Books, 1972.

Campbell, Joseph. *The Masks of God: Creative Mythology.* New York: The Viking Press, 1968.

——. *The Masks of God: Occidental Mythology.* New York: The Viking Press, 1964.

——. *The Masks of God: Oriental Mythology.* New York: The Viking Press, 1962.

——. *The Masks of God: Primitive Mythology.* New York: The Viking Press, 1959.

Capra, Fritjof. *The Tao of Physics.* Berkeley: Shambhala, 1975.

De Castillejo, Irene Claremont. *Knowing Woman, a Feminine Psychology.* New York: G. P. Putnam's Sons, 1973.

Chesler, Phyllis. *Women and Madness.* New York: Doubleday & Co., Inc., 1972.

Chuang Tsu. *Inner Chapters.* Gai-Fu Feng and Jane English, trans. New York: Random House, Vintage Books, 1974.

Cook, Roger. *The Tree of Life: Image for the Cosmos.* The Art and Cosmos Series. New York: Avon Books, 1974.

Davinci, Leonardo. *Leonardo DaVinci,* a memorial edition. New York: Reynal, 1956.

Davis, Elizabeth Gould. *The First Sex.* New York: G. P. Putnam's Sons, 1971.

Deikman, Arthur. "Bimodal Consciousness," *Archives of General Psychiatry, 25.*

Derola, Stanislas Klossowski. *Alchemy: The Secret Art.* The Art and Cosmos Series. New York: Avon Books, 1973.

Domhoff, G. William. "But Why did Tehy Sit on the King's Right in the First Place?" *Psychoanalytic Review, 56.*

Einstein, Albert. *Living Philosophies.* New York: Simon & Schuster, 1931.

Eliade, Mircea. *Images and Symbols: Studies in Religious Symbolism.* Mairet, Philip, trans. London: Harvill Press, 1961.

——— . *Mephistopheles and the Androgyne.* New York: Harper & Row, 1965.

——— . *The two and the One.* Paperback title of *Mephistopheles and the Androgyne.* New York: Harper Torchbook, 1969.

——— . *Myths, Dreams and Mysteries.* New York: Harper & Row, 1960.

——— . *Rites and Symbols of Initiation.* New York: Harper & Torchbook, 1965. Hardcover ed. is titled, *Birth and Rebirth.* New York: Harper & Brothers, 1958.

——— . *The Sacred and the Profane: The Nature of Religion.* Willard Trask, trans. New York: A Harvest Book, 1959.

——— . *Yoga: Immortality and Freedom.* New York: Pantheon, 1958.

Eliot, T. S. "East Coker," in *Four Quartets.* New York: Harcourt, Brace and World, 1943.

Fasteau, Marc Feigen. *The Male Machine.* New York: McGraw-Hill, 1974.

Ferris, Timothy. "The Universe as an Ocean of Thought: A Speculation on the Possibility of Interstellar Communication," *Harper's, July 1975.*

*Frazier, Allie, Editor. Readings in Eastern Religious Thought: Hinduism.* Volume I. Philadelphia: The Westminister Press, 1969.

Freud, Sigmund. *New Introductory Lectures in Psychoanalysis.* New York: W. W. Norton, 1933.

——— . "Some Psychological Consequences of the Anatomical Distinction Between the Sexes," *Collected Papers, 5.* London: Hogarth, 1956.

———. "The Psychogenesis of a Case of Homosexuality in a Woman," 1920. *Complete Psychological Works, Standard Edition, 18.* London: Hogarth, 1955.

———. "Analysis Terminable and Interminable," *Complete Psychological Works, 23.* London: Hogarth, 1964.

Fromm, Erich. *The Art of Loving.* New York: Harper, 1956.

Fuller, R. Buckminster, in collaboration with Applewhite, E. J. *Synergetics, Explorations into the Geometry of Thinking.* New York: Macmillan Co., 1975.

———. "Time Present," *Harper's,* March 1975.

Gamow, George. *The Creation of the Universe.* New York: The Viking Press, 1961.

Gazzaniga, Michael S. "The Split Brain in Man," *Scientific American, 217,* August, 1967.

Gidlow, Elsa. "Seventy Plus has Many Plusses," *Country Women, 11,* July 1974, San Francisco.

Gospel According to Thomas. Coptic text, A. Guillaumont, H.-Ch. Puech, G. Quispel, W. Till and Yassah 'Abd Al Masih, trans. New York: Harper & Row, 1959.

Granet, Marcel. "Le depot de l'enfant sur le sol: Rites anciens et ordalies mythiques," in the *Revue Archeologique,* 1922, republished in *Etudes Sociologique sur la Chine,* Paris, 1953.

Graves, Robert. *Adam's Rib and Other Anomalous Elements in the Hebrew Creation Myth.* First American ed. (limited). London: Thoas Yoseleff, Inc., 1958.

———. *The Greek Myths.* New York: Braziller, 1955.

Harding, M. Esther. *The Way of All Women.* New York: G. P. Putnam's Sons, 1970.

Heidel, Alexander. *The Babylonian Genesis.* Complete translation of all the published cuneiform tablets of the various Babylonian creation stories, with discussion. Chicago: University of Chicago Press, 1963.

Heilbrun, Carolyn G. *Towards Androgyny, aspects of male and female in literature.* London: Victor Gollancz, 1973.

Hillman, James. Loose Ends. Zurich: Spring Publications, 1975.

———. *The Myth of Analysis* (Studies of the C. G. Jung Institute, Zurich.) Evanston, Ill.: Northwestern University Press, 1972.

Huang, Al Chung-Liang. *Embrace Tiger, Return to Mountain.* Moab, Utah: Real People Press, 1973.

Hurwitz, Siegmund. "Psychological aspects in Early Hasidic Literature," *Timeless Documents of the Soul.* (Studies of the C. G. Jung Institute, Zürich.) Evanston, Ill.: Northwestern University Press, 1968."

Jantsch, Erich. *Design for Evolution: Self-Organization and Planning in the Life of Human Systems.* New York: George Braziller, 1975.

*Jewish Encyclopedia,* II (12 Vol.) New York and London: Funk & Wagnalls, 1901.

Jonas, Hans. *The Gnostic Religion.* Boston: Beacon Press, 1958.

Jung, Carl G. *Collected Works.* Princeton: Princeton University Press, Bollingen Series XX. Edited by Sir Herbert Read, Michael Fordham, M.D., M.R.C.P., and Gerhard Adler, Ph.D. Translated by R. F. C. Hull.
  V. 7. *Two Essays on Analytical Psychology,* 1953.
  V. 8. *The Structure and Dnamics of the Psyche,* 1960.
  V. 9, i. *The Archetypes and the Collective Unconscious,* 1959.
  V. 9, ii. *Aion: Researches into the Phenomenology of the Self,* 1959.
  V. 10. *Civilization in Transition,* 1964.
  V. 11. *Psychology and Religion: West and East,* 1958.
  V. 12. *Psychology and Alchemy,* 1953.
  V. 13. *Alchemical Studies,* 1967.
  V. 14. *Mysterium Coniunctionis,* 1963.
  V. 16. *The Practice of Psychotherapy,* 1954.

——. *Contributions to Analytical Psychology.* New York: Harcourt, Brace, 1928.

——. *Memories, Dreams, Reflections,* recorded and edited by Aniela Jaffé. New York: Random House, Pantheon Books, 1963.

——. Foreword and Commentary on *The Secret of the Golden Flower,* Richard Wilhelm's Translation into German (Rendered into English by Cary F. Baynes). New York: Harcount, Brace and World, 1965.

Kardiner, Abram. "Report on a Meeting in New York of the American Academy of Psychoanalysis," *Science News,* 102, December 16, 1972.

Kaufmann, Yehezkel. *The Babylonian Captivity and Deutero-Isaiah.* C. W. Efroymson, trans. New York: Union of American Hebrew Congregations, 1970.

Kenner, Hugh. "Bucky Fuller and the Final Exam." *The New York Times Magazine,* July 6, 1975.

Kenton, Warren. Astrology, *The Celestial Mirror.* New York: Avon Books, 1974.

Kirk, G. S. and Raven, J. E. *The Pre-Socratic Philosophers.* New York: Cambridge University Press. 1966.

Krishna, Gopi. *The Biological Basis of Religion and Genius.* New York: Harper & Row, 1972.

——. Kundalini, *The Evolutionary Energy in Man.* New Delhi: Ramadhar and Hopman, 1967.

Kuhn, Thomas. *The Structure of Scientific Revolutions.* Chicago: University of Chicago Press, 1962.

Lao Tsu. *Tao Tĕ Ching.* Gia-Fu Feng and Jane English, trans. New York: Random House, Vintage Books, 1972.

Laszlo, Ervin. *The Systems View of the World.* New York: Braziller, 1972.

Leshan, Lawrence. *The Medium, the Mystic, and the Physicist: Toward a General Theory of the Paranormal.* New York: The Viking Press, 1966.

*Les très riches heures du Duc de Berry,* French, early fifteenth century. Illustration reproduced in Kenton's Astrology, *The Celestial Mirror.*

Lovell, A. C. B. *The Individual and the Universe.* New York: Harper and Brothers, 1958.

Malamud, René. "The Amazon Problem." Zurich: Spring, 1971.

Manilius. *The Five Books of Manilius.* "T.C. Trand. Washington: National Astrological Library, 1953."

Margulis, Lynn. *Origin of Eukaryotic Cells.* New Haven: Yale University Press. 1970.

Mathers, S.L. MacGregor. *The Kabbalah Unveiled.* London: Rouledge & Kegan Paul, 1957.

Mead, G. R. S. *Fragments of a Faith Forgotten.* London: John M. Watkins, 1931.

——. *Pistis Sophia* (a Gnostic miscellany: being for the most part extracts from the books of the Saviour, to which are added extracts from a cognate literature). London: John M. Watkins, 1921.

Mellaart, James. *Catal Huyuk, a Neolithic Town in Anatolia. New York: McGraw-Hill, 1967.*

Metzner, Ralph. *Maps of Consciousness.* New York: Collier Books, 1971.

Morris, Jan. *Conundrum, from James to Jan.* New York: Harcourt, Brace, Jovanovich, 1974.

Neumann, Erich. *The Great Mother, An Analysis of the Archetype.* New York: Pantheon, 1955.

——. *The Origins and History of Consciousness.* New York: Pantheon, 1954.

Niebuhr, H. Richard. *Radical Monotheism and Western Culture.* New York: Harper, 1960.

Nin, Anais. *The Diary of Anais Nin V. 3, 1939-1944.* New York: Harcourt, Brace, Jovanovich, 1969.

D'Oliver, Fabra. *Histoire Philosophique du Genre Humain,* in Eduard Schure, *The Great Initiates, I.* New York: David McKay, 1913.

Orstein, Robert E., ed. *The Nature of Human Consciousness.* San Francisco: W. H. Freeman, 1973.

Ornstein, Robert E. *The Psychology of Consciousness.* San Francisco: W. H. Freeman, 1972.

Penfield, Wilder. *The Mystery of the Mind*. Princeton: Princeton University Press, 1975.

Plato. *Symposium (abridged)*, Benjamin Jowett, trans., *and reprinted in Great Books of the Western World*, 7. Chicago: Encyclopedia Britannica, 1952.

Poncé, Charles. "An Alchemical Allegory: Notes Toward an Understanding of Genesis," *Maitreya* 5. Berkeley, Calif.: Shambhala Publications, 1974.

——— . *The Game of Wizards*. Baltimore: Penguin Books, 1975.

——— . *Kabbalah, an Introduction and Illumination for the World Today*. San Francisco: Straight Arrow Books, 1973.

——— . "Woman, the Feminine and Alchemy: Notes for Alchemical Journal," *Maitreya* 4. Berkeley, Calif.: Shambhala Publications, 1973.

Praz, Mario. *The Romantic Agone*, Angus Davidson, trans. London, New York: Oxford University Press, 1970.

Rawson, Philip. *The Art of Tantra*. Greenwich, Conn.: New York Graphic Society, 1973.

——— . *Tantra: The Indian Cult of Ecstasy*. The Art and Cosmos Series. New York: Avon Books, 1973.

Rawson, Philip and Legeza, Laszlo. *Tao: The Eastern Philosophy of Time and Change*. New York: Avon Books, 1973.

Readm, John. *Prelude to Chemistry*. London: G. Bell and Sons, 1961.

Roszak, Betty and Roszak, Theodore, editors. *Masculine/ Feminine: Readings in Sexual Mythology and the Liberation of Women*. New York: Harper Colophon Books, 1969.

Scholem, Gershom G. *Major Trends in Jewish Mysticism*. New York: Schocken, 1954.

——— . *Zohar, The Book of Splendor, Basic Readings from the Kabbalah*. New York: Schocken, 1963.

Serrano, Miguel. *C. G. Jung and Hermann Hesse: A Record of Two Friendships*. Frank MacShane, trans. London: Rougledge & Kegan Paul, 1966.

——— . *The Serpent of Paradise: The Story of an Indian Pilgrimage*. London: Routledge & Kegan Paul, 1974.

Seznec, J. *The Survival of the Pagan Gods*. New York: Pantheon, 1953.

Shah, Idries, *The Way of the Sufi*. New York: E. P. Dutton, 1970.

Sherfey, Mary Jane. *The Nature and Evolution of Female Sexuality*. New York: Random House, 1972.

Sperling, Harry and Simon, Maurice, trans. *The Zohar*. London: The Soncino Press, 1956.

Stolier, Robert J. "Facts and Fancies: An Examination of Freud's Concept of Bisexuality," *Women & Analysis.* Jean Strouse, ed. New York: Viking Press Grossman Div., 1974."

Szent-Gyorgyi, Albert. *Introduction to a Submolecular Biology.* New York: Academic Press, 1960.

Teilhard de Chardin, Pierre. *The Prayer of the Universe.* Perennial Library, 1973.

Thass-Thienemann, Theodore. *The Interpretation of Language; Volume II: Understanding the Unconscious Meaning of Language.* New York: Jason Aronson, 1973.

Thomas, Keith. *Religion and the Decline of Magic.* New York: Scribner's, 1971.

Thompson, William Irwin. *Passages About Earth: an Exploration of the New Planetary Culture.* New York: Harper & Row, 1973.

Ulanov, Ann Belford. *The Feminine in Jungian Psychology and in Christian Theology.* Evanston, Illinois: Northwestern University Press, 1971.

*The Upanishads,* Swami Nikhilananda, ed. & trans. New York: Harper Torchbooks, 1963.

Vanggaard, Thorkil. *Phallos: A Symbol and its History in the Male World.* New York: International Universities Press, 1969.

Waley, Arthur. *The Way and Its Power, A Study of the Tao Te Ching and Its Place in Chinese Thought.* London: George Allen and Unwin, 1968.

Watson, James D. *The Double Helix: A Personal Account of the Discovery of the Structure of DNA.* New York: Atheneum, 1968.

Watts, Alan and Elisofon, Eliot. *Erotic Spirituality: the Vision of Konarak.* New York: Collier Books, 1971.

——— . *Tao: the Watercourse Way.* With the collaboration of Al Chung-Liang Huang. New York: Pantheon, 1975.

Wiener, Herbert. *9 1/2 Mystics: The Kabbala Today.* New York: Collier Books, 1973.

Whyte, Lancelot Law. *The Universe of Experience: A World View Beyond Science and Religion.* New York: Harper Torchbooks, 1974.

Wickes, Frances G. *The Inner World of Choice.* Boston: Sigo Press, 1988.

Wilhelm, Richard, trans. *The Secret of the Golden Flower, A Chinese Book of Life.* New York: Harcourt, Brace and World, 1965.

——— . *The I Ching or Book of Changes.* Cary F. Baynes, trans. New York: Pantheon, 1962.

Wosien, Maria-Gabriele. *Secret Dance: Encounter with the Gods.* London: Thames and Hudson, 1974.

Yeats, W. B. *Selected Poems and Two Plays.* New York: Macmillan, 1962.

Zimmer, Heinrich. *Myths and Symbols in Indian Art and Civilization*. New York: Harper Torchbooks, 1962.

———. *Philosophies of India*. Campbell, Joseph, ed. Bollingen Series XXVI. New York: Pantheon Books, 1951.

*The Zohar*. Five Vols. Harry Sperling and Maurice Simon, trans. London: The Soncino Press, 1956.

# Index

Blackburn, and modes of conscious-
 ness, 158
black holes, 156, 175, 230
"black sun" (sol niger), 92, 155, 241
Blake, William, 36, 75, 85, 90,
 101-102, 149, 151, 169, 173, 185,
 193 Book of Urizen, 85; Proverbs of
 Hell, 3, 227
Blofeld, John, 144
Boas, George, 40
Bogen, Joseph E., 157
Boreas, 34
Boyle, Robert, 77-78
Brahma, 122n.
Brahman, 122-124
breath/breathing, 131, 136, 146,
 234-235
Britomartis, 46
Buddhism, 132-133, 134, 148; Zen, 33,
 189
bull(s), 41, 44-45, 51. See also Taurus,
 age of

calligraphy, 151-154
Campbell, Joseph, 40
castration, 26-27, 39
"Catal Hüyük, 41, 46
celibacy, 197, 220-222, 244
Chaldea(ns), 62, 70
Chandni Chowk, 214
Chaos, 33, 34, 36-37, 54, 62, 84, 101,
 110, 123, 163, 171, 172-174, 176,
 235. See also nigredo; prima materia
Chesler, Phyllis, 26
ch'i, 144, 150-153, 180, 237
childbirth, 15, 28-29, 61, 186; and
 Eleusinian rites, 38
children, 15, 83, 93, 196-197
Christianity, 53, 58, 88-89, 122
Church, the, 93, 98
circumcision, 52, 71
clitoris, 186
closed systems, 183, 184, 193, 206,
 237, 238
Coeus, 35

coincidentia oppositorum, 132
coitus interruptus, 217
cold/heat, 78, 97, 99, 141
communication, 195-196
consciousness, 8, 14, 24, 30, 46, 52,
 58, 67-68, 139-140, 144; and
 bisexuality, 206-207; and
 masturbation, 217; and marijuana, 210; energy and evolution of,
 179-190; higher, 235; modes of,
 156-160; sexual, 194
Coomaraswamy, Ananda K., 123
Copernicus, 72, 198
copulation (see also sexual intercourse);
 self-, 90
corpus callosum, 156
Corpus Hermeticum, 88
Cosmic Egg (Orphic Egg), 37, 38, 179
courtship, 131
Creation (cosmogeny, cosmology), 6,
 33-39, 43, 53, 61-68, 70, 85-86,
 97, 123, 155, 179, 238 (see also
 alchemy; astrology, Kabbalah;
 systems theory; Taoism); and
 Gnostics, 88-93
Creation of the Universe, The, 171
Creative (hexagram), 141-142, 154
creativity, 26, 167, 215, 221, 228, 241
Crete, Cretans, 40, 44-45, 54, 55
Crius, 35
Cronus, 35, 39, 45, 92. See also Saturn
crucifixion, 91-92
Cyclopes, 39
Cyprus, 54

dance, dancing, 34, 38, 54, 62, 169,
 197; and Tai ch'i, 150, 159-160
Daniel, 71
darkness, 38, 63, 112, 113, 175 (see also
 black holes; Chaos; moon; night;
 nigredo, shadow; yin/yang); and
 Ialdabaôth, 91; and Sheba, 176
"Dark night of the soul," 101
David, 88
day, 62, 70, 153-154, 146, 159. See also

Zen, 33, 187
Zeus, 28ff, 39, 43, 44-45, 46, 52, 55,
    92; and Dionysus, 48; in Platonic
    myth, 82
Zimmer, Heinrich, 37, 47n
Zodiac, 72, 74
Zodiacal Man, 74, 86, 87. *See also*
    Primal Man
Zoë, 91, 142
*Zohar,* 65-66, 107-108